THE CHRIST OF THE COVENANTS

by

O. Palmer Robertson

PRESBYTERIAN AND REFORMED PUBLISHING CO.
PHILLIPSBURG, NEW JERSEY

ISBN: 0-87552-418-4

Fourth printing, February 1984

Scripture quotations are primarily from the
author's translation or the New American
Standard Bible.

PRINTED IN THE UNITED STATES OF AMERICA

To Judy
my invaluable helpmate
and beloved fellow-heir
of the grace of covenant life

Contents

Preface vii

PART ONE:
INTRODUCTION TO THE DIVINE COVENANTS

1. The Nature of the Divine Covenants................... 3
2. The Extent of the Divine Covenants 17
3. The Unity of the Divine Covenants................... 27
4. Diversity in the Divine Covenants 53

PART TWO:

5. The Covenant of Creation 67

PART THREE:
THE COVENANT OF REDEMPTION

6. Adam: The Covenant of Commencement.............. 93
7. Noah: The Covenant of Preservation.................. 109
8. Abraham: The Covenant of Promise 127
9. The Seal of the Abrahamic Covenant 147

10. Moses: The Covenant of Law 167
11. *Excursus:* Which Structures Scripture—
    Covenants or Dispensations? 201
12. David: The Covenant of the Kingdom 229
13. Christ: The Covenant of Consummation 271
Scripture Index 301

Preface

THIS work focuses on two areas central to the concerns of biblical interpretation today: the significance of God's covenants and the relation of the two testaments. By understanding correctly God's initiatives in establishing covenants in history, a solid foundation will be laid for unravelling the complex question of the relation of the two testaments.

Virtually every school of biblical interpretation today has come to appreciate the significance of the covenants for the understanding of the distinctive message of the Scriptures. May the Lord of the covenant bless this ongoing discussion so that a fuller love of him who has made himself to be "a covenant for the peoples" will be kindled in the hearts of men of all nations.

O. Palmer Robertson
Covenant Theological Seminary
St. Louis, Missouri
September 1, 1980

PART ONE

INTRODUCTION TO THE DIVINE COVENANTS

1
The Nature of the Divine Covenants

WHAT is a covenant?

Asking for a definition of "covenant" is something like asking for a definition of "mother."

A mother may be defined as the person who brought you into the world. That definition may be correct formally. But who would be satisfied with such a definition?

Scripture clearly testifies to the significance of the divine covenants. God has entered repeatedly into covenantal relationships with particular men. Explicit references may be found to a divine covenant established with Noah (Gen. 6:18), Abraham (Gen. 15:18), Israel (Exod. 24:8), and David (Ps. 89:3). Israel's prophets anticipated the coming of the days of the "new" covenant (Jer. 31:31), and Christ himself spoke of the last supper in covenantal language (Luke 22:20).

But what is a covenant?

Some would discourage any effort to present a single definition

3

of "covenant" which would embrace all the varied usages of the term in Scripture. They would suggest that the many different contexts in which the word appears imply many different meanings.[1]

Clearly any definition of the term "covenant" must allow for as broad a latitude as the data of Scripture demands. Yet the very wholeness of the biblical history in being determined by God's covenants suggests an overarching oneness in the concept of the covenant.

What then is a covenant? How do you define the covenantal relation of God to his people?[2]

A covenant is a *bond in blood sovereignly administered*. When God enters into a covenantal relationship with men, he sovereignly institutes a life-and-death bond. A covenant is a bond in blood, or a bond of life and death, sovereignly administered.

Three aspects of this definition of the divine covenants must be considered more closely.

A COVENANT IS A BOND

In its most essential aspect, a covenant is that which binds people together. Nothing lies closer to the heart of the biblical concept of the covenant than the imagery of a bond inviolable.

---

1. Cf. D. J. McCarthy, "Covenant in the Old Testament: The Present State of Inquiry," *Catholic Biblical Quarterly* 27 (1965): 219, 239. Delbert R. Hillers comments on the task of defining covenant in *Covenant: The History of a Biblical Idea* (Baltimore, 1969), p. 7: "It is not the case of six blind men and the elephant, but of a group of learned paleontologists creating different monsters from the fossils of six separate species."

2. The very fact that Scripture speaks of "divine" covenants, covenants made by God with his people, may be of great significance in itself. Apparently this phenomenon of divine covenants does not appear outside Israel. "Outside the Old Testament we have no clear evidence of a treaty between a god and his people," says Ronald E. Clements, *Abraham and David; Genesis 15 and its Meaning for Israelite Tradition* (Naperville, Ill., 1967), p. 83. Cf. also David Noel Freedman's comment in "Divine Commitment and Human Obligation," *Interpretation* 18 (1964): 420: "There are no convincing parallels in the pagan world . . ." to the covenants of God with man as found in the Bible.

Extensive investigations into the etymology of the Old Testament term for "covenant" (בְּרִית) have proven inconclusive in determining the meaning of the word.[3] Yet the contextual usage of the term in Scripture points rather consistently to the concept of a "bond" or "relationship."[4] It is always a person, either God or man, who makes

---

3. The inconclusive character of etymological evidence is acknowledged quite generally. Cf. Moshe Weinfeld, *Theologisches Wörterbuch zum Alten Testament* (Stuttgart, 1973), p. 783; Leon Morris, *The Apostolic Preaching of the Cross* (London, 1955), pp. 62ff. One suggestion points to the verb *barah,* which means "to eat." If this were the case, the reference would be to the sacred meal which often was associated with the covenant-making process. Martin Noth, "Old Testament Covenant-Making in the Light of a Text from Mari" in *The Laws in the Pentateuch and Other Essays* (Edinburgh, 1966), p. 122, argues against this hypothesis. He suggests that the phrase "to cut a covenant" then would involve allusions to different methods for making a covenant. On the one hand it would suggest the self-malediction of animal division. On the other hand it would point to participation in a covenant meal. Noth favors the suggestion that "covenant" derives from the Akkadian *birit,* which relates to the Hebrew preposition בֵּין "between." He constructs a multi-step process by which the term attained adverbial independence through the phrase "slay an ass in between," took on the substantival meaning of "a mediation," which consequently required the introduction of a second preposition "between" and finally evolved into the normal word for "covenant," which could be used with verbs other than "to cut" (between). A third etymological suggestion points to the Akkadian root *baru,* "to bind, to fetter," and the related noun *biritu,* "band" or "fetter." Weinfeld, op. cit., p. 783, regards this last suggestion as the most likely.

4. The recent argumentations of E. Kutsch that the term "covenant" means "obligation" or "commitment" indeed are fascinating. But they are not adequate to overthrow the basic concept that a covenant is a "bond." Kutsch argues that the definition of "covenant" as "obligation" holds whether the type covenant is one in which a person "obligates" himself, is "obligated" by a foreign power, or arrives at a mutual "obligation" with an equal party. He also notes that Hebrew parallelism frequently interchanges "covenant" with "statute" and "oath," which he feels would favor the meaning of "obligation" (E. Kutsch, "Gottes Zuspruch und Anspruch. *berit* in der alttestamentlichen Theologie," in *Questions disputées d'Ancien Testament* [Gembloux, 1974], pp. 71ff.). Cordial disagreement with Kutsch's theory as expressed in earlier articles is registered by D. J. McCarthy in "Berit and Covenant in the Deuteronomistic History," in *Studies in the Religion of Ancient Israel, Supplement to Vetus Testamentum,* 23 (1972): 81ff. McCarthy concludes that the traditional translation can stand, despite Kutsch's argumentations. While the divine covenants invariably involve obligations, their ultimate purpose reaches beyond the guaranteed discharge of a duty. Instead, it is the personal interrelation of God with his people that is at the heart of the covenant. This concept of the heart of the covenant was perceived in the history of covenant investigators as early as the work of John Cocceius, as seen by his stress on the effect of the covenant as making peace between parties. Cf. Charles Sherwood McCoy, *The Covenant Theology of Johannes Cocceius* (New Haven, 1965), p. 166.

a covenant. Still further it is another person who stands as the other party of the covenant with few exceptions.[5] The result of a covenant commitment is the establishment of a relationship "in connection with," "with" or "between" people.[6]

The formalizing element essential for the establishing of all divine covenants in Scripture is a verbalized declaration of the character of the bond being established. God speaks to establish his covenant. He speaks graciously to commit himself to his creatures, and to declare the basis on which he shall relate to his creation.

The prominence of oaths and signs in the divine covenants underlines the fact that a covenant in its essence is a bond. A covenant commits people to one another.[7]

---

5. One exception would be Gen. 9:10, 12, 17, in which God establishes a covenant with the beasts of the field. Cf. also Hos. 2:18; Jer. 33:20, 25. Despite the role of impersonal parties to the covenant in these passages, it is still a "bond" that is being established with them.

6. The prepositions בֵּין, עִם, אֶת, and לְ may be used to describe this relation.

7. Much evidence supports the significance of the oath in the covenant-making process. For a full statement of the evidence that an oath belonged to the essence of covenant, see G. M. Tucker, "Covenant Forms and Contract Forms," *Vetus Testamentum*, 15 (1965): 487–503.

While the oath repeatedly appears in relation to a covenant, it is unclear that a formal ceremony of oath-taking absolutely was essential for the establishment of a covenant relationship. Neither the Noahic nor the Davidic covenant explicitly mentions the taking of an oath at the point in history at which these covenants were inaugurated, although subsequent Scriptures mention an oath in association with both these covenants (Gen. 9; II Sam. 7; cf. Isa. 54:9; Ps. 89:34f.). In his now-classic analysis of the elements of the Hittite suzerainty treaties, George A. Mendenhall first lists the six basic elements of the treaty. The list does not include an oath. Mendenhall comments: "We know that other factors were involved, for the verification of the treaty did not take place by the mere draft in written form" ("Covenant Forms in Israelite Tradition," *The Biblical Archaeologist* 17 [1954]: 60f.). It is on this basis that Mendenhall proceeds to introduce item seven into the treaty form, which he calls "the formal oath." Yet he himself feels compelled to add: ". . . although we have no light on its form and content."

Scripture would suggest not merely that a covenant generally contains an oath. Instead, it may be affirmed that a covenant *is* an oath. The commitment of the covenantal relationship binds people together with a solidarity equivalent to the results achieved by a formal oath-taking process. "Oath" so adequately captures the relationship achieved by "covenant" that the terms may be interchanged (cf.

A binding oath of the covenant might take on a variety of forms. At one point a verbal oath could be involved (Gen. 21:23, 24, 26, 31; 31:53; Exod. 6:8; 19:8; 24:3, 7; Deut. 7:8, 12; 29:13; Ezek. 16:8). At another point some symbolic action could be attached to the verbal commitment, such as the granting of a gift (Gen. 21:28–32), the eating of a meal (Gen. 26:28–30; 31:54; Exod. 24:11), the setting up of a memorial (Gen. 31:44f.; Josh. 24:27), the sprinkling of blood (Exod. 24:8), the offering of sacrifice (Ps. 50:5), the passing under the rod (Ezek. 20:37), or the dividing of animals (Gen. 15:10, 18). In several passages of Scripture the integral relation of the oath to the covenant is brought out most clearly by a parallelism of construction (Deut. 29:12; II Kings 11:4; I Chron. 16:16; Ps. 105:9; 89:3, 4; Ezek. 17:19). In these cases, the oath interchanges with the covenant, and the covenant with the oath.

This closeness of relationship between oath and covenant emphasizes that a covenant in its essence is a bond. By the covenant, persons become committed to one another.

The presence of signs in many of the biblical covenants also emphasizes that the divine covenants bind people together. The token of the rainbow, the seal of circumcision, the sign of the Sabbath—these covenantal signs enforce the binding character of the covenant. An interpersonal commitment which may be guaranteed has come into effect by way of the covenantal bond. Just as bride and groom interchange rings as "token and pledge" of their "constant faith and abiding love," so the signs of the covenant symbolize the permanence of the bond between God and his people.

A COVENANT IS A BOND IN BLOOD

The phrase "bond-in-blood" or bond of life and death expresses the ultimacy of the commitment between God and man in the covenantal context. By initiating covenants, God never enters into a

---

Ps. 89:3, 34f.; 105:8–10). The formalizing process of oath-taking may or may not be present. But a covenantal commitment inevitably will result in a most solemn obligation.

casual or informal relationship with man. Instead, the implications
of his bonds extend to the ultimate issues of life and death.

The basic terminology describing the inauguration of a covenantal
relationship vivifies the life-and-death intensity of the divine covenants. The phrase translated "to make a covenant" in the Old
Testament literally reads "to cut a covenant."

This phrase "to cut a covenant" does not appear just at one stage in
the history of the biblical covenants. Much to the contrary, it occurs
prominently across the entire spread of the Old Testament. The law,[8]
the prophets,[9] and the writings[10] all contain the phrase repeatedly.

It might be supposed that the passage of time would have dulled
the vivid imagery of "cutting a covenant." Yet the evidence of an
abiding awareness of the full import of the phrase appears in some
of Scripture's most ancient texts as well as in passages associated
with the very end of Israel's presence in the land of Palestine. The
original record of the inauguration of the Abrahamic covenant,
laden as it is with internal signs of antiquity, first introduces the
concept of "cutting a covenant" to the biblical reader (cf. Gen. 15).
At the other extremity of Israel's history, Jeremiah's prophetic
warning to Zedekiah at the time of Nebuchadnezzar's seige of
Jerusalem literally bristles with allusions to a "cut-covenant"
theology (cf. Jer. 34).

A further indication of the permeating significance of this phrase
is found in the fact that it is related to all three of the basic
covenantal types. It is employed to describe covenants inaugurated
by man with man,[11] covenants inaugurated by God with man,[12] and
covenants inaugurated by man with God.[13]

---

8. Gen. 15:18; 21:27, 32; 26:28; 31:44; Exod. 23:32, 34; 24:8; 34:10, 12, 15, 17;
Deut. 4:23; 5:2, 3; 7:2; 9:9; 29:1, 12, 14, 25, 29; 31:16.
9. Josh. 9:6ff.; 24:25; Judg. 2:2; I Sam. 11:1, 2; II Sam. 3:12ff.; I Kings 5:12ff.;
II Kings 7:15ff.; Isa. 28:15; 55:3; Jer. 11:10; 31:31ff.; Ezek. 17:13; Hos. 2:18; Hag.
2:5; Zech. 11:10.
10. Job 31:1; Ps. 50:5; I Chron. 11:3; II Chron. 6:11; Ezra 10:3; Neh. 9:8.
11. Gen. 21:27, 32; II Sam. 3:12, 13.
12. Gen. 15:18 (Abrahamic); Exod. 24:8 and Deut. 5:2 (Mosaic); II Chron. 21:7
and Ps. 89:3 (Davidic); Jer. 31:31, 33 and Ezek. 37:26 (new). The phrase is not used
in conjunction with Noah's covenant.
13. These covenant relations initiated by man with God should be understood in

Particularly striking is the fact that the verb "to cut" may stand by itself and still clearly mean "to cut a covenant."[14] This usage indicates just how essentially the concept of "cutting" had come to be related to the covenant idea in Scripture.

This relating of a "cutting" process to the establishment of a covenant manifests itself throughout the ancient languages and cultures of the Middle East. Not only in Israel, but in many of the surrounding cultures, the binding character of a covenant is related to a terminology of "cutting."[15]

Not only the terminology, but the rituals commonly associated with the establishment of covenants reflect quite dramatically a "cutting" process. As the covenant is made, animals are "cut" in ritual ceremony. The most obvious example of this procedure in Scripture is found in Genesis 15, at the time of the making of the Abrahamic covenant. First Abraham divides a series of animals and lays the pieces over against one another. Then a symbolic representation of God passes between the divided pieces of animals. The result is the "making" or "cutting" of a covenant.

What is the meaning of this division of animals at the point of

---

a context of covenant renewal. It is only on the basis of a relation previously existing that man may presume to covenant with God. Cf. II Kings 11:17; II Kings 23:3; II Chron. 29:10.

14. I Sam. 11:1, 2; 20:16; 22:8; I Kings 8:9; II Chron. 7:18; Ps. 105:9; Hag. 2:5. Noth, op. cit., p. 111, does not regard this shorter phrase as containing an ellipsis into which the term "covenant" is to be supplied. Instead, he proposes that the phrase "to cut between" as it occurs in these passages should be regarded as a "particularly ancient and original expression" serving as the linguistic equivalent of the phrase "to slay (an ass)" as found in the Mari texts. This analysis of the phrase corresponds to Noth's rather elaborately developed hypothesis that the term "covenant" derives etymologically from the word "between," as mentioned earlier. According to his construction, the phrase "to cut between" would represent an earlier form of the phrase prior to the time in which "between" evolved into a nominal usage, thus demanding the introduction of a second "between" with the result that the phrase would read in its more familiar form "to cut a covenant between." Noth does not venture to explain why the full phrase "to cut a covenant" should appear in the most ancient texts (i.e., Gen. 15:18), or why the abbreviated form should still occur in post-exilic texts (i.e., Hag. 2:5).

15. For a full presentation of the extra-biblical evidence, see Dennis J. McCarthy, *Treaty and Covenant* (Rome, 1963), pp. 52ff.

covenantal inauguration? Both biblical and extra-biblical evidence combine to confirm a specific significance for this ritual. The animal-division symbolizes a "pledge to the death" at the point of covenant commitment. The dismembered animals represent the curse that the covenant-maker calls down on himself if he should violate the commitment which he has made.

This interpretation finds strong support in the words of the prophet Jeremiah. As he recalls Israel's disloyalty to their covenant commitments, he reminds them of the ritual by which they "passed between the parts of the calf" (Jer. 34:18). By their transgression, they have called down on themselves the curses of the covenant. Therefore they may expect dismemberment of their own bodies. Their carcasses "shall be food for the birds of the sky and the beasts of the earth" (Jer. 34:20).

It is in this context of covenant inauguration that the biblical phrase "to cut a covenant" is to be understood.[16] Integral to the very terminology which describes the establishment of a covenantal relationship is the concept of a pledge to life and death. A covenant is indeed a "bond-in-blood," or a bond of life and death.[17]

This phrase "bond in blood" accords ideally with the biblical

●————————●

    16. John Murray, *The Covenant of Grace* (Grand Rapids, 1954), p. 16, n. 19, judges that the evidence for understanding this phrase as referring to the cutting asunder of animals falls short of sure confirmation, although he acknowledges that there seems to be no other satisfactory explanation. Meredith G. Kline, *By Oath Consigned* (Grand Rapids, 1968), p. 42, accepts this explanation in the stride of his argument and cites supporting evidence from other current studies on the subject. Perhaps the "light . . . from other sources" which was lacking according to Murray's earlier judgment may be found in such a work as that of McCarthy, *Treaty and Covenant*, pp. 5ff.
    17. Recent scholarship has tended to extend the concept of "cutting a covenant" in many directions, often without adequate substantiation. Erich Isaac, "Circumcision as a Covenant Rite," *Anthropos* 59 (1961): 447, suggests that the calling of heaven and earth as witnesses to the covenant in Deut. 4:26 relates to the "cutting" of a covenant by means of allusion to the Babylonian creation myth, which involved the cleaving of a primeval being to form heaven and earth. W. F. Albright accepts the suggestion of A. Goetze that the division of the Levite's concubine (Judg. 19:29) and the hewing of the oxen by Saul (I Sam. 11:7) were intended to renew Israel's tribal covenant (review of A. Goetze's "The Hittite Ritual of Tunnawi" in *Journal of Biblical Literature* 59 (1940): 316.

emphasis that "apart from shedding of blood there is no remission" *good*
(Heb. 9:22). Blood is of significance in Scripture because it represents
life, not because it is crude or bloody. The life is in the blood (Lev.
17:11) and so the shedding of blood represents a judgment on life.

The biblical imagery of blood-sacrifice emphasizes the interrelation of life and blood. The pouring out of life-blood signifies the
only way of relief from covenant-obligations once incurred. A
covenant is a "bond-in-blood," committing the participants to loyalty
on pain of death. Once the covenant relationship has been entered,
nothing less than the shedding of blood may relieve the obligations
incurred in the event of covenantal violation.

It is just at this point that the effort to relate the "covenant" idea
in Israel's life and experience to the concept of a "last will and
testament" must be rejected. It is simply impossible to do justice to
the biblical concept of "covenant" and at the same time to introduce
an idea of "last will and testament."[18]

The major point of confusion in these two concepts of "covenant"
and "testament" arises from the fact that both a "covenant" and a
"testament" relate to "death." Death is essential both to activate a
last will and testament and to inaugurate a covenant. Because of this
similarity, the two concepts have been confused.

However, the two ideas of covenant and testament actually diverge
radically in their significance. The similarity is only formal in
nature. Both "covenant" and "testament" relate closely to "death."
But death stands in relationship to each of these concepts in two
very different manners.

In the case of a "covenant," death stands at the beginning of a
relationship between two parties, symbolizing the potential curse-
factor in the covenant. In the case of a "testament," death stands at the
end of a relationship between two parties, actualizing an inheritance.

---

18. Cf. J. Barton Payne's *Theology of the Older Testament* (Grand Rapids, 1962).
Payne has organized the entirety of his Old Testament theology on the basis of a
"last will and testament" understanding of the covenant. Notice also his argumentation in "The B'rith of Yahweh," *New Perspectives on the Old Testament* (Waco,
1970), p. 252.

The death of the covenant-maker appears in two distinct stages. First it appears in the form of a symbolic representation of the curse, anticipating possible covenantal violation. Later the party who violates the covenant actually experiences death as a consequence of his earlier commitment.

The death of the testator does not come in two stages. No symbolic representation of death accompanies the making of a will. The testator does not die as a consequence of the violation of his last will and testament.

The provisions of the "last will and testament" inherently presume death to be inevitable, and all its stipulations build on that fact. But the provisions of a covenant offer the options of life or death. The representation of death is essential to the inauguration of a covenant. The consecrating animal must be slain to effect a covenant. But it is not at all necessary that a party to the covenant actually die. Only in the event of covenant violation does actual death of the covenant-maker occur.

It is in the context of covenantal death, not testamentary death, that the death of Jesus Christ is to be understood. Christ's death was a substitutionary sacrifice. Christ died as a substitute for the covenant-breaker. Substitution is essential for the understanding of the death of Christ.

Hmm.

Yet death in substitution for another has no place whatsoever in the making of a last will and testament. The testator dies in his own place, not in the place of another. No other death may substitute for the death of the testator himself.

But Christ died in the place of the sinner. Because of covenantal violations, men were condemned to die. Christ took on himself the curses of the covenant and died in the place of the sinner. His death was covenantal, not testamentary.

Certainly it is true that the Christian is presented in Scripture as the heir of God. But he is heir by the process of adoption into the family of the never-dying God, not by the process of testamentary disposition.

On the popular level, it has been assumed that the Lord's Supper was the occasion of Christ's making his last will and testament. But it must be remembered that it was a covenantal meal that was being celebrated on this occasion. In the context of the covenantal meal of the Passover Jesus introduced the provisions of the new covenant meal. Clearly his intention was to proclaim himself as the Passover Lamb, who was taking on himself the curses of the covenant. His death was substitutionary; his blood was "poured out" for his people. His words were not those of testamentary disposition, but those of covenant fulfillment and inauguration.

The Old Testament concept of the covenant must not be reinterpreted in terms of a "last will and testament." The total perspective of the Old Testament people concerning their relation to God was consistently covenantal. A complete redirection of their thinking simply cannot be accomplished.

Even on a more modest scale, the concept of "testament" cannot be substituted for covenant in the "Old Testament" Scriptures.[19] The presence of provisions in the ancient Near Eastern treaty forms relating to succession arrangements does not provide adequate basis for imposing a "testamentary" idea on the biblical concept of covenant.[20] A treaty agreement may include succession arrangements as

---

19. The reader will appreciate the rather humorous situation of the author at this point. He is attempting to argue against the approach which would understand "covenant" as meaning "last will and testament," while being required at every turn to refer to the Old "Testament" Scriptures because of the traditional division of the Bible.

20. Cf. Meredith G. Kline, *Treaty of the Great King* (Grand Rapids, 1963), pp. 39ff. Kline notes the record of Moses' death and his blessings on the tribes of Israel as found in Deut. 33, 34. He ventures to designate these blessings as "testamentary," and suggests that they demonstrate "the coalescence of the covenantal and testamentary forms" (p. 40). However, no evidence suggests that the tribal blessing of Deut. 33 depended on the death of Moses for enactment. A blessing uttered before death is not the same thing as a testamentary disposition. Kline acknowledges that testament and suzerainty covenant are not simple equivalents (p. 40). But he then attempts to relate the two ideas on the basis of covenantal provision for dynastic succession. He suggests that the book of Deut. as a whole was "a Mosaic testament" from Joshua's perspective as Moses' appointed successor, while at the same time being a "covenant" from the people's perspective. This cannot be the case. The deuteronomic document cannot change its basic literary character just by being viewed from a different perspective. Kline has presented the most able case to date

one part of its stipulations. But the inclusion of such a section does not create a testamentary document. All the provisions of a last will and testament await the death of the testator. Certainly that is not the case with respect to the covenant commitments which God has made to his people throughout the ages.

A "covenant" may well include aspects which insure continuation of its provisions beyond those people then living. As a matter of fact, the biblical covenants extend to a "thousand generations" (Deut. 7:9; Ps. 105:8). But these provisions do not transform the covenant into a last will and testament.

A covenant is not a testament.

A covenant is a bond-in-blood. It involves commitments with life-and-death consequences. At the point of covenantal inauguration, the parties of the covenant are committed to one another by a formalizing process of blood-shedding. This blood-shedding repre-

---

for seeing the entirety of Deut. as a covenantal document. If the book does possess this basic form, it cannot suddenly transform itself into a testamentary document simply because Joshua is the one observing it. Joshua's succession to Moses is a provision of God's covenant as recorded in Deut. and not a provision of Moses' last will and testament. God as covenant lord appoints Joshua, not Moses as dying testator.

In making his case for viewing Deut. as a testamentary document, Kline cites a particular Assyrian treaty in which the entire purpose of the document is to assure the security of Ashurbanipal's regal authority over vassal nations after the death of Esarhaddon (see D. J. Wiseman, *The Vassal-Treaties of Esarhaddon* (London, 1958), pp. i, ii; 4, 5ff.; 30ff.). It does not seem quite appropriate to employ this specialized document as a means for interpreting a single provision within the book of Deut. A provision for succession within a covenantal framework simply is not the same thing as a testamentary document.

Kline also attempts to interpret the difficult passage in Heb. 9:16, 17 by reference to this supposed testamentary disposition related to dynastic succession (p. 41). The subject of Heb. 9:15–20, however, is not dynastic succession but covenant inauguration. It is the blood associated with the covenant inauguration ceremony, not the blood of a testator's death, that is in view in these verses. Heb. 9:16, 17 do not stand bracketed in a context of covenant inauguration as a "parenthetical allusion" to the dynastic testamentary aspect of the ancient suzerainty covenants. Instead, these verses rehearse vividly the principle that a "covenant" is "made firm" "over dead bodies," as verse 17a reads literally. For an extended discussion of these verses in a covenantal context, see below, pp. 141ff.

sents the intensity of the commitment of the covenant. By the covenant they are bound for life and death.

A COVENANT IS A BOND-IN-BLOOD SOVEREIGNLY ADMINISTERED

Bond in staple

A long history has marked the analysis of the covenants in terms of mutual compacts or contracts.[21] But recent scholarship has established rather certainly the sovereign character of the administration of the divine covenants in Scripture. Both biblical and extra-biblical evidence point to the unilateral form of covenantal establishment. No such thing as bargaining, bartering, or contracting characterizes the divine covenants of Scripture. The sovereign Lord of heaven and earth dictates the terms of his covenant.

The successive covenants of Scripture may emphasize either promissory or legal aspects. But this point of emphasis does not alter the basic character of covenantal administration. Whatever may be the distinctive substance of a particular covenant, the mode of administration remains constant. A covenant is a bond-in-blood sovereignly administered.

---

21. Cf. the survey of Murray, op. cit., pp. 5ff.

2

The Extent of the Divine Covenants

AMPLE biblical evidence establishes the vital role the divine covenants have played in God's dealings with man from Noah to Jesus Christ. No period in the history of redemption from Noah to Christ stands outside the realm of God's covenantal dealings with his people. The successive covenants made with Noah, Abraham, Moses, and David span the entirety of the Old Testament period. The promise concerning the new covenant, given during the time at which Israel was on the brink of being cast outside the land, finds its fulfillment in the days of Jesus the Christ and extends to the consummation of all things (Jer. 31:31ff.; Ezek. 37:26ff.; cf. Luke 22:20; II Cor. 3:6; Heb. 8:8ff.; 9:15; 10:15–18; 12:24).

The only question that remains concerning the extent of the divine covenants has to do with God's relation to man prior to Noah. May the concept of the covenant be extended legitimately to the period preceding the establishment of God's covenant with Noah? Is this earliest portion of biblical history also to be understood from the perspective of a covenantal framework?

17

A quick glance at any trustworthy concordance will make it plain
that the term "covenant" appears for the first time in Scripture in
connection with God's establishing of his bond with Noah. It is
equally obvious, however, that man sustained a relationship of one
sort or another with God his Creator in the period prior to God's
speaking to Noah concerning a "covenant." The question is whether
or not the various relationships sustained between God and man
prior to Noah legitimately may be termed covenantal.

At the outset, it should be acknowledged that the absence of the
term "covenant" before Genesis 6:18 should be given its full weight
of significance. For some reason, the formalizing term "covenant"
does not appear in the earlier narratives of Genesis. The biblical
exegete should be concerned to determine the reason for this
omission.

Yet it is not appropriate to let rest the broader question as to
whether or not God's relationship to man prior to Noah legitimately
may be considered to be "covenantal." To the contrary, several
considerations from within Scripture itself encourage the usage of
the designation "covenant" to describe the pre-Noahic situation
despite the absence of the term in the Genesis narrative.

First of all, some scriptural precedent exists for the omission of
the term "covenant" in discussing a relationship which unquestionably is covenantal. Nowhere in the original account of the establishment of God's promise to David does the term "covenant"
appear (II Sam. 7; I Chron. 17). Yet this relationship clearly is
covenantal. God's commitments to David were covenantal in nature
despite the absence of any formal application of the term "covenant"
in the original context of the establishment of the relationship.
Subsequent Scripture specifically speaks of God's "covenant" with
David (cf. II Sam. 23:5; Ps. 89:3).

The formal employment of the term "covenant" was not used in
connection with the establishment of God's bond to David. Since
such a situation existed in the case of God's relationship to David, it
also could have existed in the case of God's relationship to man
before Noah. If all the ingredients essential to the making of a

covenant were present prior to Noah, the relationship of God to man prior to Noah may be designated as "covenantal."

Secondly, two passages in Scripture appear to designate the order established by creation as covenantal. These two passages deserve closer attention.

JEREMIAH 33:20, 21, 25, 26

The first passage reads as follows:

> Thus says the Lord, "If you can break My covenant for the day, and My covenant for the night, so that day and night will not be at their appointed time, then My covenant may also be broken with David My servant that he shall not have a son to reign on his throne, and with the Levitical priests, My ministers."
> . . . .
> Thus says the Lord, "If My covenant for day and night stand not, and the fixed patterns of heaven and earth I have not established, then I would reject the descendants of Jacob and David My servant, not taking from his descendants rulers over the descendants of Abraham, Isaac, and Jacob. But I will restore their fortunes and will have mercy on them."

In these verses, Jeremiah relates the word of the Lord, who speaks of "my covenant of the day and my covenant of the night" (אֶת־בְּרִיתִי הַיּוֹם וְאֶת־בְּרִיתִי הַלָּיְלָה v. 20). He also refers to God's "covenant [with] day and night" (בְּרִיתִי יוֹמָם וָלָיְלָה v. 25).

When did God establish a "covenant" with "day and night"?

These phrases apparently refer either to God's ordinances of creation or to the ordinances of the covenant with Noah. In both instances, the regularity of day and night play a prominent role.

The stipulations of God's covenant with Noah indicate that "seedtime and harvest, and cold and heat, and summer and winter, and day and night (וְיוֹם וָלָיְלָה) shall not cease" (Gen. 8:22). Jeremiah could have reference to this aspect of Noah's covenant.

How do you want a cont. of day & nite?

But it is equally possible that the reference to a "covenant" of "day and night" might refer to the ordinances of the third day of creation. According to Genesis 1:14 God said: "Let there be lights in the expanse of the heaven, to divide between the day and the night" (בֵּין הַיּוֹם וּבֵין הַלָּיְלָה v. 14).

or neither!

To which of these passages does Jeremiah allude? Is he reflecting the language of God's covenant with Noah? Or is he alluding to a covenantal relationship that has existed since creation?

A second passage from Jeremiah may aid in determining this question. An argument basically of the same construction appears in Jeremiah 31:35f.:

> Thus says the Lord,
> Who gives the sun for light by day,
> And the fixed order of the moon and the stars for light by night,
> . . . .
>
> If this fixed order departs from before me, declares the Lord,
> Then the offspring of Israel also shall cease
> From being a nation before me forever.

This second passage from Jeremiah does not use the term "covenant." Instead, it employs the equivalent expression "statute" or "fixed-order" (חֹק). The two terms "covenant" and "statute" are used as parallel expressions elsewhere in Scripture (cf. I Kings 11:11; II Kings 17:15; Ps. 50:16; 105:10).

The closeness of parallel in argumentation with Jeremiah 33 is quite apparent. As certainly as the sun's rule over the day and the moon's rule over the night will not cease, so Israel will never cease from being God's people. But the additional particulars of Jeremiah 31 may help to resolve the question as to whether Jeremiah 33 refers to the ordinances of creation or the ordinances of the covenant with Noah.

According to Jeremiah 31:35, God gives the sun for light by day (לְאוֹר יוֹמָם), and the ordinances (חֻקֹּת) of the moon and the stars for light by night (לְאוֹר לָיְלָה). Quite interestingly, the reference to the sun and moon specifically as light-bearers for day and night is found

in the creation narrative but not in the narrative describing God's covenant with Noah. Furthermore, the narrative of the creation-activity of the third day refers to the stars as well as to the moon (Gen. 1:16), as does Jeremiah 31:35. The record of God's covenant with Noah makes no mention of the stars.

For these reasons, it seems likely that Jeremiah 31 alludes to the Genesis narrative of creation rather than to the establishment of God's covenant with Noah. His reference seems to be to the "statutes" of God's creation ordinances. → *This is similarity in some language only → No link can be demonstrated.* The term "covenant" does not occur in Jeremiah 31. But it does occur in the passage originally under discussion. Jeremiah 33 refers to God's "covenant" of day and night. Because of the similarity of argumentation in the two passages, it would seem appropriate to conclude that the "covenant" of day and night mentioned in Jeremiah 33 would be the same as the "statute" concerning day and night of Jeremiah 31.

Because of the closeness of the parallelism of the two chapters, it would seem that Jeremiah 33, which uses the term "covenant," also refers to the creational orderings of Genesis 1. If this is the case, then the term "covenant" would be applied to the orderings of creation.[1]

---

1. Rather interesting in this regard are the efforts to integrate the covenants of Noah with creational ordinances by L. DeQueker, "Noah and Israel. The Everlasting Divine Covenant with Mankind" in *Questions disputées d'Ancien Testament: Méthode et Théologie* (Gembloux, 1974), pp. 128f. DeQueker follows P. de Boer in interpreting the וַהֲקִמֹתִי of Genesis 6:18 as "I will maintain" my covenant rather than "I will establish" my covenant. He suggests that God's word to Noah presumes a covenant already to be in existence through the "divine guarantee which is embodied in creation." His conclusion is that the concept of creation provides the only adequate framework for understanding the covenant which God made ulti-mately in favor of Israel.

DeQueker may be placing excessive weight on the significance of וַהֲקִמֹתִי. But he certainly is correct in binding together God's creational and redemptive covenants. Particularly in the case of God's covenant with Noah, redemption echoes creation. This wholeness of the divine purpose lends strong support to viewing the creational ordering as a covenantal structure.

In considering the reference to the "covenant" of day and night in Jer. 33, it should not be forgotten that God's covenant with Noah in its broadest structures

It makes you wonder about ever doing it again.

HOSEA 6:7

The second passage in which the term "covenant" may be applied to the order of creation declares that the people of Israel, "like Adam," have transgressed the covenant. This statement may be understood basically in three different ways.

First of all, it has been suggested that "Adam" should be understood as designating a place. "At Adam" Israel has broken the covenant.

This interpretation is difficult to support. Only pure supposition can provide a concrete occasion of national sin at Adam, located on the Jordan about 12 miles north of Jericho. The account of the rolling back of the Jordan to Adam makes no mention of a sin on Israel's part (cf. Josh. 3:16).

Furthermore, this interpretation would seem to require an emendation of the massoretic text.[2] The verse as it stands does not read "at Adam," but "as Adam."

The more traditional interpretation has seen in the phrase "like Adam" an explicit reference to the sin of the first man.[3] This

---

reflects on creational ordinances. The ordering of day and night under Noah presumes creational ordinances. This fact means that whether Jeremiah alludes to the time of creation or to Noah's day, the ultimate reference must return to creation's orderings. The regularity of day and night appropriately is characterized by the prophet as "covenantal."

2. Cf. H. W. Wolff, *Dodekapropheton I, Hosea*, in *Biblischer Kommentar, Altes Testament*, Band XIV/1 (Neukirchen, 1961): 134; James Luther Mays, *Hosea. A Commentary. The Old Testament Library* (Philadelphia, 1969), p. 100. Mays' argument that the substitution of בְּאָדָם for כְּאָדָם is supported by the parallel measure, "*there* they betrayed me," is not conclusive. The emphatic "there" could represent a dramatic gesture toward the place of Israel's current idolatry rather than requiring a poetic parallel to the location at which Israel had sinned in the past.

3. A. Cohen, *The Twelve Prophets, Hebrew Text, English Translation and Commentary. The Soncino Books of the Bible* (London, 1948), p. 23, notes that Jewish commentators traditionally have referred this phrase "to the disobedience of Adam in the Garden of Eden." Cf. C. F. Keil, *The Twelve Minor Prophets* (Grand Rapids, 1949), 1: 99f.; C. Von Orelli, *The Twelve Minor Prophets* (Edinburgh, 1897), p. 38: L. Berkhof, *Systematic Theology* (Grand Rapids, 1946), p. 214.

interpretation is the most straightforward, and offers the fewest difficulties. As Adam transgressed the covenant arrangement established by creation, so Israel has transgressed the covenant appointed at Sinai.

The third possible way of reading this phrase suggests that Israel has broken the covenant "like man," or "like mankind."[4] "After the manner of men," Israel has broken the covenant.

It is difficult to settle on one of these last two interpretations. But in either case, something would be implied about the relation of non-Israelite man to his Creator-God.

The point of the passage rests on a comparison. Israelite man (cf. v. 4: "Ephraim and Judah") in his relation to God is compared to non-Israelite man in his relation to God.[5] Israel has transgressed the covenant. In this respect, Israel is "like man" in general or "like Adam" in particular. In either case, it would be implied that a covenantal relationship existed between God and non-Israelite man. As non-Israelite man has broken the covenant, so Israelite man has broken the covenant.

In what sense may it be affirmed that non-Israelite man stands in a covenantal relationship with God that may be broken? No specific covenant with man outside Israel finds any mention in Scripture other than God's covenant with Noah, which lacks adequate emphasis on specifics of covenantal obligation for Hosea to say with convincing clarity that man has "broken" the covenant.

Apparently Hosea intends to suggest that God has established a

4. The Septuagint reads ὡς ἄνθρωπος, which clearly favors this interpretation. Cf. also John Calvin, *Commentaries on the Twelve Minor Prophets* (Edinburgh, 1846), 1: 233, 235; William Rainey Harper, *A Critical and Exegetical Commentary on Amos and Hosea. The International Critical Commentary* (New York, 1905), p. 288.

5. The suggestion that "like man" is to be interpreted as meaning "as non-Israelite man is in the habit of breaking the covenants he may make with other men" forces too much into this brief phrase. It appears much more appropriate in light of the explicit reference to the breaking of a covenantal relationship with God on Israel's part to assume that "man" (or "Adam") also is guilty of breaking a (covenantal) relationship with God.

covenant relationship with man outside Israel through creation. If "Adam" is taken individually, the term would refer to the original representative man. His violation of the covenant would refer to the specific breaking of the test of probation described in the early chapters of Genesis. If "Adam" is taken generically, the term would refer to the broader covenantal obligation that falls on man as he has been given solemn responsibilities in God's world by creation. In either case, Hosea 6:7 would appear to apply covenantal terminology to the relation of God to man established by creation.[6]

To summarize the argument in favor of seeing God's relation to man prior to Noah as covenantal despite the absence of the actual usage of the term "covenant" in the early chapters of Genesis, two points have been noted thus far: first, the relation of God to David was not designated as "covenantal" originally, but nonetheless was covenantal in substance; and secondly, Jeremiah 33:20ff. and Hosea 6:7 apparently refer to God's original creational relationship in covenantal terms.

Thirdly, those elements essential to the existence of a covenant were present in God's relationship to man prior to Noah despite the absence of the term "covenant" in the early chapters of the Genesis narrative. It is the presence of these elements which, after all, is determinative for the question. Messianic prophecies appear in Scripture long before the term "messiah" occurs. The realities of the kingdom of God on earth manifest themselves thousands of years before the terms "king" and "kingdom" appear in Scripture to designate God's relationship to his creation.

---

6. Patrick Fairbairn, "Covenant," *Imperial Bible Dictionary* (London, 1890), 2: 71 does not regard this verse as proving that a "covenant" existed with Adam. He observes correctly that the "covenant" to which the prophet alludes is the Sinaitic law-administration. He proceeds to suggest that if the allusion is to the original "Adam," it would indicate no more than that as "Adam" has transgressed against one divine ordination, so had Israel against another. However, it should be noted that Fairbairn has chosen to speak of a "divine ordination" as that which is common to God's dealings with "Adam" and with Israel. Having granted this commonness of relationship to God, and having noted that the relationship to Israel is specifically designated as "covenantal" by Hosea, little would remain to prevent the suggestion that God's relationship to "Adam" also was "covenantal."

The same situation prevails with respect to the term "covenant." If those elements essential for the characterization of a relationship as "covenantal" are present, the relationship under consideration may be designated as covenantal despite the formal absence of the term.

It is just this circumstance that appears in the early chapters of Genesis. A bond of life and death clearly is present between God and man newly created (Gen. 2:15–17). If Adam would refrain from eating the forbidden fruit, he would live. But if he would eat of the tree of the knowledge of good and evil, he would die. This relationship of God to man is administered sovereignly.

Subsequently a bond of life and death was established between God and man after the fall into sin. The Lord sovereignly committed himself to establish enmity between the seed of the woman and the seed of Satan (Gen. 3:15). This divine commitment set the stage for a life-and-death struggle. God's bond with fallen man resulted in life for the seed of the woman, and death for the seed of Satan.

The presence of all elements essential to the existence of a covenant in these relationships of God to man prior to Noah provides adequate basis for the designation of these circumstances as "covenantal." Although the term "covenant" may not appear, the essence of a covenantal relationship certainly is present.

Ultimately it is this basically covenantal substance of man's created status that justifies the usage of covenantal terminology to describe man's relationship to God prior to Noah. In full sovereignty God established a relationship. That relationship involved a commitment for life and death.

By creation God bound himself to man in covenantal relationship. After man's fall into sin, the God of all creation graciously bound himself to man again by committing himself to redeem a people to himself from lost humanity. From creation to consummation the covenantal bond has determined the relation of God to his people. The extent of the divine covenants reaches from the beginning of the world to the end of the age.

3

The Unity of the
Divine Covenants

SCRIPTURE obviously presents a series of covenantal relationships instituted by the one true living God. The primary covenants in Scripture are those made with Noah, Abraham, Moses, David, and the new covenant.[1] In addition, strong evidence favors viewing the original creation relationship between God and man, as well as the first bond established by God with man after the fall, as covenantal.

How do these various covenants relate to one another? If the interjection of divine initiative into human history comes by way of the covenants, how do these covenants coordinate?

Obviously an element of freshness and newness will emerge each time the Lord God constitutes a distinctive relation to his people.

---

1. The covenants with Isaac and Jacob represent renewals of the Abrahamic promise. The covenant with Phineas (Num. 25:12, 13) appears as an adjunct to the Mosaic covenant, developing one specific aspect of the priestly legislation given to Moses. These covenants do not possess the same epoch-making character as the ones noted above.

But does some unity bind together the various covenantal administrations spread across human history? Are the covenants to be
viewed as successive and distinctive commitments that replace one
another in temporal sequence? Or do the covenants build the one on
the other so that each successive covenant supplements its prede-
cessors without at the same time supplanting the continuing role of
the more ancient bond between God and his people?

Hmm.
this will
be tough

The cumulative evidence of the Scriptures points definitely toward
the unified character of the biblical covenants. God's multiple bonds
with his people ultimately unite into a single relationship. Particular
details of the covenants may vary. A definite line of progress may be
noted. Yet the covenants of God are one.

This unity of the covenants may be seen from two perspectives.
First, God's covenants manifest a structural unity; and secondly,
God's covenants manifest a thematic unity.

STRUCTURAL UNITY OF THE DIVINE COVENANTS

In considering the unity of the various covenantal administrations,
a beginning may be made by examining first the covenants made
with Abraham, Moses, and David.

Unity of the Abrahamic, Mosaic, and Davidic Covenants

The Abrahamic, Mosaic, and Davidic covenants do not present
themselves as self-contained entities. Instead, each successive covenant builds on the previous relationship, continuing the basic
emphasis which had been established earlier. The unity of these
three covenants is seen particularly in the historical experience of
Israel, and in the genealogical emphasis of Scripture.

A unity in historical experience. As the history of God's dealing
with his people progresses, the unity of the covenantal bond becomes

apparent. God initiates distinctive covenants through Abraham, Moses, and David. Yet ~~the history surrounding these various cove~~nants emphasizes the unity and continuity of the relationship. The overarching unity of these bonds is established in two ways:

1. The points of covenantal inauguration demonstrate unity.

To set aside a people to himself, God established his covenant with Abraham. Subsequently Abraham's descendants lived also under the Mosaic and Davidic covenants. At those points in history in which God initiated the new covenantal relationships under Moses and David, evidence indicates that God was intending to bring to a further stage of development the same redemption that had been promised earlier. Instead of "wiping clean the slate" and beginning anew, each successive covenant with Abraham's descendants advanced the original purposes of God to a higher level of realization. This principle manifests itself in the history surrounding the inauguration of both the Mosaic and the Davidic covenants.

When Israel cried to God because of the Egyptian bondage, Scripture says that "God heard their groaning; and God remembered his covenant with Abraham, Israel, and Jacob" (Exod. 2:24). Out of the context of the Abrahamic covenant and its promises God began to move toward the deliverance of Israel under Moses. Says John Murray: "The only interpretation of this is that the deliverance of Israel from Egypt and the bringing of them into the land of promise is in fulfillment of the covenant promise to Abraham respecting the possession of the land of Canaan (Exod. 3:16, 17; 6:4–8; Ps. 105:8–12, 42–45; 106:45)."[2] A passage such as Exodus 6:4–8, set in the context of the origination of God's relationship to Israel under Moses, particularly unites the provisions of the Abrahamic and Mosaic covenants:

> 4. And I also established My covenant with them [i.e., with Abraham, Isaac, and Jacob] to give them the land of Canaan, the land in which they sojourned.
> 5. And furthermore I have heard the groaning of the sons of

---

2. Murray, *The Covenant of Grace,* p. 20.

Israel, because the Egyptians are holding them in bondage; and I have remembered My covenant.

6. Say, therefore, to the sons of Israel, "I am the Lord and I will bring you out from under the burdens of the Egyptians, and I will deliver you from their bondage. I will also redeem you with an outstretched arm and with great judgments.

7. Then I will take you for My people, and I will be your God; and you shall know that I am the Lord your God, who brought you out from under the burdens of the Egyptians

8. And I will bring you to the land which I swore to give to Abraham, Isaac, and Jacob, and I will give it to you for a possession; I am the Lord (Exod. 6:4–8).

God had made a covenantal commitment to the patriarchs. He had promised them the land of Canaan. Because of this promise, God acted sovereignly in Moses' day to deliver Israel from Egypt.

It is true that this reference to the Abrahamic covenant in the context of God's deliverance of Israel out of Egypt precedes the formal inauguration of the Mosaic covenant. It might therefore be argued that this earlier reference cannot have the effect of binding the Abrahamic covenant and its provisions with the Mosaic.

However, the sequence of historical anticipation of a covenantal relation followed by a formalizing ceremony of covenant inauguration finds repeated manifestation in Scripture. God called Abraham out of Ur of the Chaldees and declared to him all the promises that belonged to the covenant (Gen. 12:1ff.). But only subsequently did God formally institute his covenantal bond with the patriarch (cf. Gen. 15:18). In David's experience, God designated him as the anointed king of Israel long before the official sanctions of a covenantal relationship had been inaugurated (I Sam. 16:12; cf. II Sam. 7:1ff.). Christ's incarnation and public ministry ought to be regarded as a vital part of the realization of the promise concerning the new covenant. By his being clothed in human flesh, the Immanuel principle of the covenant achieved its fullest realization. By his ministry of miracles, the covenantal kingdom of God had come. Yet the formal inauguration of the new covenant era occurred after this period of historical anticipation of the realities that the covenant assured (Luke 22:20).

With that pattern in mind, it seems quite appropriate to regard God's dealings with Israel in Egypt prior to Sinai as historical anticipation of the Mosaic covenant. Quite significantly, the covenantal meal of the passover was instituted in association with the Exodus rather than with the events of Sinai.

At any rate, the promises of the Abrahamic covenant provide the historical impetus for the institution of the Mosaic covenant. God remembers his covenant with Abraham, and God acts for Israel.

Even more explicitly, the events associated immediately with the covenant inauguration at Sinai clearly connect to the deliverance from Egypt, which had preceded the formal assembly. Because of God's promises to Abraham he delivered Israel from Egypt. This fact of deliverance from the house of bondage became the basis for the decalogue (Exod. 20:1). The Ten Commandments or "ten words," which form the heart of the Mosaic covenant, rest solidly on the deliverance from Egypt achieved in fulfillment of the commitment made to Abraham.

The altar Moses built in association with the inauguration of the covenant at Sinai provides further evidence that the Mosaic covenant was bound inseparably to the Abrahamic. Moses constructs the altar "with twelve pillars for the twelve tribes of Israel" (Exod. 24:4). The tribal structure of the patriarchal era thereby finds solemn representation at the time of the inauguration of the Mosaic covenant.

This same picture of continuity emerges at the time of the inauguration of the Davidic covenant. The promises come to David not as words novel or discontinuous with the past. Instead, both God's words to David and David's response to the Lord reflect on the past experience of God's delivering Israel out of Egypt as a people for himself. The God who institutes his covenant with David is the same God who "brought up the sons of Israel from Egypt" (II Sam. 7:6; cf. v. 23).

Still further, David in his deathbed charge to Solomon explicitly gives recognition to the Mosaic foundation of his covenant. He directs Solomon to keep God's laws, "according to what is written in the law of Moses . . . so that the Lord may carry out His promise which He spoke concerning me" (I Kings 2:3f.).

Thus the crucial points of covenantal inauguration under Moses and David reflect the continuity of the covenants. As God institutes a fresh covenant with the nation of Israel, he orders the occasion so that it reflects specifically a continuity rather than a discontinuity with the past.

2. The history of life under the covenants demonstrates unity.

Israel's actual experience under the various covenants also reflects the continuity rather than the discontinuity of these relationships. Once the Mosaic covenant has been inaugurated, it is not as though the Abrahamic covenant were "shelved" for the duration. Much to the contrary, the history after Sinai continues to center on the old original promises to the patriarchs.

In reaction to the golden calf, Moses bases his plea for the mercy of God squarely on the promises of the Abrahamic covenant:

> Remember Abraham, Isaac, and Israel, Thy servants to whom Thou didst swear by Thyself, and didst say to them, "I will multiply your descendants as the stars of the heavens, and all this land of which I have spoken I will give to your descendants, and they shall inherit it forever." So the Lord changed His mind about the harm which He said He would do to His people (Exod. 32:13, 14).[3]

The plea of Moses rests on the promises of Abraham. Despite the emergence of the Mosaic covenant, the significance of the Abrahamic covenant continues.

Still later, the possession of the land under Joshua represents a fulfillment of the ancient promise to Abraham as well as the promise to Moses (cf. Gen. 15:18; Exod. 23:31; Josh. 1:3). Integral to the narrative of the establishment of the Abrahamic covenant itself may

---

3. The threat of God to annihilate Israel and to raise up a seed through Moses should not be understood as a potential severing of God's covenant with Israel. Moses himself was of the seed of Abraham. The potential judgment was to fall appropriately on the disobedient seed currently involved in apostasy.

be found a prophetic anticipation of the course of the history which found realization only after the Mosaic covenant had been introduced. Abraham received the covenantal oath sealing the promise concerning the possession of the land by his seed (Gen. 15:18). But he also was told that the possession of the land would occur only after a 400-year interlude (Gen. 15:13, 14).

The fulfillment of the promise concerning the possession of the land occurs after the Mosaic covenant of law has been instituted. This fact clearly supports Paul's later judgment that the law, coming 400 years after, could not annul the promise (Gal. 3:17).

Thus the history of Israel supports the unity of these two covenants. The Mosaic covenant did not annul or interrupt the Abrahamic covenant. The Abrahamic covenant continued to function actively after the institution of the Mosaic covenant. In the context of the history of the Mosaic covenant, the Abrahamic covenant found a basic fulfillment.

Subsequent history indicates that the Davidic covenant in its turn did not annul or interrupt the Mosaic covenant. Each of the basic triumphs and tragedies of David and his sons may be seen as the outworking of the stipulations of the Mosaic covenant.

First, Israel's monarchy moves toward localization of worship and rule. Why?

This movement toward localization must not be understood primarily as a consequence of David's political sagacity. Instead, the movement toward localization represents a consequence of the Mosaic legislation concerning a centralized sanctuary (Deut. 12:5, 11, 14, 18 etc.). This significant development under the auspices of the Davidic covenant actually roots in the previous legislation of the covenant with Moses. David permanently established the place of worship because Moses anticipated just such a development.

Even further, David's song at the time of the bringing of the ark to Jerusalem identifies this event as a fulfillment of God's covenant promises to Abraham:

Remember His covenant forever,
The word which He commanded to a thousand generations,
The covenant which He made with Abraham,
And His oath to Isaac.
He also confirmed it to Jacob for a statute,
To Israel as an everlasting covenant,
Saying, 'To you I will give the land of Canaan,
As the portion of your inheritance' (I Chron. 16:15–18).

The coronation of God as king in Zion is to be understood as a fulfillment of God's covenant promises to Abraham. The events in Davidic history which symbolize the establishment of God's throne in the land of promise relate immediately to the commitment concerning the land made to Abraham.

Subsequently, Israel's monarchy moves toward devastation at the hands of the nations. Why?

Israel's national devastation may be understood only in terms of the Mosaic covenant. The Davidic covenant indeed was in effect. But it was Israel's violation of the stipulations of the Mosaic covenant that finally determined the inevitability of their captivity. Because Israel would not keep God's commandments and statutes according to the law of Moses, exile occurred (cf. II Kings 17:13ff.).

The history of God's covenant people indicates that the covenants basically are one. The Abrahamic, Mosaic, and Davidic covenants do not supplant one another; they supplement one another. A basic unity binds them together.

A unity in genealogical administration. An additional factor emphasizes the unity of the Abrahamic, the Mosaic, and the Davidic covenants. The genealogical administration of the covenant underscores the connection of each successive covenant with previous administrations.

A wealthy individual might make an arrangement with his bank in which he would receive $1,000 per month for the rest of his life. When he died, the same payments would be made to his son. If it were possible legally, he might arrange to have the same payments made to his yet unborn grandson. Thus a line of continuity on the basis of genealogy would be established.

When God determined to relate to a people covenantally, he made his arrangement a genealogical one. This genealogical aspect of the covenant is present in the Abrahamic, the Mosaic, and the Davidic covenants. It is manifested specifically in the reference to the "seed"-concept (cf. Gen. 15:18; Exod. 20:5, 6; Deut. 7:9; II Sam. 7:12). David's son is not simply heir of the covenant promise made to David. He is heir also of the covenant promises made to Moses and Abraham. The genealogical promises of God's covenants assure his participation in the blessings of the Abrahamic and the Mosaic as well as the Davidic covenant.

This principle of the unity of the covenants established by a genealogical relationship finds rather dramatic expression in certain passages of Scripture. Two points in the renewal of the Mosaic covenant as recorded in Deuteronomy particularly may be noted. One passage occurs early in this covenant-renewal document, and one passage occurs near the end of the document.

Deuteronomy 5:2, 3 read as follows:

> The Lord our God made a covenant with us at Horeb. The Lord did not make this covenant with our fathers, but with us, with all those of us alive here today.

The original text is particularly emphatic.[4] It stresses the fact that it was the people standing in the plains of Moab at the end of the forty years in the desert who were involved in the covenant-making ceremony at Sinai (Horeb). This affirmation is particularly striking in the light of the earlier statement of Deuteronomy that all the generation of those present at Sinai finally had perished in the wilderness (Deut. 2:14, 15; cf. Num. 14:28–35; 26:63–65).

Some of those assembled in the plains of Moab had been among the juveniles at Sinai and thus had been present personally when the covenant originally was made. But the great majority of those with

---

4. The Hebrew text of Deut. 5:3b reads: כִּי אִתָּנוּ אֲנַחְנוּ אֵלֶּה פֹה הַיּוֹם כֻּלָּנוּ חַיִּים

whom the covenant was renewed in Moab were not even born when God appeared as covenant Lord at Sinai. Yet Moses affirms with startling emphasis that all of them indeed were "present" at Sinai. Because of solidarity with their forefathers by genealogical continuity they were involved in the covenant-making ceremony of Sinai.[5]

this is absurd

To dramatize Moses' words at this point, the text of Deuteronomy 5:3 might be read: ". . . with us, the Christians of the twentieth century, all of us alive in Christ today, God made the covenant at Sinai." Every generation of subsequent believers was present at the time of the making of the ancient covenant by the genealogical principle. The covenant of God to redeem a people to himself is indeed a unified whole.

The second passage emphasizing the genealogical aspect of the covenant is found in Deuteronomy 29:14f. (Heb., vv. 13f.):

> Now not with you alone am I making this covenant and this oath, but both with those who stand here with us today in the presence of the Lord our God and with those who are not with us here today.

All Israel then living had been assembled by Moses in the plains of Moab, including women and children (v. 11). Only those not yet born could not be present for the covenant renewal ceremony. But as Moses renews the covenant in Moab, he is not content to indicate merely the role of the members of the nation then living. He extends the provisions of Deuteronomy to include peoples yet to be born. Says one commentator:

> . . . it was to embrace not only those who were living then, but their descendants also. . . .[6]

---

5. This principle holds true whether the reference to the "fathers" of Deut. 5:3 be interpreted as referring to the patriarchs or to the adult generation which actually was alive at Sinai when the covenant was made. In Deut. 4:37, the reference definitely is to the patriarchal fathers. But that verse specifically proceeds to underline the role of the genealogical principle in God's covenants. Because God loved the patriarchal fathers, he chose their (lit., his) seed after them and delivered them out of Egypt.

6. C. F. Keil & F. Delitzsch, *Biblical Commentary on the Old Testament. The Pentateuch* (Edinburgh, 1880), 3:448. The reference to "those who are not with us

How far may the "generation principle" be extended legitimately? How many generations may be included?

Scripture itself answers this question. Psalm 105:8–10 celebrates the covenantal faithfulness of God toward the Abrahamic promise:

> He has remembered His covenant forever,
> The word which He commanded to a thousand generations,
> The covenant which He made with Abraham,
> And His oath to Isaac.
> Then He confirmed it to Jacob for a statute,
> To Israel as an everlasting covenant (Ps. 105:8–10).

According to this Scripture, it is to a thousand generations that the covenant promise extends. This reference to a thousand generations implies an eternal covenant. But it suggests more. The genealogical emphasis contains the idea of eternal *succession*. Never will the line of the faithful be cut off completely. In every generation the line of God's covenant people shall be maintained.

The same perspective is found in Deuteronomy 7:9:

> Know therefore that the Lord your God, He is God, the faithful God, who keeps His covenant and His lovingkindness to a thousandth generation with those who love Him and keep His commandments (Deut. 7:9).

This passage is particularly valuable for the light it gives to the decalogue in its role as summation of the Mosaic covenant. According to Exodus 20:5, 6, God will visit the iniquity of the fathers on the children to the third and fourth (generation) of those that hate him, and will show lovingkindness to "thousands" of those that love him and keep his commandments. The phrasing in the original text of

---

here today" could be understood on the surface as referring to people spatially not present. But the context clearly indicates that the whole nation had been gathered for this significant occasion. Only unborn Israelites were absent from the covenant-renewal ceremony.

this last line is almost identical to that of Deuteronomy 7:9.[7] As enlightened by the parallelism of Deuteronomy 7:9, it would appear that Exodus 20:6 refers to thousands of generations.[8] God will show the lovingkindness of the Mosaic covenant to a thousand generations.

Clearly the reference to a "thousand" generations intends to depict the concept of an eternal covenant. But just to out-literalize the literalist interpreter for the moment, some quick calculations may be made on the assumption that God's covenant promises extend to a "thousand" generations. Figuring on the basis of a modest 20 years per generation, the covenant promises would extend to 20,000 years. Since Abraham lived only 4000 years ago, at least the next 16,000 years are "covered" by the promises of the Abrahamic covenant!

It is in the context of the genealogical principle that Peter's words to the Israelites of his day are to be understood: "It is you who are the sons of the prophets, and of the covenant which God covenanted with your fathers" (Acts 3:25). The genealogical provisions of the covenants with Abraham, Moses, and David extend even into the new covenant.

One additional passage bearing on the genealogical significance of the covenant promises may be noted. This passage indicates that the covenant in its genealogical dimension does not relate merely to externalities. Instead, it includes the gift of the Spirit to God's people. Says the prophet Isaiah:

"And as for me, this is My covenant with them," says the Lord: "My Spirit which is upon you, and My words which I have put in your mouth, shall not depart from your mouth, nor from the mouth of

---

7. The two passages compare as follows:

(וְעָשָׂה) Exod. 20:6   חֶסֶד (לַאֲלָפִים לְאֹהֲבַי וּלְשֹׁמְרֵי מִצְוֹתָי

(שֹׁמֵר הַבְּרִית וְהַחֶסֶד) Deut. 7:9   לְאֹהֲבָיו וּלְשֹׁמְרֵי מִצְוֹתוֹ לְאֶלֶף דּוֹר

8. S. R. Driver, *A Critical and Exegetical Commentary on Deuteronomy* (New York, 1902), p. 102, indicates that he regards Deut. 7:9 as "a rhetorical amplification, rather than an exact interpretation, of the אלפים of Exodus 20:6." But C. F. Keil and F. Delitzsch, *Biblical Commentary on the Old Testament. The Pentateuch* (Edinburgh, 1880), 2: 116f. evaluate Exod. 20:5 differently: "The cardinal no. is used here for the ordinal, for which there was no special form in the case of אלף."

your offspring, nor from the mouth of your offspring's offspring," says the Lord, "from now and forever" (Isa. 59:21).

This text concerning the gift of the Spirit in a genealogical line finds further light from the New Testament, which indicates that the blessing of Abraham is to be related to the receiving of the Holy Spirit. According to Paul, the gift of the Spirit to new covenant believers comes in fulfillment of the covenant promises to Abraham: "Christ redeemed us from the curse of the law . . . in order that in Christ Jesus the blessing of Abraham might come to the Gentiles, so that we might receive the promise of the Spirit through faith" (Gal. 3:13f.).

As the genealogical dimension of God's covenant promises is being considered, two corollary principles must be kept in mind.

First of all, the "grafting" principle must be remembered. From the most ancient history of the Abrahamic covenant, the "in-grafting" of those not of natural Israelite birth was made a possibility (Gen. 17:12, 13). Through the incorporation of the proselyte, peoples of any nation could become Israelites in the fullest sense.

Any definition of the biblical significance of "Israel" must not fail to include this dimension. "Israel" cannot be restricted in its essence to an ethnic community. Israel must include the proselyte who does not belong to "Israel" according to the flesh, but is absorbed into Israel by process of ingrafting.

The New Testament displays an awareness of this principle when it speaks of the "ingrafting" of the Gentiles (Rom. 11:17, 19). People from all nations may become a vital aspect of the branch of God's people by faith.

Full appreciation must be given to the "ingrafting" concept as it relates to the genealogical principle. By the process of "ingrafting," the Gentile becomes an "Israelite" in the fullest possible sense (cf. Gal. 3:29). From the point of ingrafting, his subsequent seed becomes heir to the promises given to Abraham. His line now stands as legitimate heir to the genealogical promises given to the patriarch.

Secondly, and from the opposite perspective, the "pruning" principle must be noted. Not only is it possible for a new branch to be
grafted into genealogical relation to Abraham. It is also possible for
a natural seed of Abraham to be removed from its position of
privilege. This principle also may be traced back into the earliest
experience of the line of promise. To demonstrate the sovereignty of
God in the electing process, it was said, "Jacob have I loved, and Esau
have I hated" (Rom. 9:13; cf. Mal. 1:2, 3; Gen. 25:23).

This concept of pruning also must be given full weight in the
definition of "Israel." Again, "Israel" cannot be identified merely as
ethnic descendants of Abraham, for "they are not all Israel who are
descended from Israel" (Rom. 9:6). It is those who, in addition to
being related to Abraham by natural descendency, also relate to him
by faith, plus those Gentiles who are ingrafted by faith, that constitute the true Israel of God.[9]

As the concept of "pruning" is being considered, it must be
understood that this possibility does not have the effect of nullifying
the genealogical principle of natural descendency. Isaac, the chosen
seed, was a natural descendant of Abraham, as were Moses, David,
Christ, and Paul. While the "pruning" principle may threaten any
who would be presumptuous, it does not intend to suggest that
God's grace works against the natural order of creation. The grace of
God in salvation is not against creation's order; it is against sin. The
Christian must avoid being lured into a nature/grace dichotomy as
he considers the working of God in salvation. Redemption has the
effect of restoring the order of creation, and the solidarity of the
family is one of the greatest of creation's ordinances. The genealogical character of redemption's activity underscores the intention
of God to work in accord rather than in discord with this creational
ordering.

In any case, the genealogical principle of God's covenantal activity
stresses the unity of the covenants. "Unto a thousand generations"
God abides faithful to his covenanting promises. This faithfulness

---

9. See, in this regard, Paul's careful delineation of the twofold fatherhood of
Abraham in Romans 4:11, 12.

across generations serves to bind each of the successive covenants to one another. The covenants of Abraham, Moses, and David actually are successive stages of a single covenant.

Unity Incorporating the New Covenant

The new covenant, promised by Israel's prophets, does not appear as a distinctive covenantal unit unrelated to God's previous administrations. Instead, the new covenant as promised to Israel represents the consummate fulfillment of the earlier covenants.

This organic relation of the new covenant to the covenants of Abraham, Moses, and David finds explicit development both in the Old Testament prophecies concerning the covenant and in the New Testament realizations of this consummating covenant. From either perspective, the new covenant may be understood in no other way than as a realization of the prophetic projections found in the Abrahamic, Mosaic, and Davidic covenants.

Jeremiah's classic prophecy clearly relates the new covenant to its Mosaic predecessor (cf. Jer. 31:31ff.). This "new covenant" with the "house of Israel and with the house of Judah" will not be like the Mosaic covenant in its externalistic features. But the law of God as revealed to Moses shall be written on the heart. While the substance of the law will be the same, the mode of its administration will be different. The form may change, but the essence of the new covenant of Jeremiah's prophecy relates directly to the law-covenant made at Sinai.

In the following chapter, Jeremiah combines a reference to the new covenant with allusion to the ancient covenant made with Abraham. God will "faithfully plant" his people "in this land" (Jer. 32:41). But at the same time he will "give them one heart and one way" that they may fear him always (Jer. 32:39, 40).

By the intertwining of these references, the prophet combines the Abrahamic with the new covenant. These two covenants unite to form a single expectation for God's people.

The prophet Ezekiel also relates the new covenant to God's previous dispensations. Ezekiel 34:20ff. refers to a "covenant of peace" which God yet was to establish with Israel. God will set over them one shepherd, his "servant David," who will be prince over them (Ezek. 34:23, 24). Thus the prospect of the new covenant merges with the Davidic covenant of old.

In a second most remarkable passage, the prophet Ezekiel combines allusions to the Abrahamic, Mosaic, and Davidic covenants with a word of prophecy concerning Israel's future covenantal expectations. He anticipates by divine inspiration the day in which

> *not reel.* my servant David will be king over them, and they will have one shepherd [an allusion to the Davidic covenant], and they will walk in my ordinances, and keep my statutes, and observe them [an allusion to the Mosaic covenant]. And they shall live on the land that I gave to Jacob My servant, in which your fathers lived [an allusion to the Abrahamic covenant] . . . and I will make a covenant of peace with them; it will be an everlasting covenant with them [an allusion to the new covenant] (Ezek. 37:24–26).

Now all three ancient covenants combine into a single divine ordering. By the new covenant, all the promises of God find their consummation.

These prophetic passages relate the Abrahamic, Mosaic, and Davidic covenants to Israel's future covenant expectation. The new covenant does not appear in the promises of the Old Testament as some novelty previously unknown to God's people. Instead, the new covenant represents the collation of all the old covenant promises in terms of a future expectation.

So far as the history of the Old Testament people of God is concerned, the provisions and expectations of the new covenant never found realization. Prophecies concerning restoration to the land of promise received a "mini-realization" at the point of return after exile. Israel did return to the land after the 70 years of prophesied captivity had transpired. Yet this small-scale restoration, significant though it may have been, hardly could be understood as fulfilling the magnificent expectations described by Israel's prophets.[10]

It was not until the glories of the New Testament era that the new covenant received its formal inauguration. By the ministries of the incarnated son of God the new covenant finally brought to fruition the promises of the Abrahamic, the Mosaic, and the Davidic covenants.

Jesus Christ indicates the point of formal inauguration of the new covenant at the institution of the covenantal meal of the Lord's Supper. Having taken the cup, he declares: "This cup which is poured out for you is the new covenant in My blood" (Luke 22:20). At that crucial moment, Jesus communicates by word and deed that the distribution of the cup representing his blood is to be understood as the inauguration ceremony of the new covenant. No longer is the covenant a promise to be anticipated. It is a reality to be enjoyed.

The Christian celebrates the reality of this new covenant relationship each time he participates in the Lord's Supper. Paul the apostle recognizes this supper to be a covenantal feast in that he echoes the words of the Lord Jesus concerning the "new covenant" (I Cor. 11:25).

The writer to the Hebrews also recognizes the fulfillment of these new covenant promises for the present age by citing Jeremiah's prophecy at two points (Heb. 8:6-13; 10:15-18). In his contextual comments, the writer relates the "better" covenant of the present age to the "new" covenant prophesied by Jeremiah (cf. Heb. 8:6 with 9:15). In a most pointed fashion, he indicates that Jeremiah's word concerning the "new" covenant is the Holy Spirit's bearing witness to "us" (Heb. 10:15).

---

10. In explaining the prophecy of Jeremiah 32, Calvin says: "When Christians explain this passage and the like, they leave out the liberation of the people from Babylonish exile, as though these prophecies did not belong at all to the time; in this they are mistaken. And the Jews, who reject Christ, stop in that earthly deliverance. But the Prophets, as I have said, begin with the return of the people, but they set Christ also in the middle, that the faithful might know that the return was but a slight taste of the full grace, which was alone to be expected from Christ; for it was then, indeed, that God really planted his people" (*Commentaries on the Book of the Prophet Jeremiah and the Lamentations,* [Grand Rapids, 1950], 4: 220f.).

Thus it may be concluded that the covenants of Abraham, Moses, and David find fulfillment in the reality of the new covenant of the present day. God's covenants throughout the ages are one. This oneness finds splendid testimony in the consummating character of the new covenant.

Unity Extending to the Covenants Made with Noah and Adam

To this point, the covenants of Abraham, Moses, and David have been viewed as organically related. These three covenants have been seen as finding their combined consummation in the new covenants.

Now the question must be asked: How do the covenantal administrations prior to Abraham relate to these later covenants? Does the unity of God's covenant include these earlier administrations? Answering this question rather concisely, the following may be noted.

The covenant with Noah provides the preservative structure by which God's purpose to redeem a people to himself may be realized. "So long as the earth remains," the provisions of God's longsuffering to sinful man as delineated in the covenant with Noah continue to be in effect (Gen. 8:22). Even today, the regularity of seasons remains established because of God's covenanting word with Noah. This ancient bond still provides the framework in which redemption may be accomplished.

In a similar manner, the curse pronounced soon after the fall of man was at the same time a commitment by the Almighty to redeem a people to himself. This commitment made to Adam in sin continues to have significance. Quite dramatically in his letter to the Romans, the apostle Paul alludes to the covenantal commitment of God to guarantee the triumph of the seed of the redeemed over Satan: "And the God of peace will soon crush Satan under your feet" (Rom. 16:20; cf. Gen. 3:15). God's word of commitment spoken first to the serpent has abiding significance today.

Finally, the question of the relation of the covenant established at creation to God's redemptive covenant must be raised. It must be acknowledged that certain key aspects of God's bond with pre-fallen man came to an end with the entrance of sin. For example, "Adam" does not equal "Everyman" in his original state of innocence, so that every subsequent man faces the same option to choose for or against eating the forbidden fruit. Nevertheless, man continues to exist throughout the ages as a being made in God's image with certain obligations to the Creator. He still has the responsibility to multiply, to subdue the earth, and to offer the work of his hands to the glory of the Creator/Redeemer.

Because of this continuing relationship of creature to Creator, it may be said also of the original bond of God to man that it continues to have abiding significance. The covenantal relation established by creation permeates the whole history of God's forming a people for himself.

Conclusion

The covenant structure of Scripture manifests a marvelous unity. God, in binding a people to himself, never changes. For this reason, the covenants of God relate organically to one another. From Adam to Christ, a unity of covenantal administration characterizes the history of God's dealing with his people.

THEMATIC UNITY OF THE DIVINE COVENANTS

The divine covenants of Scripture are bound together not only by a structural unity. They manifest also a thematic unity. This unity of theme is the heart of the covenant as it relates God to his people.

Throughout the biblical record of God's administration of the covenant, a single phrase recurs as the summation of the covenant relationship: "I shall be your God, and you shall be my people." The constant repetition of this phrase or its equivalent indicates the unity of God's covenant. This phrase may be designated as the "Immanuel principle" of the covenant. The heart of the covenant is the declaration that "God is with us."

Several aspects of this unifying theme of God's covenant may be noted:

1. First of all, *this theme appears explicitly in connection with the Abrahamic, the Mosaic, the Davidic, and the new covenant.* The words of this formula consistently manifest themselves as the heart of the covenant.

The first occurrence of the phrase is found in Genesis 17:7 in connection with the establishment of circumcision as the seal of the Abrahamic covenant. God reassures Abraham of the settled character of his covenantal commitment. The Lord affirms his intention "to be God to you and to your seed after you." The connection of the phrase to the genealogical promise emphasizes the abiding significance of this relationship.

Under the Mosaic covenant, the phrase appears frequently with pointed emphasis. The essence of the covenant mediated through Moses has to do with the deliverance of Israel from the bondage of Egypt. Israel must be freed from the pollution of the Egyptians in order to become the Lord's people. In reference to this redemption, God says: "I will take you for my people, and I will be your God" (Exod. 6:6, 7).

Essentially the same note is struck at the point of covenantal inauguration at Sinai. God reminds Israel that he delivered them from Egypt, bore them on eagles' wings, and brought them to himself. If they continue in obedience, they will be his "special treasure among all the peoples" (Exod. 19:4, 5).

This same connection between the formula summarizing the essence of the covenant and the deliverance from Egypt is found elsewhere in the Pentateuch. God says, "I am the Lord, who brought you up from the land of Egypt, *to be your God*" (Lev. 11:45). At another point, Moses reminds the people: "the Lord has taken you and brought you out of the iron furnace, from Egypt, *to be a people for His own possession"* (Deut. 4:20).

As Israel stands before God in the plains of Moab to renew the bonds of the covenant, Moses indicates the express purpose of their gathering. They are "to enter into the covenant with the Lord your God . . . in order that he may establish you today as His people and that He may be your God, just as He spoke to you and as He swore to your fathers, to Abraham, Isaac, and Jacob" (Deut. 29:13, NASB; Heb. v. 12). The very purpose of the covenant (לְמַעַן) consists of God's intention to make a people to be his own.

Thus the identical summary of the essence of covenant is found in the Mosaic and the Abrahamic covenants. This fact binds these two epochs together. In each case, God's purpose is to make a people for himself.

The same formula of covenantal summation appears in the Davidic covenant. At one crucial point in the history of the monarchy, the covenant with David is related explicitly to the essence of God's covenantal commitment. The high priest Jehoiada is replacing the corrupted Queen Athaliah with seven-year-old Jehoash, in order to maintain the line of David. The narrative of Kings indicates the significance of the event:

> And Jehoiada cut the covenant between Yahveh and between the king, and between the people to be a people for Yahveh; and between the king and between the people (II Kings 11:17).

The parallel account in II Chronicles 23:16 reads as follows:

> And Jehoiada cut a covenant between him [self] and between all the people, and between the king, to be a people for Yahveh.

Several points of interest arise when these two passages are studied in conjunction with one another. Did Jehoiada institute two, three, or four covenantal relations? How do these various covenants relate to one another? These questions deserve careful consideration.

For the present, it is sufficient to note that the essence of the

David substitutes for all the people

divine covenant finds explicit expression in the Davidic covenant. The maintenance of the Davidic line in covenantal relation with Yahveh is related specifically with Israel's being "a people for Yahveh."[11]

The prophet Ezekiel also discusses God's commitment to David in terms of the essential theme of the covenant. Ezekiel modifies the normal formula. As the full phrase generally occurs in Scripture, it contains two elements: (1) I shall be your God, and (2) you shall be my people. But Ezekiel dramatizes the relation of the covenantal formula to the Davidic covenant. The prophet declares: "I Yahveh will be their God, and my servant David prince in their midst" (Ezek. 34:24). As covenantal representative, David substitutes for the whole of the people. Because he belongs to the Lord, all the people belong to the Lord. The essence of the covenant finds its fulfillment through God's intimate relation with the heir to the Davidic throne.

The new covenant also is interpreted in its essence by the use of this phrase "to be a people for the Lord."[12] Some rather interesting dimensions of the future covenantal expectations for God's people in Old Testament times may be found particularly in the prophecies of Zechariah.

In Zechariah 2:11 (in Heb., v. 15), the prophet anticipates the day in which "many nations" will be joined to Yahveh. "In that day," says the Lord, "they will be to me for a people, and I shall dwell in your midst." Now the essence of covenantal relationship explicitly is being extended to the inclusion of Gentiles.

In Zechariah 8:8, the prophet develops the ethical significance of the essence of the covenantal bond. The Lord declares that in the day of the full restoration of the people of God, "they will be my people and I will be their God in truth and righteousness." On the basis of this promise, Zechariah's contemporaries are admonished to "speak

---

11. These verses represent the only instance in which it is stated that the essence of the covenant is making a people for Yahveh. In all other cases, so far as the present writer has observed, the formula speaks of making a people for _Elohim_.

12. Cf. Jer. 24:7; 31:33; 32:37f.

the truth to one another" (Zech. 8:16). Quite interestingly, this verse finds explicit application to God's new covenant people as they enjoy the unity of the body of Christ. The people of the new covenant are to "speak truth, each one of you, with his neighbor, for we are members of one another" (Eph. 4:25).

Explicit application of the essence of the new covenant to God's people in the present age is found in Hebrews 8:10 and II Corinthians 6:16. In the words of Paul to the Corinthians, Christians are to separate from unbelievers, for God has said: "I will be their God, and they shall be my people" (II Cor. 6:16). This call to a separated holiness represents a most appropriate application of the covenant formula, since Moses originally related the phrase to Israel's separation from the uncleanness of Egypt (see particularly Lev. 11:44ff.).

It may be affirmed, therefore, that the summarizing essence of the covenant is applied explicitly in Scripture to the Abrahamic, the Mosaic, the Davidic and the new covenants. The uniformity of application of this single theme binds the covenants together.

2. Secondly, *the theme* "I shall be your God and you shall be my people" *is developed particularly in association with God's actually dwelling in the midst of his people.* The reality of God's residing among his people displays an ever-increasing significance throughout Scripture. It moves from the figure of the tabernacle to the figure of the temple to the figure of the city of God. It involves the incarnate Christ, the church of Christ, and the final glorification of God's people. In each case, God's dwelling among his people is related directly to the heart of the covenant concept: "I shall be your God and you shall be my people." By dwelling in their midst, God seals the reality of the fact that he indeed is their God and they indeed are his people.

The essence of the covenantal relation found its initial fulfillment in the form of the tabernacle. God commanded Israel to construct the tabernacle that he might dwell among them (Exod. 25:8). The tabernacle was to be the place of God's meeting with his people (Exod. 29:42–44). The effect of the consecration of the tent of meeting was that God would dwell among the sons of Israel, *and would be their God* (Exod. 29:45; cf. Lev. 26:9–13).

The emphasis throughout the book of Deuteronomy on "the place" in which the Lord was to "choose for his name to dwell" anticipates the centralization of God's dwelling in Zion in the midst of his people.[13] At the heart of the theocracy is the principle of God's being with his people.

Projections concerning the future also relate God's dwelling in the midst of his people to covenant fulfillment. The prophet Ezekiel expands on the figure of God's tabernacle:

> I will make a covenant of peace with them; it will be an everlasting covenant with them. And I will place them and multiply them, and will set My sanctuary in their midst forever. My dwelling place also will be with them; and I will be their God, and they will be My people. And the nations will know that I am the Lord who sanctifies Israel, when My sanctuary is in their midst forever (Ezek. 37:26–28).

The summarizing formula of the covenant is related directly to future expectations concerning the sanctuary. "I shall be their God and they shall be my people" finds its realization in the form of the temple.

In terms of the consummate experience of the new covenant, the theme of Immanuel as the sum of the covenant also plays a central role. God "tabernacles" in human flesh by the presence of the incarnate Son (John 1:14). God's people are the temple of the Lord, "being built together into a dwelling of God in the Spirit" (Eph. 2:21f.). The great multitude of the redeemed which no one can number serve the Lord day and night in his temple, having God's tabernacle spread over them (Rev. 7:15).

The final echo of the covenantal formula in Scripture is found in Revelation 21:3:

> And I heard a loud voice from the throne, saying, "Behold, the tabernacle of God is among men, and He shall dwell among them, and they shall be His people, and God Himself shall be among them."

---

13. Deut. 12:5, 11, 14; 14:22; 16:2, 6, 7, 11, etc.

Quite interestingly, the context of this passage relates closely to the creation-ordering of things. A "new heaven and a new earth" prepare the way for the consummate dwelling of God among his people (Rev. 21:1).

This echo of creation in relation to the theme of the covenant supports the suggestion that the Immanuel principle binds the whole of Scripture together. At the heart of the covenant may be found the substance that unifies the long history of God's dwelling with his people.

3. Finally, *the theme* "I shall be your God and you shall be my people" *reaches its climax through its embodiment in a single person*. Not in the tabernacle, but in Christ the covenant theme finds consummate fulfillment.

The prophet Isaiah explicitly develops this particular theme. Thus the essence of the covenant concept unites with Israel's messianic expectations. The anticipation of the future focuses on a single individual who shall embody in himself the essence of the covenant, while at the same time functioning as messianic head.[14]

This most significant individual fulfills his role as embodiment of the covenant through suffering in behalf of others. He is the servant of the Lord, regal in character, but destined to suffer. He is God's special instrument, appointed to be in himself "a covenant to the people, and a light to the nations" (Isa. 42:6; cf. Isa. 49:8; 55:3, 4).

In this single person all God's purposes find climactic fulfillment. He is the head of God's kingdom and the embodiment of God's covenant. In his person "I shall be your God and you shall be my people" achieves incarnated reality.

Because the various strands of hope for redemption converge on this single person, He becomes the unifying focus of all Scripture. Both "kingdom" and "covenant" unite under "Immanuel." It is not "the" blood of the covenant that he administers, as does Moses (Exod. 24:8). Instead he solemnly declares "this is *my* blood of the covenant . . ." (Matt. 26:28, cf. Luke 22:20). As kingly covenant-

---

14. Cf. W. Eichrodt, *Theology of the Old Testament* (Philadelphia, 1961), 1: 61f.

mediator, he does not administer merely the laws of the kingdom. It is himself that he administers to the people.

The covenants of God are one. The recurring summation of the essence of the covenant testifies to this fact.

In the person of Jesus Christ, the covenants of God achieve incarnational unity. Because Jesus, as the Son of God and mediator of the covenant, cannot be divided, the covenants cannot be divided. He himself guarantees the unity of the covenants, because he himself is the heart of each of the various covenantal administrations.

4
Diversity in the Divine Covenants

BOTH structurally and thematically the covenants of God are one. A covenantal unity characterizes God's dealings with men from creation to consummation.

But the various covenants administered throughout history do not appear as monotonous duplications of one another. A luxuriant diversity of covenantal administration emerges as history progresses.

Three basic structural distinctions have been suggested by various theologians with respect to covenantal diversity. All three of these distinctions deserve consideration.

PRE-CREATION/POST-CREATION COVENANTS

Since the Reformation, distinctions have been made between a pre-creation covenantal bond among the persons of the Trinity and a historical covenant between God and men. The pre-creation covenant between Father and Son has been designated variously as the "covenant of redemption," the "eternal covenant," the "counsel of peace," or the "counsel of redemption."[1] This particular "covenant" finds no specific development in the classic creeds of the Reformers of the sixteenth and seventeenth centuries. But it has been recognized broadly among covenant theologians since that time.

The intention of God from eternity to redeem a people to himself certainly must be affirmed. Before the foundation of the world God set his covenantal love on his people.

But affirming the role of redemption in the eternal counsels of God is not the same as proposing the existence of a pre-creation covenant between Father and Son. A sense of artificiality flavors the effort to structure in covenantal terms the mysteries of God's eternal counsels. Scripture simply does not say much on the pre-creation shape of the decrees of God. To speak concretely of an intertrinitarian "covenant" with terms and conditions between Father and Son mutually endorsed before the foundation of the world is to extend the bounds of scriptural evidence beyond propriety.

It should be noted further that most of the discussion in this area built on the assumption that a covenant was to be defined as a mutual contract, not as a sovereignly administered bond. In view of more recent light on the character of the biblical covenants, the feasibility of a "covenant" among members of the Trinity appears even less likely.

COVENANT OF WORKS/COVENANT OF GRACE

The second structural distinction among the divine covenants which generally is recognized has greater scriptural support.

---

1. For a historical survey of the various approaches to this pre-creation covenant, see Charles Hodge, *Systematic Theology* (Grand Rapids, 1952), 2: 354ff.; L. Berkhof, *Systematic Theology* (Grand Rapids, 1972), pp. 265ff.; and Ken M. Campbell, *God's Covenant,* unpublished Th.M. thesis, Philadelphia: Westminster Theological Seminary (1971), pp. 6ff.

Classically, covenant theology has spoken of a "covenant of works" and a "covenant of grace."[2]

The term "covenant of works" has been applied to God's relation to man prior to his fall into sin. This relationship has been characterized as a covenant of "works" in an effort to emphasize the testing period of Adam. If Adam should "work" properly, he would receive the blessings promised by God.

The phrase "covenant of grace" has been used to describe the relationship of God to his people subsequent to man's fall into sin. Since man became incapable of works suitable for meriting salvation, this period has been understood as being controlled primarily by the grace of God.

This division of God's covenant dealings with men in terms of a "covenant of works" and a "covenant of grace" has much to commend it. It emphasizes properly the absolute necessity of recognizing a pre-fall relationship between God and man which required perfect obedience as the meritorious ground of blessing. In this structure, Adam cannot be regarded purely as a mythical figure. In real history God bound himself to the man he had made to be "very good."

This distinction also provides an overarching structure to unite the totality of God's relation to man in his fallen state. Because of its inherent emphasis on the unity of God's redemptive program, this structure delivers the church from the temptation to draw too strongly a dichotomy between old and new testaments.

However, the terminology traditionally associated with this scheme has significant limitations.[3] No criticism may be offered with respect to the general structure of this distinction. Two basic epochs of God's dealing with man must be recognized: pre-fall and post-fall. All the dealings of God with man since the fall must be seen as possessing a basic unity.

---

2. Cf. *The Westminster Confession of Faith*, VII, 1–6; *The Westminster Larger Catechism*, Questions 30–35; *The Westminster Shorter Catechism*, Question 20.

3. See in this connection the treatment of Meredith G. Kline, *By Oath Consigned* (Grand Rapids, 1968), p. 32.

Yet the nomenclature chosen to designate these two epochs suffers from a lack of preciseness. To speak of a covenant of "works" in contrast with a covenant of "grace" appears to suggest that grace was not operative in the covenant of works. As a matter of fact, the totality of God's relationship with man is a matter of grace. Although "grace" may not have been operative in the sense of a merciful relationship despite sin, the creational bond between God and man indeed was gracious.

This terminology further suggests that works have no place in the covenant of grace. But from the biblical perspective, works play a most essential role in the covenant of grace. Christ works for the salvation of his people. His accomplishment of righteousness for sinful men represents an essential aspect of redemption. Still further, those redeemed in Christ certainly must work. They are "created in Christ Jesus unto good works" (Eph. 2:10). Scripture consistently indicates that the final judgment of man shall be according to works. While salvation is by faith, judgment is by works.

Furthermore, the covenant of "works" terminology has tended to concentrate attention on one single element of the creational bond between God and man. The non-eating of the tree of the knowledge of good and evil has been viewed as that one "work" which man as created had to perform. Rather than seeing the broader implications of man's responsibility to his Creator, attention has been directed more exclusively toward Adam's probation-test.[4]

---

4. The contrast between giving full expression to the broader responsibilities of man at creation and concentrating more particularly on the probation-test may be illustrated by a comparison of question 20 of *The Westminster Larger Catechism* and the corresponding statement (question 12) of *The Westminster Shorter Catechism. The Larger Catechism* delineates rather fully God's providence toward man at creation:

"Q. 20. What was the providence of God toward man in the estate in which he was created?

"A. The providence of God toward man in the estate in which he was created was, the placing him in paradise, appointing him to dress it, giving him liberty to eat of the fruit of the earth, putting the creatures under his dominion, ordaining marriage for his help, and instituting the Sabbath; entering into a covenant of life with him, upon condition of personal, perfect, and perpetual obedience, of which the tree of life was a pledge; and forbidding to eat of the tree of the knowledge of good and evil, upon pain of death."

Because of these limitations in the terminology "covenant of works" and "covenant of grace," different designations for these two great covenantal epochs are desirable. The terms "covenant of creation" and "covenant of redemption" may serve much more appropriately as categorizations of God's bond with man before and after the fall.[5] The "covenant of creation" refers to the bond which God established with man by creation. The "covenant of redemption" encompasses the various administrations by which God has bound himself to man since the fall.

OLD COVENANT/NEW COVENANT

The third distinction among God's covenants relates to the diversity of administration within the framework of God's dealings with fallen man. The incarnation of Christ represents the most basic differentiation-point in this history. The bond of God with man before Christ may be called "old covenant" and the bond of God with man after Christ may be called "new covenant." The "old covenant" may be characterized as "promise," as "shadow," as "prophecy"; the "new covenant" may be characterized as "fulfillment," as "reality," as "realization."

The *Shorter Catechism* directs attention in question and answer to the "special" act of providence toward man at creation:

"Q. 12. What special act of providence did God exercise toward man, in the estate wherein he was created?

"A. When God had created man, he entered into a covenant of life with him, upon condition of perfect obedience; forbidding him to eat of the tree of the knowledge of good and evil, upon pain of death."

The catechisms clearly indicate self-consciousness in treating either the more general "providence of God toward man" at creation (*The Larger Catechism*) or God's "special act of providence" concerning the test of probation (*The Shorter Catechism*). Concentration on the probation-test certainly is justified in the light of the pivotal role of this test in God's original relationship to man. Yet the inherent possibility of failing to remember the broader context of creational obligations ought to be noted.

5. These categories are suggested by Meredith G. Kline, *By Oath Consigned* (Grand Rapids, 1968), p. 37.

The entire structure of the letter to the Hebrews builds on this basic distinction. Essential to the total presentation of the Christian gospel in that Epistle is the concept of promise in the old covenant achieving fulfillment in the new.

In his letter to the Galatians, the apostle Paul sets several dynamic concepts over against one another. Central among contrasting covenantal perspectives is his development of the distinction between the old covenant and the new.

Paul's ultimate purpose in the entire discussion is to contrast the legalism of current Judaizers with the graciousness of the new covenant (Gal. 2:14–16; 3:1; 4:31–5:2). But in order to heighten that distinction, he sets up several secondary contrasts.

To avoid a blatant misreading of the apostle's primary intention, it is essential to consider these secondary contrasts as they relate to his primary purpose. Unless the central argument of the apostle is kept in view, an absolutizing of relative contrasts may mislead the reader seriously.

The apostle himself modifies each of the contrasts he sets up, with one exception. Sometimes explicitly, sometimes implicitly, he tempers the absoluteness of his antitheses. However, one contrast he maintains resolutely. No compromise whatever may be made between the destructive proposals of the Judaizers and the gospel of Christ. Every other contrast developed by the apostle enforces the absoluteness of this essential distinction.

First of all, Paul contrasts the whole of the historical period before the coming of Christ with the age of the new covenant. The period "before faith came" contrasts drastically with the time in which "faith has come" (Gal. 3:23, 25). The coming of Christ, and his consequent position as object of faith, has altered the entire course of history. God's dealings with men cannot return to the old patterns once the Christ has come. The Judaizers are in error because they have not taken into account adequately the radical difference Christ's coming has made for history.

Yet with all the force of the absolutes involved in the apostle's presentation, an inherent modification also is present. For the very same gospel was "preached beforehand" to Abraham (Gal. 3:8). It is along with Abraham the believer that the Christian today enters into his state of blessedness (Gal. 3:9). From one perspective an absolute antithesis may be drawn between the periods of history before and after the coming of Christ. The old covenant and the new covenant are radically distinct from one another. But from another perspective a single way of salvation always has been present.[6]

Secondly, Paul contrasts the Abrahamic and the Mosaic periods of the Old Testament (Gal. 3:15–19). The apostle makes it plain that the inheritance of God's blessing is not based on law, but on promise. By such an antithesis, he sets the Mosaic covenant of law over against the Abrahamic covenant of promise.

Yet it must be recognized again that Paul's ultimate purpose in this entire discussion is to distance the true gospel of Christ from every approximation of the Judaizers' false gospel. His discussion focuses on law as isolated from promise and its fulfillment in Christ. Law under Moses never was intended to function apart from promise. Separated from its promise-dimension, which reached its fulfillment in Christ, law never could provide a way for making sinners righteous. Promise as under Abraham was the only effective way by which sinners could be justified before God throughout the history of the old covenant.

While the apostle quite vigorously sets promise over against law, he actually sees a basic unity between the Abrahamic and the Mosaic covenants in contrast with the legalistic proposals of the Judaizers. He emphatically focuses on the legal requirement of circumcision as that point which distinguishes the anti-gospel of the Judaizers from

---

6. The primary reference to the period "before faith came" in Gal. 3:23 contrasts specifically the Mosaic period with the present age. But this fact does not permit the marking off of the Mosaic period so that it stands alone in old covenant history as a time in which "faith" had not "come." Clearly men were saved by grace through faith alone in Moses' time as well as in Abraham's time. The phrase must include the Abrahamic period as well, even though "law" was not functioning in the same manner under Abraham as it was under Moses. The coming of "faith" in Gal. 3:23, whether it be understood objectively or subjectively, sets the historical period after the coming of Christ over against the historical period before his coming.

the true gospel of Christ. If the Galatians should receive circumcision, Christ will not benefit them (Gal. 5:2). Yet circumcision, it must be remembered, historically found its initial institution under the provisions of the Abrahamic covenant of promise rather than the Mosaic covenant of law. This fact clearly indicates that the ultimate contrast in Paul's mind is not between the Abrahamic and the Mosaic covenants, but between the way of justification advocated by the Judaizers and the way of justification provided by Christ. So long as God's people lived in the age of shadowy rituals and revelations, circumcision served a proper function. The "husk" of externalities had a useful purpose. But now that the reality has appeared in history, insistence on continuation of the husk-forms insults and nullifies the reality.

Thus the emphatic antithesis in Paul between the "law-covenant" and the "promise-covenant" must not be allowed to detract from the unity of God's dealings under the covenant of redemption.[7] Elsewhere Paul clearly affirms that the law-covenant did not annul the covenant of promise (Gal. 3:17). Ultimately in Galatians 4, Paul specifically traces the antithesis which he has in mind to the contrast between the "present Jerusalem" and the "Jerusalem above" (Gal. 4:25f.). By his reference to the "present Jerusalem," Paul alludes to the understanding of the Mosaic law-covenant maintained by the contemporary Judaizers. The new covenant obviously stands in starkest contrast with the legalism of the Judaism current in Paul's

---

7. Cf. the statement of Meredith G. Kline that the Sinaitic covenant as such ". . . made inheritance to be by law, not by promise—not by faith, but by works" (*By Oath Consigned,* [Grand Rapids, 1968], p. 23). Kline is to be commended for his effort to capture the historical distinctiveness of the law-covenant. He does acknowledge that Paul ultimately blends law and promise under a single program for man's salvation.

Yet it simply is not true that under the Mosaic law-covenant inheritance was "not by faith, but by works." Indeed, the law was calculated to amplify the radicalness of sinful man's inclination toward self-trust. But the law never was intended to offer an alternative way of salvation. Kline's appeal to Christ as ultimate law-fulfiller certainly is true. But this affirmation does not bridge adequately the principial chasm between law and promise which he has created. Rather than affirming alternative ways of achieving inheritance by law and by promise, the relative emphasis of both law and promise in both covenants must be clarified.

day. But this misappropriation of the Mosaic law-covenant certainly cannot be equated with God's original intention in the giving of the law. The Judaizers of Paul's day were not correct in their understanding of Mosaic law. The full force of the apostle's polemic is directed against their misunderstanding. Here is the key question: Were the Judaizers correct in their understanding of Mosaic law?

Indeed, it should be acknowledged that law in distinction from promise was given to reveal sin (Gal. 3:19). The radicalness of this exposure of human depravity is seen in the fact that the law, by its very form, was calculated to uncover sinful man's inclination to self-trust. In this respect, Sinai represents a covenantal administration in sharpest contrast with Abraham's promise-covenant. But this contrast must not be understood as rupturing the unity and progress of the revelation of the covenant of redemption.

Old and new covenants merge into a basic harmony. Abrahamic and Mosaic covenants unite in the purposes of God's grace. But no unifying factor whatsoever arises to harmonize the message of the Judaizers with the message of Christ. This antithesis is absolute.

Diversity indeed exists in the various administrations of God's covenants. This diversity enriches the wonder of God's plan for his people. But the diversity ultimately merges into a single purpose overarching the ages.

Having considered the basic options for denoting diversity among God's covenants, the various historical manifestations of the covenant of redemption may be categorized according to their specific emphases:

> Adam: the covenant of commencement
> Noah: the covenant of preservation
> Abraham: the covenant of promise
> Moses: the covenant of law
> David: the covenant of the kingdom
> Christ: the covenant of consummation

The relation of the various covenants to one another may be diagrammed as follows:

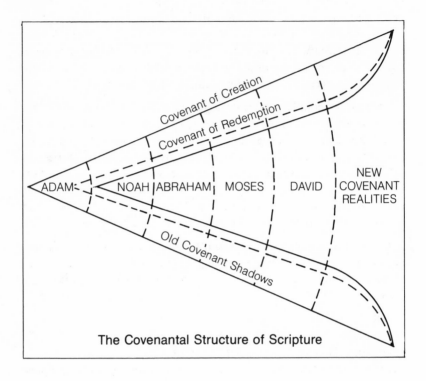

The Covenantal Structure of Scripture

Features in the diagram intend to represent several significant aspects of the divine covenants in their diversity:

1. The ultimate purpose of the covenant of creation finds realization in the covenant of redemption. The intended goals of the two covenants correspond. By redemption, the original purposes of creation are achieved—or even excelled.

2. The various administrations of the covenant of redemption relate organically to one another. They do not replace one another chronologically. Instead, each successive covenant expands on previous administrations.

3. Each of the shadowy, prophetic administrations of the covenant of redemption (dotted lines) finds its fulfillment in Christ, the personal embodiment of the new covenant. In him is found the fulfillment of all God's covenant purposes.

PART TWO

5

The Covenant
of Creation

BY the very act of creating man in his own likeness and image, God established a unique relationship between himself and creation. In addition to this sovereign creation-act, God spoke to man, thus determining precisely the role of man in creation.

Through this creating/speaking relationship, God established sovereignly a life-and-death bond. This original bond between God and man may be called the covenant of creation.

The creation bond between God and man may be discussed in terms of its general and its focal aspects. The general aspect of the covenant of creation relates to the broader responsibilities of man to his Creator. The focal aspect of the covenant of creation relates to the more specific responsibility of man arising from the special point of probation or testing instituted by God.

The recognition of both these aspects in the covenant of creation has far-reaching implications. Because of an exclusive concentration on the specific test concerning the tree of the knowledge of good and evil, the broader responsibilities of man as created in God's image frequently have been ignored. This narrowed perspective has been extended into considerations of the redemptive purposes of God. The result has been the development of a gaping deficiency in the church's concept of man's redemption. By thinking too narrowly about the covenant of creation, the Christian church has come to cultivate a deficiency in its entire world-and-life view. Instead of being kingdom-oriented, as was Christ, it has become exclusively church-oriented.

THE COVENANT OF CREATION: ITS GENERAL ASPECT

Man, as part of creation, is responsible to obey the ordinances embedded in creation's structure. Three ordinances, inherent in God's creational orderings, deserve particular attention. They are the Sabbath, marriage, and labor. Each of these creational orderings stands as an inviolable principle inherent in the structure of the world as God has ordained it.

The Sabbath

The institution of the Sabbath roots in the pattern of God's creative activity. By following the order of six and one in his making of the world, God established a structural pattern for his creation.

The significance of the Sabbath principle for the ordering of creation appears not only in the pattern of six days of creative activity followed by a day of rest. It also appears explicitly in the statement that God "blessed the sabbath day and sanctified it" (Gen. 2:3).

When Scripture records that God "blessed" the Sabbath day in conjunction with his creational activity, it obviously cannot mean that God spoke meaninglessly into a vacuum. His blessing of this day had a significant effect on the world. Furthermore, the reference to God's blessing the day should not be interpreted as meaning that

God blessed the day with respect to himself. It was with respect to his creation, and with respect to man in particular that God blessed the Sabbath day. As Jesus indicated pointedly, "the Sabbath came into being (ἐγένετο) for the sake of man (διὰ τὸν ἄνθρωπον) (Mark 2:27). Because it was for the good of man and the whole of creation, God instituted the Sabbath.

Neither antinomianism nor dispensationalism may remove the obligation of the Christian today to observe the creation ordinance of the Sabbath. The absence of any explicit command concerning Sabbath-observance prior to Moses does not relegate the Sabbath principle to temporary legislation of the law-epoch. The creational character of God's sabbath-blessing must be remembered. From the very beginning, God set a distinctive blessing on the Sabbath.

The fourth commandment of the decalogue appeals to the creational character of the sabbath-structure as the basis for its particular requirements. Because of the Lord's work-and-rest pattern in creation, man must "remember the sabbath day to sanctify it" (Exod. 20:8, 11). Even the beasts of the field are to participate in this rest (v. 10), indicating God's intention to bless the whole of creation by this institution.

God blessed man through the Sabbath by delivering him from slavery to work. By the grace of God, provision for seven days of livelihood would come from only six days of labor. Freely God gave relief from work 52 days out of the year, one and one-half months out of the 12. Just as God chose to rest from his labor on the seventh day, so man must choose to cease from his. On this day, the Lord rested from all his creational labors, and "refreshed himself" in them (Exod. 31:17). In the same way, God's people are to "refresh themselves" in association with this day (Exod. 23:12).

The sanctifying of the Sabbath indicates that the Lord of creation has established the pattern by which he is to be honored as Creator. Certainly it is appropriate that times should be appointed for men to worship God. By sanctifying the Sabbath, God has indicated that he expects men regularly to bring themselves as well as the fruit of their labor to be consecrated before him.

Subsequent revelation in Scripture indicates that this Sabbath principle manifested itself in a variety of ways among God's people. Not only did Israel celebrate a weekly Sabbath. The nation was instructed in addition to celebrate both a Sabbath year and a jubilee Sabbath.

Once every seven years, the land of Israel was to celebrate a Sabbath to the Lord (Lev. 25:1-7). The purpose of this rest was to protect the land from abuse as well as to provide refreshment for man. The land itself was to enjoy a Sabbath rest, a "sabbath to the Lord" (Lev. 25:4). Although the land was at man's disposal, it was not at his disposal without restriction. In a most unique sense, the land was the Lord's.

At the same time, the Sabbath year indicated something about man in relation to the world. Man was not to be captive to the creation. The great purpose for which God's people existed was not to be found in the "uninterrupted tilling" of the ground. Instead, God's people were to live in "the peaceful enjoyment of the fruits of the earth."[1]

Israel also was to celebrate the jubilee year. At the end of seven groups of seven years, a special Sabbath celebration was to be held. Each fiftieth year had a unique sabbatical significance (Lev. 25:8-22). In this year the trumpet was to sound and liberty was to be proclaimed throughout all the land (v. 9). All debts were to be cancelled.

Interestingly, the prophet Isaiah subsequently employed this sabbatical imagery to describe the proclamation of liberty associated with the coming of the anointed Messiah (Isa. 61:1-3). Christ himself chose this prophetic message to characterize his personal ministry as he began to preach in Nazareth (Luke 4:18, 19).

This larger usage of the sabbatical concept as it relates to the ministry of Christ may serve to introduce a further aspect of the Sabbath in Scripture. Not only does the Sabbath relate to the repetitive and sacral patterns of God's people, such as the weekly Sabbath,

---

1. C. F. Keil and F. Delitzsch. *Biblical Commentary on the Old Testament. The Pentateuch* (Grand Rapids, 1949-50), 1:457.

the seventh-year Sabbath and the year of jubilee. The Sabbath also relates to the linear dimension of history. In the Sabbath may be seen the pattern of progress in God's dealings with his people through the entire extent of human history.

The "rest" of Israel's conquest under Joshua accords with this Sabbath principle. Israel moves from captivity in Egypt through wandering in the wilderness toward "rest" in Canaan. Moses anticipates the "rest" which God was to give Israel from all its enemies (Deut. 12:9, 10). The psalmist subsequently refers to God's denial of "rest" for Israel because of their sin in the wilderness (Ps. 95:11). The New Testament interprets this history explicitly in terms of the Sabbath principle. Because Joshua could not give Israel "rest," a "Sabbath" yet remains for the people of God (Heb. 4:8, 9). The "Sabbath" thereby provides a significant key to the understanding of the history of God's people. Not only in Israel's repetitive patterns of weekly worship, but also in God's ordering of history, the Sabbath plays a prominent role in determining Israel's history.

Israel's 70 years of captivity also are interpreted by Scripture in terms of the Sabbath principle. Because of their sin, the land of Israel had to observe an enforced accumulation of Sabbaths during the people's exile (Lev. 26:33-35). The years of captivity had to compensate for Israel's neglect of the sabbatical principle.

Other Scripture interprets Israel's captivity in terms of the same principle. According to the book of Chronicles, Israel must remain expelled from their land until the reign of the king of Persia

> to fulfill the word of the Lord by the mouth of Jeremiah, until the land had enjoyed its sabbaths. All the days of its desolations it kept sabbath until seventy years were complete (II Chron. 36:21).

These considerations indicate that the Sabbath-principle structures history. In a most dramatic fashion, the law of the Sabbath determines the years of Israel's captivity.

Eschatological expectations for God's people also relate to the Sabbath principle. As Daniel contemplates the end of the 70 Sabbaths of Israel's captivity, he receives his revelation concerning the "seventy sevens" yet to come (Dan. 9:1, 21, 24–27). These 70 sevens structure the eschatological expectations of God's people along sabbatical lines.[2]

This broader understanding of the role of the Sabbath in the origin, the history, and the eschatology of the world provides the framework for understanding the significance of the Sabbath for the new covenant. To speak of the "abolishment" of the Sabbath under the new covenant does not involve merely the denial of the continuing significance of the Mosaic decalogue. It involves a breach of the very orders of creation, history, and consummation as revealed in Scripture. Instead of resisting the role of the Sabbath in redemption, the participant in the new covenant should rejoice in the privileges associated with God's consummating Sabbath-ordinance.

While the line of continuity between old covenant and new covenant Sabbath ought to be noted, something of the freshness of the new situation must be captured. The entirety of history under the old covenant moved toward a goal. Rest always remained ahead of the people of God. The very pattern of six days of work moving toward a day of rest aptly depicted the "anticipating" character of life under the old covenant. Not only did this pattern reflect the order of creation. It also made graphic the stance of futuristic hope which stylized the life-perspective of the old covenant believer.

Appropriately the Sabbath principle under the old covenant was associated with redemption as well as with creation. The forward-looking character of a seventh-day Sabbath anticipated the day of redemption's consummate restoration.

Even more explicitly, the second giving of the law intertwines the Sabbath with redemption. The single most significant modification of the decalogue in Deuteronomy 5 relates to the reason given for the celebration of the Sabbath:

---

2. See in particular the stimulating article by M. G. Kline entitled "The Covenant of the Seventieth Week," in *The Law and The Prophets. Old Testament Studies Prepared in Honor of Oswald Thompson Allis*, ed. John H. Skilton (Nutley, N.J., 1974), pp. 452–69.

And you shall remember that you were a slave in the land of Egypt, and the Lord your God brought you out of there by a mighty hand and by an outstretched arm; therefore the Lord your God commanded you to observe the sabbath day (Deut. 5:12, NASB).

Now the reason for Sabbath-observance relates not only to creation but also to redemption. Because God gave rest by redemption, Israel must observe the Sabbath.

The two alternative reasons for keeping the Sabbath focus on the two great pivots of God's historical dealings with his people. These two events have equal significance. Creation originates a people of God. Redemption recreates a people of God. In each case, the Sabbath plays a vital role.

When the place of the Sabbath under the new covenant is considered, this perspective must not be forgotten. By his resurrection from the dead, Jesus Christ consummated God's redemptive purposes. His coming forth into new life must be understood as an event as significant as the creation of the world. By his resurrection, a new creation occurred.

To be more precise, the resurrection of Christ signified an event which even surpassed God's original creative activity. In the resurrection, God brought to final fulfillment his creative/redemptive program. The original creation launched the world. But the resurrection-creation brought the world to its destined perfection.

For this reason, the Christian perceives history differently. He does not only look forward to a redemption yet to come. He does not merely hope for a future Sabbath rest. He looks back on a redemption fully accomplished. He stands confidently on the basis of what the past already has brought.

Therefore, it is fitting that the new covenant radically alters the Sabbath perspective. The current believer in Christ does not follow the Sabbath pattern of the people of the old covenant. He does not first labor six days, looking hopefully toward rest. Instead, he begins the week by rejoicing in the rest already accomplished by the cosmic event of Christ's resurrection. Then he enters joyfully into his six days of labor, confident of success through the victory which Christ already has won.

In considering the significance of Old Testament Sabbath legislation for the New Testament believer, some distinction must be made between the abiding kernel of Old Testament realities and the temporary husk which surrounded them. Because of its position in the substance of the "Ten Commandments," the weekly Sabbath retains its binding character on the recipient of the new covenant in a manner which does not apply to the sabbatical year or the year of jubilee. Although the day on which the celebration is to be held has been changed from the seventh to the first day of the week, the Christian is obligated to remember the Sabbath day, to keep it holy, to refrain from work, and to restrain himself from employing others. The "ten words" derive their binding power from the fact that they reflect the nature of God himself. As the central core of the Mosaic phase of the covenant of redemption, the "Ten Commandments" retain just as binding a character on the new covenant believer as does the principle of faith which formed the central core of the Abrahamic phase of the covenant of redemption.

At the consummation, God's people shall enter completely into the rest that shall experience no interruption. There "yet remains" a rest for the people of God. As they enter into the resurrection state with Christ, they shall know the consummational Sabbath of the new creation (cf. Heb. 4:9, 10).

In summary, the Sabbath principle of creation's ordering manifests itself in a variety of ways throughout Scripture. Both in the repetitive patterns of the worship experience and in the consummative patterns of history, the Sabbath ordinance plays a determining role. This ordinance clearly affects the structure of history. Having been blessed of God in creation, the Sabbath consummates God's purposes in redemption.

Marriage

A second creational ordinance of God that has affected the total life of man is marriage. In the ordering of creation, God himself indicated: "it is not good that man should be alone" (Gen. 2:18).

So God created a helper who corresponded appropriately to the man.

The creational origin of the marriage relationship has far-reaching implications. By tracing this ordinance to the sovereign creative act of God himself, Scripture removes all doubt with respect to the sanctity of marriage. The Lord-Creator ordained marriage from the time of man's creation.

Several significant conclusions may be reached concerning the creational ordinance of marriage on the basis of the testimony of Scripture.

First, the wonder of interpersonal fusion involved in the marriage bond should be noted. The oneness realized in marriage relates to the intimate process by which the woman came into being. Because the original woman was formed from a part of her husband, each subsequent man must leave his parents and cleave to his wife, thus constituting these two people as one (Gen. 2:22–24).

The "being one flesh" described in Scripture does not refer simply to the various moments of marital consummation. Instead, this oneness describes the abiding condition of union achieved in marriage.

Implicit in this interpersonal fusion as ordered in creation is the fact that two and only two may enter such a relationship. The text in Genesis says that a man shall cleave to his wife, and they shall be one flesh (Gen. 2:24). The most obvious sense of this statement is "that one man is to be joined to one woman and that the two become one flesh."[3]

While the Genesis text itself does not insert the term "two," Jesus interprets the passage explicitly as conveying precisely this thought. In dealing with the question of divorce, Jesus appeals to the order established by the Creator. "He who did the creating" says Jesus, "from the beginning made them male and female . . . for this cause a man shall leave his father and his mother and shall be joined to his wife, and the two shall be one flesh" (οἱ δύο εἰς σάρκα μίαν; Matt.

---

3. John Murray, *Principles of Conduct* (Grand Rapids, 1957), p. 29.

19:4, 5; cf. Mark 10:6–8; Eph. 5:31). Jesus explains that the man and
the woman are no longer two, but one flesh, because God the
Creator has joined them together (Matt. 19:6).

These texts emphasize the interpersonal fusion achieved by marriage. By the ordering of creation, marriage unites persons.

Secondly, creation's ordering determines the internal structuring
that characterizes God's institution of marriage. Because it is not
good for the man to be alone, God declares that he shall make
עֵזֶר כְּנֶגְדּוֹ, "a helper corresponding to him" (Gen. 2:18).

According to this phrase, the woman was created by God to be a
helper to the man in the marriage relationship. This internal order
of the marriage relationship finds explicit confirmation in the New
Testament. Paul states that the man was not created for the woman.
Instead, the woman was created for the man (I Cor. 11:9). The
purpose of the man's existence as created is not to be a help to the
woman. But the purpose of the woman's existence as created is to
glorify God in being a help to the man.

A significant balancing element must be noticed in the scriptural
presentation of the role of the woman in marriage. Indeed, the
woman is to be helper to the man. But she is to be a helper
"corresponding to him." The whole of God's creation could serve as
help to the man in one way or another. But nowhere in creation
could be found a helper "corresponding to" the man (Gen. 2:20).
Only the woman as created from the man corresponded to him in a
way that made her the appropriate help he needed.

This distinctiveness of the woman indicates that she is no less
significant than the man with respect to her person.[4] Equally with
the man she bears in herself the image and likeness of God (Gen.
1:27). Only as equal in personhood could the woman "correspond
to" the man.

Further revelation in Scripture seems to indicate that the woman

---

4. The term "corresponding to him" derives from the word נֶגֶד, which conveys
the idea of something that is "in front of" or "face to face with" something else. In
this context, the term suggests the idea of equality of person.

is helper to the man specifically for the purpose of bringing all creation to its consummation-goal. In heaven, men neither marry nor are given in marriage (Matt. 22:30). Once the consummate state has been realized, the woman's role as helper to the man will come to an end. Bearing God's image in her own person, the woman shall enjoy consummation in her own completeness. For the present, the woman shares with the man the responsibility to subdue the earth to the glory of God. She joins with him in his task of forming a culture glorifying to God the Creator.

The ultimate condition of the woman finds eschatological anticipation in the equality of men and women with respect to the gospel. There is "neither . . . male nor female" with respect to the privilege and responsibility of responding in faith to the gospel (Gal. 3:28).

Furthermore, the distress of the present hour may lead to the man's or woman's remaining outside the marriage bond. While God's admonition to multiply and replenish the earth still applies to men today, and marriage still stands as the creationally ordered intention for man, no contradiction must be seen when the apostolic "it is good that a man not marry" (I Cor. 7:1) is set beside the creational "it is not good that man should be alone" (Gen. 2:18). On the basis of the necessary "gift" to remain in the single state (I Cor. 7:7), and due to the present distress (I Cor. 7:26), a man or a woman may remain unmarried.[5]

At creation, God admonished man to multiply and to fill the earth. This commandment contains significant implications about the role of the man in the marriage relationship. The man must love and cherish his wife. He must care for her, particularly as she fulfils her role in bearing children. As Paul the apostle subsequently admonishes, the husband is to love his wife, even as Christ loved the church and gave himself for it (Eph. 5:25). He indeed has the responsibility of functioning as head in the marriage relationship. Yet he must function not as a "bloated" head or a "domineering" head, but as a "saving" head. Particularly, he must remember that

---

5. For a most helpful discussion of these questions, see John Murray, *Principles of Conduct* (Grand Rapids, 1957), pp. 58ff.

. . . in the Lord, neither is woman independent of man, nor is man independent of woman. For as the woman originates from the man, so also the man has his birth through the woman; and all things originate from God (I Cor. 11:11, 12).

Far from being independent of the woman, the man owes his existence to her. In the Lord, these two forms of man's being merge in a mutual dependence which acknowledges that all of creation originates from God.

In any case, the internal order for the marriage relationship is determined by creation. The woman is "helper corresponding to" the man. The man is head over the wife, loving her as himself.

Thirdly, the effect of the creational ordinance of marriage on various sexual abberations ought to be noticed. Because an order has been established for the relation of men and women by creation, this order cannot be ignored or supplanted.

Polygamy contradicts the creational order of marriage. The creation of a single woman from the original man emphasizes the wholeness and exclusiveness of the union achieved in the marriage relationship. A third party never can be introduced without destroying the union which already exists. "From the beginning," God indicated that the two, and only two, should be one flesh.

Divorce contradicts the creational order of marriage. The Creator yokes men and women together. No one may break asunder what God has joined. Only in cases of unchastity, in which the marriage union already has been broken (Matt. 5:32), or of "such wilful desertion as can no way be remedied by the Church, or civil magistrate" may divorce be allowed (*Westminster Confession of Faith*, XXIV, 6; cf. I Cor. 7:15).

Homosexuality contradicts the creational order of marriage. According to the ordinances of creation, a man is to leave father and mother that he may cleave to his wife. No latitude for cleaving to someone of the same sex may be found in this creational structure. Only as one man joins to one woman has God's ordering been observed. The apostle Paul does not hesitate to condemn sexual

abberations both as originating and as resulting in judicial abandon-
ment by God:

> For this reason God gave them over to degrading passions; for their
> women exchanged the natural function for that which is unnatural,
> and in the same way also the men abandoned the natural function of
> the woman and burned in their desire towards one another, men with
> men committing indecent acts and receiving in their own persons
> the due penalty of their error (Rom. 1:26, 27).

God's creational orderings for marriage and the family have
continuing significance in the purposes of redemption. The propagation of the race through the institution of marriage indicates a
primary means by which God's purposes in redemption find realization. Not by a method contrary to the structures of creation, but by a
method in conformity with creation, God accomplishes his purposes
of redemption.

Marriage, therefore, may be regarded as a most significant
dimension in God's creational ordering. This ordinance continues to
have binding significance on man-in-redemption.

Labor

The solidarity of God's ordinance of labor with the creation order
may be seen in its immediate connection with the Sabbath principle.[6]
Meaningful rest may be experienced by the creation only in the
context of meaningful labor. One day's rest in seven clearly implies
six days of labor. By God's own pattern of creation, and by his
blessing the creation in terms of this pattern, man's order for labor
is established.

It should be noted well that it is not merely labor in rather
undefined terms that God commands. Instead, it is six days of labor,
according to the pattern of creation. As John Murray has indicated so
aptly:

---

6. Ibid., p. 35.

The stress laid upon the six days of labour needs to be duly appreciated. The divine ordinance is not simply that of labour; it is labour with a certain constancy. There is indeed respite from labour, the respite of one whole day every recurring seventh day. The cycle of respite is provided for, but there is also the cycle of labour. And the cycle of labour is as irreversible as the cycle of rest. The law of God cannot be violated with impunity. We can be quite certain that a great many of our physical and economic ills proceed from failure to observe the weekly day of rest. But we can also be quite sure that a great many of our economic ills arise from our failure to recognize the sanctity of six days of labour. Labour is not only a duty; it is a blessing. And, in like manner, six days of labour are both a duty and a blessing.[7]

The explicit command given to man concerning his responsibility toward the creation enforces the implication concerning labor in the Sabbath ordinance. Made in God's own image, man has a unique responsibility to "subdue" the earth and rule over every living creature (Gen. 1:27, 28). This subduing involves the bringing out of all the potential within the creation which might offer glory to the Creator.[8] Such an ordinance, embedded in the creational responsibilities of man, clearly intends to affect his entire life-pattern.

Even more specifically, the charge given to man to cultivate and to keep the garden underscores the role of the creational ordinance of labor (Gen. 2:15). Indeed, man is to enjoy his life in the context of God's creation. But as a matter of fact, labor is to be seen as a principal means by which man's enjoyment of the creation is assured.

---

7. Ibid., p. 83.
8. Francis Schaeffer in his *Pollution and the Death of Man* (Wheaton, 1970), p. 12, cites a significant scientist who blames the ecological crisis on Christianity's teaching that man was to have dominion over the world. This scientist suggests that the biblical teaching concerning man's lordship over creation has encouraged selfish exploitation. Such a viewpoint fails completely to see the responsibility of man to subdue the earth to the glory of the Creator. The biblical pattern clearly stresses that man's labor always is to be consummated by the consecration of the fruit of his work to the Creator. The setting of six days of labor in the context of one day of worship and rest indicates the true perspective from which man's dominion over the earth is to be viewed.

The creational ordinance of labor finds specific support in the legislation of the new covenant. The apostle Paul made it quite plain that good standing within the Christian community hinged in part on a proper respect for work:

> For even when we were with you, we used to give you this order: If anyone will not work, neither let him eat.
>
> For we hear that some among you are leading an undisciplined life, doing no work at all, but acting like busybodies.
>
> Now such persons we command and exhort in the Lord Jesus Christ to work in quiet fashion and eat their own bread (II Thess. 3:10–12).

Instead of being a legal aspect of the old covenant, labor belongs integrally to the role of man made in God's image. This creation-ordinance joins with the Sabbath and marriage to provide meaningful structure to man's existence under the general provisions of the covenant of creation.

THE COVENANT OF CREATION: ITS FOCAL ASPECT

In addition to these general provisions of the covenant of creation, man made in God's image also had responsibility for a more specific command addressed to him. He was not to eat of the tree of the knowledge of good and evil (Gen. 2:16, 17).

In considering the prohibition of Genesis 2:17, it is essential to appreciate the organic unity between this commandment and the total responsibility of man as created. The requirement concerning the tree of the knowledge of good and evil must not be conceived of as a somewhat arbitrary stipulation without integral relation to the total life of man. Instead, this particular prohibition must be seen as the focal point of man's testing.

Lacking this awareness of the total unity of man's responsibilities under the covenant of creation, an extremely dangerous dualism will develop between man's "religious" or "spiritual" responsibilities and his "cultural" or "work-a-day" responsibilities. Adam under the covenant of creation did not have one set of duties relating to the created world, and another more specific duty of an entirely different nature which could be designated as "spiritual." All that Adam did had direct bearing on his relation to the covenant God of creation. The creational ordinances of marriage, labor, and Sabbath did not have a distinctive existence separated from Adam's responsibility to refrain from eating of the tree of the knowledge of good and evil. His life as a covenant creature must be viewed as a unified whole.

This same unity of covenantal relationship subsequently characterized the various administrations of the covenant of redemption. Always the total life of the participant in the divine covenant finds its ordering through the covenantal bond. God's covenant with Noah embraces the total orientation of man to the creation. Under the Abrahamic covenant, the promises of land, seed, and blessing, coupled with the all-inclusive demand for Abraham to walk before God in "completeness" (Gen. 17:1) involve the broadest possible dimensions of human life. The summation of the Mosaic law in terms of whole-souled love to God and neighbor depicts a covenantal relationship which encompasses every thought and action. The kingdom-covenant under David obviously intends to order the entire realm of existence of the servants of the King. Covenant-relationship involves total-life relationship. Rather than addressing itself to some ill-conceived "religious" aspect of man, the covenant of God is all-inclusive.

If the covenant of creation is thought not to exceed Adam's probation-test, a curious brand of Christianity ultimately emerges. It is a brand of Christianity greatly at odds with that in which the probation-test is understood as the focal point of a total life-embracing covenantal relationship. The difference between the two views is the difference between "fundamentalism" narrowly conceived and the broader covenantal theology of Scripture.

The "fundamentalist" may conceive of the significance of Christianity more narrowly in terms of the salvation of the "soul." Too often he may fail to consider adequately the effect of redemption on the total life-style of man in the context of an all-embracive covenant. That view results frequently in a by-passing of the responsibility of redeemed man to carry forward the implications of his salvation into the world of economics, politics, business, and culture.

The total life-involvement of the covenant relationship provides the framework for considering the connection between the "great commission" and the "cultural mandate." Entrance into God's kingdom may occur only by repentance and faith, which requires the preaching of the gospel. This "gospel," however, must not be conceived of in the narrowest possible terms. It is the gospel of the "kingdom." It involves discipling men to Jesus Christ. Integral to that discipling process is the awakening of an awareness of the obligations of man to the totality of God's creation. Redeemed man, remade in God's image, must fulfil—even surpass—the role originally determined for the first man. In such a manner, the mandate to preach the gospel and the mandate to form a culture glorifying to God merge with one another.

In a somewhat similar fashion, the prohibition concerning the tree of the knowledge of good and evil and the more general demands on man must be seen to relate to one another. It is not that man had fulfilled all his obligations under the covenant of creation by refusing to eat of the tree. He had larger demands on his life as well.

Yet the response to the particular prohibition concerning the tree was crucially determinative. The focal point of the covenant rested specifically on this single test. If Adam succeeded in submitting to God at this point, his blessing under the larger provisions of the covenant of creation was assured.

As the test concerning the tree is examined, the radicalness of the obedience demanded stands out boldly. Contrary to the normal order which pervaded the garden scene, man was not to eat of this single tree.

Man had been given the privilege of eating from every tree of the garden. As God's vice-gerent, all was his. Yet now, one marked exception is introduced. One tree stands in the midst of the garden as symbolic reminder that man is not God. All has been given to him graciously; but the one exception reminds him that he must not confuse his bountiful blessedness with the state of the Creator. He is creature; God is Creator.

In this particular situation, man had nothing to indicate the exceptional nature of this one tree other than the word of God. This point emphasizes the radical nature of the obedience required. Acting as a free agent, endued with natural powers beyond all of God's creation, man nonetheless must humble himself beneath the word once spoken by his sovereign Creator.

As has been indicated, man was required to do many things under the provisions of the covenant of creation. But the probationary test concerning the tree established a focal point at which man's submission to the Creator could be scrutinized. Now the point of testing reduces itself to man's willingness to choose obedience for the sake of obedience alone. The raw word of God in itself must become the basis of man's action.

When this focal character of the probationary test is appreciated, something of the reality of the entire scene becomes apparent. The narrative does not recount a silly story about a stolen apple. Instead, a most radical test of the original man's willingness to submit to the specific word of the Creator is involved.

Furthermore, it should be clear that the narrative does not intend to depict the experience of "Everyman." No one but the original "Adam" had the choice described in these verses.[9] He faced a decision concerning willingness to submit to God's word that was absolutely unique.

Additional insight into this crucial point of man's testing may be found in the parallel experience of God's people under the covenant

---

9. The argument that Adam equals "Everyman" because the Hebrew term for "Adam" elsewhere is used in Scripture for man in general continues to recur, even in the most scholarly circles. Cf. more recently B. W. Anderson, *Creation versus Chaos: The Reinterpretation of Mythical Symbolism in the Bible* (New York, 1967), p. 86. Obviously subsequent men would be called generically according to the name assigned the first man. Jews today still are called "Israelites," according to their forefather's name. The original man could have been called "Snark" or "Boojum," *a la* Lewis Carroll; then where would be man's come-of-age dignity?

of redemption. Israel, the prophetic shadow of the second Adam, underwent testing regarding eating during its wandering in the wilderness. The purpose of this testing was to teach man that he does not live by bread only, but by every word that proceeds from the mouth of God (Deut. 8:3). Even the providential ordering of God which deprives of bread may become a source of life if Israel will learn that existence does not depend primarily on the consumption of the material substance of the creation. It depends instead on fellowship with the Creator, which arises from an acceptance in joyful trust of all that he orders for life.

Similarly, Christ the second Adam experienced deprivation of material sustenance in the wilderness (Matt. 4:1ff.). Satan tempted him to exercise his rightful powers in order to alleviate his discomfort arising from God's providential orderings. Christ repulsed this temptation by reaffirming the principle indicated in Deuteronomy. Man does not live by bread only, but by every word that proceeds from the Creator's mouth. Even the divine word that deprives will be a source of life, since it awakens the creature to full awareness that life depends always on the Creator.

Radical obedience therefore provides the key to blessing under the covenant of creation. If man will acknowledge fully the lordship of the Creator by obeying his word purely for the sake of obedience, he shall experience the consummate blessing of the covenant. Life in perpetuity shall be his.

Appropriately, a comparable emphasis on the role of obedience is found in association with the covenant of redemption. Restoration of fallen man hinges on the one act of obedience of Christ, the second Adam:

> So then as through one transgression there resulted condemnation to all men, even so through one act of righteousness there resulted justification of life to all men. For as through the one man's disobedience the many were made sinners, even so through the obedience of the One the many will be made righteous (Rom. 5:18, 19).

Only radical obedience may provide a proper basis for restoration of men guilty of radical disobedience. Herein lies the significance of the ultra-drama enacted in Gethsemane. Christ, the second Adam, genuinely grappled with the demand for radical obedience. Three times in great agony Christ struggled with this ultimate of decisions (cf. Matt. 26:39; 26:42; John 18:11). In evident progress of obedience he moves from: "If it is possible, let this cup pass from me," to: "If this cannot pass away unless I drink it, thy will be done"; to: "The cup which the Father has given me, shall I not drink it?" Though he was a son, he learned obedience through the things which he suffered (Heb. 5:8). As obedient unto death, he is able to save all that come to God by him.

The ultimate alternatives of the covenant of creation are spelled out quite explicitly. Clearly this relationship between man and his Creator may be described as a "bond of life and death sovereignly administered."

Cursing and blessing, life and death—these are the alternatives faced by man under the covenant of creation. The outcome focuses on the probation test.

In the day that man eats of the forbidden fruit, he shall surely die (Gen. 2:17). Violation of the stipulations of the covenant of creation cannot but result in death.

The alternative of blessing is related inherently to the presence of the tree of life in the garden (Gen. 2:9). The precise role of this tree in the probation experience of man is difficult to determine. But when it is noted that man is denied the privilege of eating from this tree as a consequence of his fall, it would seem that the tree of life represented the power to sustain in a particular condition (Gen. 3:22).

Apparently the tree of life symbolized the possibility of being sustained in the condition of covenantal blessing and life. If man would pass the test of probation, he would live forever. This sign of perpetual blessing reappears in the biblical imagery of consummation. The tree of life appears once more. This time 12 different varieties of fruit appear, providing freshness of life according to each month of the year (Rev. 22:2).

CONCLUSION

Generally the emphasis on blood in the biblical faith is regarded as an element of primitivism that must be excused. But the pledge-to-death involved in the covenant of creation makes mandatory just such an emphasis. Once this initial covenant has been violated, no way of relief from the death-curse may be found other than a bloody substitution. Only as Jesus the lamb of God bears in himself the ultimate curse of the creation covenant may restoration be accomplished.

PART THREE

THE COVENANT OF REDEMPTION

THE covenant of redemption is established immediately in conjunction with man's failure under the covenant of creation. God had bound himself to man by the special orderings of creation. Man ruptured that relationship by eating the forbidden fruit.

However, God's relation to his creature did not terminate with man's sin. The wonder of the gracious character of the Creator manifests itself immediately. Judgment indeed must fall. But even in the midst of judgment hope for restoration appears. God binds himself now to redeem a people to himself. The very words that pronounce the curse of the covenant of creation also inaugurate the covenant of redemption.

This inseparable connection of the covenant of creation with the covenant of redemption stresses the restoration goal of the covenant of redemption. From the very outset, God intends by the covenant of redemption to realize for man those blessings originally defaulted under the covenant of creation.

A further overlapping of these two covenantal administrations may be seen in that man continues to be responsible to function in the context of the original responsibilities given him at the time of his creation. The particular test of probation is present no longer. Yet man still remains responsible to consecrate the whole of creation to the Creator. Marriage, labor, and the ordinance of the Sabbath continue as principal responsibilities for man despite his fallen character.

The remainder of human history finds its key in the provisions made by God under this original covenant of redemption. The divine commitment in this hour solidifies the significance of history from this point onward.

As history progresses, the fuller implications of the covenant of redemption become manifest. Ultimately this redemptive purpose reaches its consummation in the appearance of Jesus Christ "in the fulness of time" (Gal. 4:4).

The unified purpose of the covenant of redemption binds together the gradual unfolding of the varied aspects of this single bond. At the same time, the progress of history clearly manifests significant diversity in covenantal administration. The first of these administrations may be designated as Adam: The Covenant of Commencement.

6

Adam:
The Covenant of Commencement

THE first declaration of the covenant of redemption contains in seed form every basic principle which manifests itself subsequently. God reveals in a most balanced fashion the various elements constituting his commitment to redeem his fallen creation.

Genesis 3:14–19 records the provisions of the Adamic administration of the covenant of redemption. God speaks to Satan, to the woman, and to the man, following the order of their defection from loyalty to the Creator. Elements of curse and blessing are found in each address, thus serving structurally to bind inseparably the covenant of creation with the covenant of redemption.

THE WORD TO SATAN (GEN. 3:14, 15)

The curse of God's judgment falls first on Satan, the first of offenders. Initially the word of curse addresses primarily the serpent as tool of Satan:

And the Lord God said to the serpent,
"Because you have done this,
Cursed are you more than all cattle,
And more than every beast of the field:
On your belly shall you go,
And dust shall you eat
All the days of your life;
And I will put enmity
Between you and the woman,
And between your seed and her seed;
He shall bruise you on the head,
And you shall bruise him on the heel" (Gen. 3:14, 15).

Notice first that God's word concerning man's redemption is addressed to the serpent. This factor may be evaluated in either of two ways.

On the one hand, it could be suggested that God's address to the serpent emphasizes the mythical character of the narrative. G. von Rad asserts that all the penalties described in these verses are to be interpreted aetiologically.[1] They simply represent an ancient effort to provide answers to perplexing questions about life. The crawling motion of the colorful snake needed an explanation in an ancient cultural context. So the story of the curse of this beautiful beast was invented.

Sigmund Mowinckel interprets the narrative basically in the same manner. He regards these verses as

a quite general statement about mankind, and serpents, and the struggle between them which continues as long as the earth exists. The poisonous serpent strikes at man's foot whenever he is unfortunate enough to come too near to it; and always and everywhere man tries to crunch the serpent's head when he has a chance.[2]

As in most cases with such misappropriations of Scripture, half-truths blur the wholeness of reality. The natural animosity between

---

1. G. von Rad, *Genesis* (Philadelphia, 1961), p. 89.
2. Sigmund Mowinckel, *He That Cometh* (Oxford, 1954), p. 11.

men and snakes does indeed find its explanation in these verses. The instrument used by Satan to deceive man did receive a particularly humbling curse. Symbolic of the arch-enemy's ultimate defeat, his tool in temptation habitually licks the dust of defeat.

However, the whole context makes it clear that the primary purpose of these words is not simply to explain why snakes crawl. The entire framework of the narrative is set on a much more significant level.

A cosmic drama is being enacted. The history of man's redemption involves the totality of man and his created environment. The animal world as well as the human world must feel the effects of man's fall into sin.

But redemption for man is not limited to this world's confines. God's ultimate enemy does not reside in the material creation. As Paul the Apostle later emphasized:

> Our struggle is not against flesh and blood, but against the rulers, against the powers, against the world-forces of this darkness, against the spiritual forces of wickedness in the heavenly places (Eph. 6:12).

Clearly redemption cannot be understood in a man-centered fashion. God's glory as the great Creator has been assaulted. His handiwork has been disharmonized. Not simply for the sake of man, but for the glory of God redemption is undertaken.

God says to the serpent, "Because you have done this, you are cursed above all cattle." Satan had deceived the woman by convincing her that the ordering of creation as declared by God was not true. Satan's accomplishment as tempter was to mislead the woman with respect to God's truth.³

---

3. This particular role of the serpent as deceiver is underscored by the New Testament texts which allude to this narrative. According to the Septuagint, the woman says: ὁ ὄφις ἠπάτησέ με, "the serpent deceived me" (Gen. 3:14). Paul declares that ὁ ὄφις ἐξηπάτησεν Εὔαν, "the serpent deceived Eve" (II Cor. 11:3). At another point, he indicates that Adam οὐκ ἠπατήθη, "was not deceived," but the woman, ἐξαπατηθεῖσα, "having been deceived," came into transgression (I Tim.

The Lord rightfully curses the serpent. More than all the other creation he is humbled. The snake must crawl. As tool of Satan he bears in himself the symbolic reminder of ultimate defeat.

Yet the curse certainly goes beyond the serpent to Satan himself. Only as the serpent represents Satan does its humiliation-posture possess real significance. The Satan-directed character of the curse appears more explicitly in verse 15:

> And I will put enmity
> Between you and the woman,
> And between your seed and her seed;
> He shall bruise you on the head,
> And you shall bruise him on the heel (Gen. 3:15).

The divine initiative in this establishment of animosity must be underscored. God himself shall perpetuate a continuing warfare.

Now that man has fallen into sin, the last thing that might be expected would be enmity between himself and Satan. The two have sided in their opposition against God and his purposes.

But God shall intervene sovereignly to assure conflict between Satan and mankind. These verses guarantee that God himself shall impose a continuing opposition between mankind and Satan.[4]

The enmity established by God occurs on three fronts. In each case, the precise identification of the antagonists is difficult. Yet some positive assertions may be made.

First, God says that he shall establish enmity between Satan and the woman.

2:14). In each case, it is the deceiving role of Satan with respect to the woman that is emphasized.

4. The word for enmity in Genesis 3:15 (אֵיבָה) appears only four other times in Scripture (Num. 35:21, 22; Ezek. 25:15; 35:5). But the related verb (אָיַב) in participial form occurs repeatedly, alluding frequently to the very struggle between God's and Satan's people discussed in this verse. Abraham is to possess the gate of his enemies (Gen. 22:17); Judah shall have his hand on the neck of his enemies (Gen. 49:8); God's right hand shatters his enemies at the Red Sea (Exod. 15:6); God shall be an enemy to Israel's enemies (Exod. 23:22); Balaam cannot curse Israel as the enemies of Balak (Num. 24:10); the Canaanites occupy the land of promise as Israel's enemies (Deut. 6:19); etc.

Why does God designate the woman specifically as the source of opposition to Satan? Why does he not begin with the man? Several factors may explain this divine ordering:

1. The woman was the first to be seduced. Appropriately therefore God mentioned her first. By the divine initiative, she shall be set at enmity against Satan.

2. The pride of man might lead him to disparage his wife, particularly since she was the first to fall. But now it becomes quite obvious that redemption will not be accomplished apart from the woman.[5]

3. The woman may be mentioned first because of an intention to focus on her role as bearer of the child that ultimately was to deliver man from the forces of Satan.[6] Through the woman God shall provide One who will save his people from their sins.

So God first establishes enmity between Satan and the woman. But who is the "woman" to whom God refers?

Eve herself could be meant. If such were the case, stress would be placed on the fact that this enmity would begin immediately.

However, it seems more likely that the "woman" set in opposition to Satan refers to womankind in general rather than to Eve in particular. Without implying necessarily that all women universally shall participate in the enmity against Satan, the text affirms the basic principle that womankind shall have a most significant role in this cosmic struggle.

The second level of antagonism is set between Satan's seed and

---

5. It is rather interesting to note the balance of Scripture between men and women in their faith-response to the promises concerning God's supernatural provision of a seed to conflict with Satan. In Genesis 18, Sarah laughs at God's promise concerning a seed, while Abraham believes. But in Luke 1, Zechariah the father of John the Baptist is struck dumb for his unbelief concerning his God-provided child, while Mary the mother of Jesus quietly believes.

6. It is at least possible that the reference in I Tim. 2:15 to the woman's being "saved in childbearing" may allude to this promise of Gen. 3:15. Cf. Wm. Hendriksen, *Exposition of the Pastoral Epistles. New Testament Commentary* (Grand Rapids, 1957), pp. 111f.

the woman's seed. This enmity between the seeds grows out of the enmity between Satan and the woman. But who is meant by the "seed" of the woman?

The woman's seed could be identified with the totality of humanity. However, the immediately succeeding section in Genesis narrates Cain's murder of his brother Abel (Gen. 4). The New Testament explicitly determines the significance of these two persons in the cosmic struggle between God and Satan. Cain originates from "the evil one" (I John 3:12). Though descended from Eve just as his brother, he cannot be regarded as belonging to the "seed" of the woman as described in Genesis 3:15. Instead of being opposed to Satan, he is the seed of Satan. The "seed" of the woman cannot be identified simply with all physical descendants of womankind.

The key to identifying the "seed" of the woman in this conflict resides in the God-originating character of the enmity described. God himself sovereignly sets enmity within the heart of the natural descendants of the woman. By the process of natural birth, the fallen woman brings forth a depraved seed. But by grace God establishes enmity within the heart of particular descendants of the woman. These individuals may be designated as the woman's "seed."

Now the other side of the conflict between the seeds must be considered. The seed of the serpent cannot be identified rather naively with "snakes." The conflict envisioned describes something much more crucial.

Satan also has his associates, his "angels" (cf. Matt. 25:41; Rev. 12:7-9). Although not materially descended from the devil, they may be regarded figuratively as his "seed."[7]

At the same time, Scripture indicates that within humanity itself is a "seed" of Satan set against God and his purposes. Cain was "of the evil one" (I John 3:12). John the Baptist described his hypocritical contemporaries as a "generation of vipers" (Luke 3:7). The Lord himself explicitly indicated that his opponents were of their "father the devil," and would join him in his murderous works (John 8:44).

---

7. Cf. G. Vos, *Biblical Theology* (Grand Rapids, 1959), p. 54.

Among humanity, the physical descendants of the woman, exists a seed of Satan. This "seed" stands in opposition to God and his purposes.

The introduction of conflict on the level of the two "seeds" anticipates the long struggle that ensues in the history that follows. "Seed of woman" and "seed of Satan" conflict with one another throughout the ages.

Yet a third level of enmity manifests itself in these verses. Womankind struggles with Satan; woman's seed struggles with Satan's seed; and "he" struggles with Satan.

The identification of the person designated by the pronoun "he" raises several difficult problems. The Hebrew pronoun in this case is masculine in gender, singular in number. The most natural grammatical construction would refer the term to the "seed" of the woman, which also is masculine in gender and singular in number. The "he" who is destined to bruise Satan's head would refer to the "seed" of the woman mentioned in the immediately preceding phrase. Although singular in number, this "he" could refer to a multiple of persons just as the singular "seed."

Precisely this interpretation is found in Romans 16:20: "the God of Peace shall bruise Satan under your [plural] feet shortly." Paul sees the ultimate realization of this earliest word of prophecy in the destruction of Satan under the feet of believers at the end of the age.

However, the pronoun "he" deserves further consideration. Some differentiation must be made to distinguish between the conflict of "seed" with "seed" and the conflict of "he" with Satan himself. The struggle in this last instance is not between "seed" and "seed," as in the previous phrase. Satan himself as an individual has been reintroduced into the conflict. As the prince of his people, he stands as representative of their cause.

To correspond to the narrowing from "seed" to "Satan" on one side of the enmity, it would appear quite appropriate to expect a similar narrowing from a multiple "seed" of woman to a singular "he" who would champion the cause of God's enmity against Satan. A single representative hero shall descend from the woman to join the conflict. The pronoun "he" may involve the whole of the woman's seed. But involvement shall be by the representative principle.

This "individual hero" interpretation finds ancient support by those who were responsible for translating the Old Testament into Greek almost two hundred years before Christ was born. Since the Greek word for "seed" ($\sigma\pi\acute{\epsilon}\rho\mu\alpha$) is neuter, it would have been quite appropriate that it be followed by the neuter pronoun "it" ($\alpha\mathring{v}\tau\acute{o}$). "It," the seed of the woman, would bruise the head of the serpent. But instead of following the neuter "seed" with a neuter "it," the Septuagint translators chose a distinctively masculine "he" ($\alpha\mathring{v}\tau\acute{o}\varsigma$). "He," the seed of the woman, shall crush the head of the serpent.[8]

The Latin Vulgate translation renders the pronoun as feminine (*ipsa*): "she" will crush the head of the serpent. This translation finds no support in the Hebrew text.[9] While Mary the mother of Jesus may be regarded as playing a significant role in this struggle, she should not be regarded as the specific object of the pronoun under consideration.

The respective seeds assault one another with the purpose of "bruising" or "crushing."[10] The context would suggest that a fatal wound seems clearly intended. Each antagonist attacks with the same determination of purpose. One strikes at the head, the other strikes at the heel, but each has the settled purpose to destroy.

The passage provides a fitting description of Satan's ways. The heel may not represent as crucial a point of attack as the head. But it indicates fittingly the subversiveness of the Deceiver.[11]

---

8. Cf. R. A. Martin, "The Earliest Messianic Interpretation of Genesis 3:15," *Journal of Biblical Literature,* 84 (1965): 425ff.; Martin Woudstra, "Recent Translations of Genesis 3:15," *Calvin Theological Journal,* 6 (1971): 199f.

9. The alteration of the Hebrew pronoun from "he" (הוא) to "she" (היא) is quite simple. But consistency with the text would also involve alteration of יְשׁוּפְךָ "he will bruise you" to תְּשׁוּפְךָ "she will bruise you" and of תְּשׁוּפֶנּוּ "you will bruise him" to תְּשׁוּפֶנָה "you will bruise her."

10. The term (שׁוּף) occurs only two other times outside this verse. In Job 9:17, the reference is to God's breaking Job with a tempest, which is a rather violent figure. Psalm 139:11 depicts a darkness "overwhelming" or "covering" the psalmist.

11. According to Ps. 56:6(7), the enemy watches for the "heels" of the psalmist.

If the heel may be regarded as the object of subversive attack and partial wound (despite a fatal intention), the head represents the object of open attack and mortal wound. The seed of the woman shall crush the serpent's head. Satan shall be bruised mortally, defeated totally.

The crushing of God's enemies under foot quickly captures the imagination of God's people. After the routing of the first major Canaanite coalition, Joshua triumphantly presents before Israel the five kings who have been enclosed in a cave. He summons the chiefs of his men of war, and directs that they place their feet on the necks of the humbled monarchs. Then Joshua charges the people to take great courage: "for thus shall the Lord do to all your enemies against whom you fight" (see Josh. 10:22–25).

In Psalm 110, destined to become one of the passages from the Old Testament most frequently quoted by the New Testament, vigorous imagery describes the triumph of the coming messianic Lord. Triumphantly he will "smash the head" of his enemies in a broad land (Ps. 110:6).

Ironically, the passage which subsequently is quoted by Satan as a means for tempting Christ bears testimony to the Lord's sure victory over his enemies in language strongly reminiscent of Genesis 3:15. Satan urges Christ to cast himself from the pinnacle of the temple on the basis of God's promise that God's angels shall keep him even from dashing his foot against a stone (Ps. 91:11, 12). Apparently the Tempter failed to consider fully the clear enunciation of anticipated victory by Messiah in the very next verse of the same psalm:

You will tread upon the lion and cobra,
The young lion and the serpent you will trample down (Ps. 91:13).

Ultimately, the promised seed of the woman did come. He entered

---

Note also Gen. 25:26 which describes Jacob as being born with his hand on his brother's heel, and fittingly called Jacob, "he who will (seize by the) heel." By natural birth, he belongs to the seed of the Supplanter. Only by grace is he made to be "prince with God."

into mortal conflict with Satan. Though suffering on his cross the wound of Satan, he "despoiled the principalities and powers" and "made a show of them openly," triumphing over them in it (Col. 2:14, 15).

Inherent in this imagery of the accomplishment of redemption through the victorious overthrow of the seed of Satan lies a principle of God's dealings which has continued throughout the ages. The deliverance of God's people always comes through the destruction of God's enemies.

This basic principle supplies the only adequate solution to some of the most difficult problems of Old Testament interpretation. What is the justification of the *cherem*-warfare of Joshua's day, in which whole cities including women and children were devoted to destruction? Once it is recognized that interspersed among humanity is a seed of Satan hostile to all God's righteous purposes, the intrusion of God's just judgments must be acknowledged as the only appropriate means of salvation for God's people.[12]

How is a Christian to view the imprecatory Psalms of the Old Testament, in which the psalmist calls down curses on his enemies? If the principle is recognized that salvation from God comes only through the destruction of his enemies, the Christian may join the psalmist in his solemn prayer. Indeed, he may not presume to identify finally those among men who are the seed of Satan. Yet he may pray with the sorrowful certainty that Satan's seed lives among men, and that God's purposes shall be realized only through the destruction of these "vessels of wrath fitted for destruction" which God has "endured with much longsuffering" (Rom. 9:22).[13]

---

12. For a fuller treatment of this question, see Meredith G. Kline, *The Structure of Biblical Authority* (Grand Rapids, 1972), pp. 158ff.

13. The recent treatment of Derek Kidner, *Psalms 1-72. An Introduction and Commentary on Books I and II of the Psalms* (London, 1973), pp. 25ff., must be regarded as inadequate. He reduces the earnest confrontation of reality by the psalmist as an exaggerated expression of emotion. The imprecatory Psalms are depicted as having "the shocking immediacy of a scream, to startle us into feeling something of the desperation which produced them" (p. 28). Instead of providing a vent for overworked emotions, these Psalms serve to encourage a sober sense of the stark reality of the struggle between Satan's forces and Christ's.

No word of blessing is addressed to Satan in these verses. He stands enveloped under the condemning curse of God.

Yet blessing is inherent in these words for the seed of the woman. An ultimate victory over the Wicked One shall be achieved.

THE WORD TO THE WOMAN (GEN. 3:16)

The word to the woman includes both curse and blessing. The woman shall have children, which constitutes a most significant blessing. This beneficent word to the woman should not be understood simply in terms of an assurance of fruitfulness in a domestic setting. A seed will be provided for the sake of entering into conflict with the satanic seed. God's promise to bless the woman relates to her role in God's redemptive program.

Yet curse also is involved. God will multiply greatly the woman's sorrow, particularly with reference to her conception. It is not the woman's conception in itself that is being multiplied excessively.[14] Later this identical phraseology is used of the blessing spoken over Abraham and his seed: "multiplying I will multiply your seed" (Gen. 22:17). But the woman is cursed particularly by all the various sorrows associated with her bringing children into the world.

The curse pronounced on the woman also affects her marital relationship toward her husband. The Lord declares: "Unto your husband shall be your desire, and he shall rule over you."

Generally this "desire" of the woman is interpreted as a curse of excessive dependence or longing with respect to her husband. The

---

14. Gesenius, 154, n(b) analyzes the grammatical significance of the conjunction in the phrase, "I shall greatly multiply your sorrow *and* your conception." He concludes by classifying the "and" as a *waw explicativum*. John Calvin, *Commentaries on the First Book of Moses called Genesis* (Edinburgh, 1847), 1: 172, speaks of "the pains which they endure in consequence of conception." E. A. Speiser, *Genesis* (Garden City, 1964), p. 24 interprets the phrase as meaning "your pangs that result from your pregnancy." Cf. also Keil and Delitzsch, op. cit., p. 103.

phrase is understood to mean that the woman lives under the curse of having her life excessively directed toward her husband.[15]

However, an extensive parallelism of phraseology in the very next chapter of Genesis warrants the serious consideration of another possible interpretation.[16] In this related passage, God warns Cain that the "desire" of sin shall be to dominate him. But Cain must rule over sin instead. Sin crouches at the door, "and unto you shall be his desire, but you shall rule over it" (Gen. 4:7).

The interplay of phraseology parallels exactly the word to the woman in Genesis 3:16. The "desire" of the woman shall be to the husband, but he shall rule over her. Not in the sense of excessive dependence, but in the sense of excessive determination to dominate, the woman shall "desire" her husband. Her longing shall be to possess him, to control him, to dominate him. Just as personified sin's desire was directed toward the possession of Cain, so the woman's desire shall be directed toward the possession of her husband.

The statement concerning the man's "rule" over the woman may not require the concept of oppressive domination. But the context strongly suggests it. God pronounces a curse over the woman because of a situation that arose originally from her usurpation of her husband's prerogative. Now it is indicated that habitually she shall display this tendency in her "desire" toward her husband. But he, in reaction, shall "rule" over her.

The curse of marital imbalance settles into the woman's life-style. As she perpetually attempts to possess her husband, he responds by dominating excessively.

---

15. If this interpretation is correct, a partial alleviation may be found in the later biblical hymn to married love. The Shulamite maiden declares: "I (am) for my beloved, and unto me is his desire" (Song 7:11). Now the longing desire of the married relationship belongs to the man.

16. Cf. in particular Sue T. Foh, "What Is the Woman's Desire?," *Westminster Theological Journal*, 37 (1975): 376ff.

THE WORD TO THE MAN (GEN. 3:17-19)

The word to the man also contains curse and blessing. As God introduces his covenantal commitment to redeem a people to himself, he simultaneously pronounces the curses of the covenant of creation.

The blessing is found in the fact that man will eat bread (Gen. 3:17). The sustenance essential for maintaining life shall be provided.

The gracious character of these simple words must not be overlooked. Already the curse of death hovered over man the sinner. He had brought the whole of creation under curse, and so deserved to die. Yet God graciously promises to sustain life for him. Adequate provision of food shall maintain man, so that God's purposes to redeem a people to himself may be realized.

This gracious provision of God characterizes the totality of human history from the first day of its announcement until the present. Jesus' reference to the God who causes his rain to fall on just and unjust testifies to the consistency of God's common grace (Matt. 5:45)

But curse also is involved. "In the sweat of your face you shall eat bread . . ." (Gen. 3:19). The self-sustaining effort of man shall be marred by excessive labor.

Man's curse does not reside in the requirement that he work. Labor also undergirded the creation bond between God and man. Instead, the curse of man resides in the excessive requirement of labor for the fruit produced.

Man's ultimate curse consigns him to the grave: "for dust thou art, and unto dust shalt thou return" (Gen. 3:19). The threat of the creation covenant finds an awesome fulfillment in the dissolution of man's person. Adam had been created to rule the earth. Now the earth's dust shall rule him.

In conclusion, some aspects of this original bond between God and man in sin may be noted. These points emphasize in particular the organic relation of this covenant to the entire history which follows.

First of all, the continuing operation of the provisions of this covenant in the realm of God's common grace may be noted. If, as the unbelieving mind of man has suggested, these verses were written as a tale to explain why snakes crawl, they must have been composed by a genius indeed. For with all the refinements of modern life, the principles laid down in these brief verses continue to characterize man's total existence. Even today, the basic struggles of mankind involve the questions of providing bread, relieving pain, performing labor, bearing children, and dealing with the inevitability of death.

Secondly, God's words to Adam foreshadow the subsequent history of redemption. In organic relation with all subsequent administrations of the covenant of redemption, these verses anticipate both the method by which redemption is to be accomplished and the mystery of redemption's application.

In due time, one representative man was born of woman. This single man entered into mortal conflict with Satan. Though bruised himself, he nonetheless destroyed Satan's power. By this struggle, he accomplished redemption.

Some men respond in faith to God's gracious provision of salvation and find deliverance from sin's corruption. Others continue in the stubbornness of their hearts as the enemies of God.

Why do some men receive the gospel of Christ, while others reject its saving offer? The ultimate answer to this question is found in the distinction among men made in these verses. God sovereignly sets enmity against Satan in the hearts of some. These individuals represent the seed of the woman. Other men continue in their fallen condition. These people represent the seed of Satan. Progress in the history of God's program to redeem a people to himself may be traced along the line of the enmity between these two seeds.

Finally, this covenant with Adam anticipates the consummation of God's purposes in redemption. Adam's requirement to labor echoes the original cultural mandate of the covenant of creation, with its charge to bring the whole earth into subjection to the glory of God.

The ultimate goal of redemption will not be realized merely in a return to the pristine beginnings of the garden. A new imagery of paradise arises in Scripture—the imagery of a city, of a hustling, bustling center of activity for the redeemed.

This glorious consummation focuses on the redemption of man in the context of his total potentialities. In the wholeness of a creature made in God's image, man shall be brought to redemption by realizing the fulness of possibilities available to him.

To this point, we do not see all things subjected to man. The creation in its totality has not released its full potential to the redeemed.

Yet the hope of the future remains sealed in certainty. For we do see Jesus now crowned with glory and honor. Seated at God's right hand, he has all things subjected to him (Heb. 2:8, 9). From his exalted position of power, he ultimately shall bring all things into the service of men who have been redeemed by him to the glory of God.

7

Noah:
The Covenant of Preservation

IN God's covenant with Adam the first reference to the two lines of development among humanity appears. One line belongs to the seed of Satan, one line belongs to the seed of the woman. Genesis 4-11 sketches the early development of these two divergent lines.[1]

The covenant with Noah appears in the context of the unfolding of these two lines, and manifests God's attitude toward both. Total and absolute destruction shall be heaped on the seed of Satan, while free and unmerited grace shall be lavished on the seed of the woman.

Primarily four passages present the nature of the covenant established with Noah: Genesis 6:17-22; Genesis 8:20-22; Genesis 9:1-7;

---

1. Gerhard von Rad, *Old Testament Theology* (New York, 1962), 1: 154 refers to Genesis 3-11 as "the Jahwist's great hamartiology." While von Rad has seen correctly the emphasis on the development of the line of Satan, he has failed to note the parallel maintenance of the line of "the woman."

and Genesis 9:8–17.[2] The following characteristics of the covenant with Noah may be noted on the basis of these passages:

1. The covenant with Noah emphasizes the close interrelation of the creative and redemptive covenants. Much of God's bond with Noah entails a renewal of the provisions of creation, and even reflects closely the language of the original covenant. The reference to the "birds . . . cattle . . . [and] creeping things" of Genesis 6:20 and 8:17 compares with the similar description in Genesis 1:24, 25, 30. God's charge to Noah and his family to "be fruitful, and multiply, and fill the earth" (Gen. 9:1, 7) reflects the identical command given at creation (Gen. 1:28).

Still further, the cultural mandate to "subdue" the earth (Gen. 1:28) finds a close parallel in the covenant with Noah. God's judgment on sin brought a disharmony into man's ruling role over creation. As a consequence, the fear and terror of man was to fall on every beast, bird, and fish of creation (Gen. 9:2). Man's rule shall be exercised in an unnatural context of "terror" and "dread." Yet he continues to maintain his created position as "subduer."

The explicit repetition of these creation mandates in the context of the covenant of redemption expands the vistas of redemption's horizons. Redeemed man must not internalize his salvation so that he thinks narrowly in terms of a "soul-saving" deliverance. To the contrary, redemption involves his total life-style as a social, cultural creature. Rather than withdrawing narrowly into a restricted form of "spiritual" existence, redeemed man must move out with a total world-and-life perspective.

---

2. The pre-diluvian and post-diluvian covenantal commitments of God to Noah fit the frequent pattern of covenantal administration in Scripture. It is not necessary to posit two covenants with Noah, one preceding the flood and one following the flood. Preliminary dealings precede formal inauguration procedures. God's commitment to "preserve" Noah and his family prior to the flood relates integrally to the "preservation" principle, which forms the heart of God's covenantal commitment after the flood. Cf. D. J. McCarthy, "Berît and Covenant in the Deuteronomistic History," *Supplements to Vetus Testamentum* (1972), p. 81. McCarthy notes several instances in Scripture in which a covenantal bond seals a relationship already existing.

At the same time, these broader implications of God's covenant with Noah must be viewed in a distinctively redemptive rather than in a more generalized context.[3] God does not relate to his creation through Noah apart from his on-going program of redemption. Even the provision concerning the ordering of seasons must be understood in the framework of God's purposes respecting redemption.

One of the earliest writings of Israel's prophets rather forcefully emphasizes the unity of these broader dimensions of the covenant with Noah to God's redemptive purposes. Hosea expresses himself in the language of God's covenant with Noah on questions relating to God's ongoing purposes of redemption for Israel.[4] God will "cut a covenant" with the created universe, including the beast of the field, the birds of the heaven, and the creeping things of the ground (Hos. 2:18; cf. Gen. 6:20; 8:17; 9:9, 10). In anticipation of future redemptive activity for Israel, Hosea employs the distinctive categories of the universe found in God's covenant with Noah.[5]

Thus Hosea anticipates the continuing significance of God's broader covenant commitments squarely in the context of God's purposes to redeem a people to himself. The sustaining of all God's creatures by the grace of the Noahic covenant relates immediately to God's reestablishing of Israel in a fruitful relation to himself.

The covenant with Noah binds together God's purposes in creation with his purposes in redemption. Noah, his seed, and all creation benefit from this gracious relationship.

2. A second distinctive of the covenant with Noah relates to the particularity of God's redemptive grace. Prior to the flood, the wickedness of man provoked God's decision to destroy him from the

---

3. Cf. in particular the discussion of L. Dequeker, "Noah and Israel. The Everlasting Divine Covenant with Mankind," in *Questions disputées d'Ancien Testament. Méthode et Théologie* (Gembloux, 1974), p. 119.

4. Cf. specifically Hos. 2:18-23 (Heb. 2:20-25).

5. Essentially these same categories describing the universe are found in God's original ordering of the world (cf. Gen. 1:20, 24-26, 28, 30). God's covenant with Noah thus emphasizes that the present continuation of creation's order rests on the covenanting word spoken to Noah.

face of the earth (Gen. 6:5–7).[6] In contrast to this solemn determination, God expressed a gracious attitude toward Noah: "But Noah found grace in the eyes of the Lord" (Gen. 6:8). From among the mass of depraved humanity, God directed his grace toward one man and his family.

It may be that God's grace had kept Noah from sinking to the levels of depravity found among his contemporaries. But nothing indicates that Noah's favored position arose from anything other than the grace of the Lord himself. The term "grace," which describes God's attitude to Noah, occasionally refers to something other than a response of mercy to a sinful situation (cf. Gen. 39:4; 50:4; Num. 32:5; Prov. 5:19; 31:30). But when describing God's response to fallen man, "grace" depicts a merciful attitude to an undeserving sinner. In Noah's day, every initial formation of the thoughts of man's heart (וְכָל־יֵצֶר מַחְשְׁבֹת לִבּוֹ, Gen. 6:5) were only evil all the day. But Noah found grace in the eyes of the Lord.[7]

Although Genesis 6:9 affirms that Noah was a "righteous man," structural considerations characteristic of the book of Genesis forbid the conclusion that Noah received "grace" because of a previously existing righteousness. The phrase "these are the generations

---

6. The rendering of Genesis 6:6 in the Authorized Version frequently causes undue distress. The translation reads: "And it *repented* the Lord that he had made man on the earth." The problem with this translation arises from the current limitation in the usage of the term "repent." Today this term is used only to describe changing one's mind with respect to wrongdoing.

Certainly God had done no moral wrong in his making of man from which he needed to "repent," and the Hebrew term employed (נָחַם) does not involve such a connotation. But God did respond appropriately to the historical development of human depravity. He was "moved to sorrow" that he had made man on the earth in the light of developing circumstances. This statement in no way implies that God had erred in creating man, or that he was caught by surprise over the development of sin. But it does indicate that God responds meaningfully to developing circumstances in human history.

7. W. Zimmerli, "Χαρις [etc.]" in *Theological Dictionary of the New Testament,* ed. Gerhard Friedrich (Grand Rapids, 1974), 9: 380 says of this text: "Undoubtedly there is implied here the mystery of the free divine decision whereby Noah came to have this attractiveness for God." He defines חֵן as the "kind turning of one person to another as expressed in an act of assistance" (p. 377), noting that it is "always God's free gift" (p. 378) and often is coupled with רָחַם.

of . . ." which begins Genesis 6:9 occurs 10 times in Genesis. Each time the phrase indicates the beginning of another major section of the book.[8] This phrase decisively separates the statement that "Noah found grace" (Gen. 6:8) from the affirmation that Noah was a "righteous man" (Gen. 6:9). God's grace to Noah did not appear because of this man's righteousness, but because of the particularity of God's program of redemption.

The principle of particularity as seen in God's favor toward Noah represents an early manifestation of a theme which continues throughout the covenant of redemption. As stressed by the apostle Paul, the whole by-grace-through-faith salvation-experience comes as a gift of God to those who are dead in trespasses and sins (cf. Eph. 2:1, 2, 8–10).

3. A third principle inherent in the establishment of the covenant with Noah relates to God's intention to deal with families in his covenant relationships. God will destroy all the earth. But to Noah God says:

> I will establish my covenant with you; and you shall enter the ark,—you and your sons and your wife, and your sons' wives with you (Gen. 6:18).

The repetition of this theme of God's dealing with the family of Noah throughout the narrative indicates the significance of the concept for the Noahic covenant.[9] One text in particular may be noted:

> And Yahveh said to Noah, "Go, you and all your house, into the ark; for you [singular] I have seen as righteous before me in this generation" (Gen. 7:1).

---

8. Gen. 2:4; 6:9; 10:1; 11:10; 11:27; 25:12; 25:19; 36:1; 36:9; 37:2. For a discussion of the significance of the phrase, see William Henry Green, *The Unity of the Book of Genesis* (New York, 1895), pp. 9ff.; Martin H. Woudstra, "The Toledot of the Book of Genesis and their Redemptive-Historical Significance," *Calvin Theological Journal*, 5 (1970): 184–191.

9. Cf. Gen. 7:1, 7, 13, 23; 8:16, 18; 9:9, 12.

The righteousness of the single head of the family serves as the basis for including the whole of his descendants in the ark. Because Noah is righeous, his entire family experiences deliverance from the flood.

4. Fourthly, the covenant with Noah primarily may be characterized as the covenant of preservation. This dimension of the Noahic covenant becomes evident in God's response to Noah's thank-offering after the flood-waters had subsided:

> And the Lord smelled the soothing aroma; and the Lord said to Himself, "I will never again curse the ground on account of man, for the intent of man's heart is evil from his youth; and I will never again destroy every living thing, as I have done. While the earth remains, seedtime and harvest, and cold and heat, and summer and winter, and day and night shall not cease" (Gen. 8:20–22).

By this decree, God binds himself to preserve the earth in its present world-order until the time of the consummation.

In some respects, the reason given for God's affirmation never again to curse the earth appears to be a *non sequitur.* "Because the imagination of man's heart is evil from his youth," God will not again curse the ground. It might be expected that God would determine to curse the ground repeatedly because of man's persistent depravity.

However, God understands that the sin-problem never will be cured by judgment and curse. If appropriate relief from sin's corruption is to appear, the earth must be preserved free of devastating judgments such as the flood for a time.

God exercised his prerogative of just judgment in the days of Noah not because he was ignorant of the inability of judgment to cure sin. The Lord knew precisely the state of man's heart before the flood, and certainly understood the limitations of judgment's power to change the heart of man (cf. Gen. 6:5–7).

However, to provide an appropriate historical demonstration of the ultimate destiny of a world under sin, God consumed the earth with the flood. This cataclysmic event later became the model of

God's final judgment of the earth, and the basis for refuting the argument of scoffers who would mock the certainty of an ultimate accounting-day (cf. II Pet. 3:4–6).

The divine dealing with man after the flood must be viewed with this overall perspective in mind. Man is totally depraved, inclined toward self-destruction, and worthy of judgment. But God in grace and mercy determines to preserve the life of man, and promotes the multiplication of his descendants.

God's commitment to preserve man subsequent to the flood also becomes evident in the provisions of Genesis 9:3–6:

> Every moving thing that is alive shall be food for you; I give all to you, as I gave the green plant. Only you shall not eat flesh with its life, that is, its blood. And surely I will require your lifeblood; from every beast I will require it. And from every man, from every man's brother I will require the life of man. Whoever sheds man's blood, by man his blood shall be shed, for in the image of God He made man (Gen. 9:3–6).

All created life is sacred. Yet the highest value must be attached to the life of man. To sustain life, man may eat of all the beasts of God's creation (v. 3). Yet reverence must be shown for the life-principle of the creature, symbolized by his blood (v. 4).[10]

More particularly, the man or beast that commits murder stands under special sanctions (vv. 5f.). God requires that the life of the manslayer must be taken by the hand of man.

Preservation of mankind is not stated explicitly as the reason for this requirement. The reason goes deeper. Because God's own image is stamped in man, the murderer must die.[11]

---

10. The subsequent biblical elaboration on this topic indicates that because "blood" was a symbol of "life" it belonged to God. This principle finds vivid representation in the requirement that the (flowing) blood of animals must not be eaten, but must be presented on God's altar (Lev. 17:10–14).

11. For a discussion of the two primary ways by which this phrase may be interpreted, see John Murray, *Principles of Conduct* (Grand Rapids, 1957), pp. 111ff. Meredith Kline, "Genesis," *New Bible Commentary Revised* (Grand Rapids, 1970),

Yet preservation of the race plays a major role in this legislation. The immediately succeeding verse reiterates the earlier command to Noah and his family to "be fruitful and multiply and fill the earth" (v. 7; cf. Gen. 9:1). If this divine mandate of multiplication is to be realized, humanity must be preserved from the murderous forces of man and beast, which so obviously are present in a depraved world. The taking of the life of the manslayer enforces the sanctity of human life, and preserves the race for future multiplication.

Earlier, God had reserved for himself alone the right to deal with the manslayer. In the case of Cain, God spoke judgment against the one who dared touch him (Gen. 4:15). But now God deliberately places the responsibility for the execution of the wrongdoer on man himself. If the degenerating character of man is to be stopped short of total self-destruction, adequate curbs to the advancement of wickedness must be erected. In the wisdom of God, the execution of the manslayer provides a major curb to overflowing wickedness.

While the words spoken to Noah do not present an elaborately developed theology of the role of the state, the seed-concept certainly is present.[12] In effect, God institutes the temporal power of the state as his instrument in the insistent necessity of controlling evil. This power of the sword, now for the first time placed in the hands of men, terrifies the potential evildoer and restrains his conscious activity of wickedness.[13]

---

p. 90, merges both possible understandings of the phrase: "This (i.e., the fact that man is made in God's image) could explain both the enormity of murder and the dignity of man that justified assigning him so grave a judicial responsibility."

12. John Calvin, *Commentaries on the First Book of Moses Called Genesis* (Grand Rapids, 1948), 1: 295, judges that the verse anticipates the later development of the power of the state, but that the scope of the statement includes even more. By a variety of providential orderings, God will see to it that the one who sheds blood does not go unpunished.

13. "If God on account of the innate sinfulness of man would no more bring an exterminating judgment upon the earthly creation, it was necessary that by commands and authorities He should erect a barrier against the supremacy of evil, and thus lay the foundation for a well-ordered civil development of humanity, in accordance with the words of blessing which are repeated in v. 7, as showing the intention and goal of this new historical beginning" (C. F. Keil and F. Delitzsch, *Biblical Commentary on the Old Testament: The Pentateuch*, [Grand Rapids, 1949–50], 1: 153).

Generally, commentators tend to modify the reference to capital punishment in the covenant with Noah. Either they deny the presence of such a reference, or they oppose the application of the principle to current societal structures.

A series of questions addressed to the issue may aid in clarifying the problem:

First question: Does God's covenant with Noah sanction the taking of the life of a murderer under any circumstances?

This question may be asked without entering immediately into the particular problems involved in determining the current relevance of this provision to the new covenant believer. Does the covenant with Noah in itself offer divine sanction to capital punishment?

Genesis 9:5, 6 might be interpreted simply as stating a fact that shall occur. If a man sheds blood, his blood shall be shed. On the other hand, the verse might be understood as offering divine sanction for the taking of the life of a murderer.

The first consideration in deciding between these optional understandings relates to the precise meaning of the phrase which may be rendered literally "from the hand of (man or beast) I shall require it." The phrase could mean: "By the instrumentality (of man) I shall demand an accounting." In this case, man would be the instrument by which God would bring the murderer to account. Thus the principle of capital punishment would be established.

However, this interpretation of this particular phrase runs into immediate difficulty. For the verse says that "by the hand of beast" as well as "by the hand of man" God will require life. It would be rather difficult to imagine a wild beast serving as instrument of God's judgment in the same sense in which a man would function in this regard.

The more likely interpretation of this phrase "by the hand of (man or beast) I shall demand an accounting" is: *"From* (man or beast) I shall demand an accounting." That is, God will exact justice from either man or beast that murders.

This interpretation of the phrase "from the hand of (man or beast) I shall require" is supported elsewhere in Scripture. The prophet Ezekiel states that God shall "require from" the hand of the watchman the blood of the unwarned, using the identical phraseology found in Genesis 9:5, 6 (Ezek. 33:6; 34:10).

Genesis 9:5 in itself would not appear to settle the question as to whether or not God intends man to be his instrument in the execution of justice on the murderer. Indeed, God shall require the life of the manslayer. But does he require it specifically from the hand of another man?

Genesis 9:6 answers this question in the affirmative. Both the parallelism in the structure of the verse and the indication of the instrument for executing justice point in this direction.

The parallelism of phraseology as found in the original text of Scripture may be represented as follows in English translation:

> a He who pours out
> b   the blood of
> c   man,
> c   by man
> b   his blood
> a shall be poured out (Gen. 9:6).

The structure of the verse suggests in itself the *lex talionis*, the law of an eye for an eye, a tooth for a tooth. The one who sheds man's blood shall have his blood shed by man. More specifically, man is indicated as the agent by which the murderer's blood shall be shed. When this thought is combined with the affirmation in verse 5 that God shall "demand an accounting" of the murderer, it becomes clear that the intention of the passage is to designate man as God's agent in the execution of justice on the murderer.

This conclusion is supported by subsequent scriptural legislation. Exodus 21:28 indicates that the animal that takes the life of a man must have its life taken by man. In addition, Israel is charged explicitly with the responsibility of executing capital punishment on the murderer (Exod. 21:12; Num. 35:16–21).

In conclusion, this text indicates that man has a responsibility respecting the murderer given to him by God. The requirement is unmistakable. The person who takes the life of a man must have his life taken by man.[14]

Second question: May the covenant with Noah be regarded as the first revelation of this requirement?

Those who work from the framework of a critical reconstruction of the text of Genesis would have genuine difficulty with this question. Much of the narrative concerning Noah is attributed by critical scholars to the "priestly" school, and dated into the sixth century B.C. or later. If such were the case, the material relating to capital punishment in the covenant with Noah very possibly would follow chronologically the stipulations regarding capital punishment found in the Mosaic covenant.

However, the prominence in Hosea of material strongly reminiscent of God's covenant with Noah raises serious doubts concerning the sixth-century "priestly" character of the material under discussion. Hosea, writing in the eighth century, echoes the language of a covenantal relationship enacted prior to his own day.[15] On the basis of a covenantal relationship preceding his own time, Hosea anticipates Israel's future situation. In this light, it is hardly appropriate to suggest that the distinctive provisions of the covenant with Noah did not appear until some 200 years after Hosea.

On an even more basic level, it is essential to accept the Scriptures as reporting faithfully the character of God's covenant with Noah. From this perspective, the covenant with Noah must be regarded as the first revelation of the sanction of capital punishment. The concept did not arise in the legislation given for Israel in the days of Moses, which subsequently was projected into a legendary past. Instead, it originated at the point of humanity's new beginning with the family of Noah.

---

14. Von Rad, op. cit., p. 129, does not hesitate to affirm that these verses indicate that man is to be the executor of the death penalty. He suggests that this responsibility conveys the "strong legal tone accompanying the gracious Noahic dispensation."

15. See above, p. 111.

Third question: Is this injunction concerning capital punishment limited in a temporal or ethnic sense, or universally binding in its requirements?

Obviously the provisions concerning the execution of the murderer have no ethnic limitations. Noah's covenant does not speak narrowly to one race. The first father of the new humanity, together with his entire family, constitutes the human party of this covenant. God makes his covenant to sanction life with "every living creature" (Gen. 9:9, 10).

Quite interestingly, ethnically universal legislation concerning the sanctity of life reappears at a later turning-point in the history of redemption. At the time of apostolic confirmation of the extension of the gospel to Gentile as well as Jew the law concerning the non-eating of blood reappears. The decision of the Jerusalem council frees Gentiles from the ritualistic laws of Moses. But they must abstain ". . . from what is strangled and from blood" (Acts 15:20, 29).

Apparently this passage alludes to the Noahic covenant.[16] The entry of the gospel into the broadstream of humanity passes once more through the provisions of the covenant with Noah. It is not necessary to retain up to the present the letter of the ritual laws of the Noahic covenant to appreciate their significance as transitional legislation. To avoid unnecessary stumbling among Jewish converts to Christ, this broader Old Testament legislation taken from God's covenant with Noah was enforced for a period, although later New Testament evidence points to its early repeal (Rom. 14:14; I Cor. 10:25f.).

The question of a temporal limitation of the specific legislation concerning capital punishment is a more disputable point. Primarily,

---

16. Cf. Claus Westermann, *Genesis, Biblischer Kommentar Altes Testament* (Neukirchen-Vluyn, 1974), p. 628; F. F. Bruce, *Commentary on the Book of the Acts, New International Commentary on the New Testament* (Grand Rapids, 1954), p. 312. For a discussion of the rabbinic tradition concerning the seven laws of the covenant with Noah, and their application to the Gentile world, see *Encyclopaedia Judaica* (New York, 1971), 12: cols. 1189f.

the problem centers on the relation of the legislation concerning the non-eating of blood to the requirement that the life of a man-slayer be taken from him. If one aspect of the legislation is temporally limited, could it not indicate a temporal limitation for the entirety of Noahic legislation? In response to this question, two points may be noted:

First, the possible presence of some temporally limited elements in a divine covenant does not automatically temporalize every element of the covenant.[17] The covenant with Abraham had its circumcision rite. The covenant with Moses had its sacrificial system. Yet the essence of both these covenants continues to play a vital role in the life of God's people.

Secondly, the sanctity of the life of man finds abiding reinforcement through the recognition of the power granted to the state in Scripture (cf. Rom. 13:1ff.; I Pet. 2:13, 14). Civil authorities continue to bear the sword on behalf of God.

In any case, the preservative character of the covenant with Noah plays a central role in the progress of redemptive history. Men today still live under the provisions inaugurated in this covenant. The regularity of the seasons derives directly from God's determination to preserve the earth until deliverance from sin can be accomplished. The institution of the state indicates the purpose of God to restrain the evil inherent in humanity.

5. Fifthly, the covenant with Noah possesses a distinctively universalistic aspect. The particular stress on the cosmic dimensions of the covenant with Noah should be noted in this regard. The whole of the created universe, including the totality of humanity, benefits from this covenant. Not only Noah and his seed, but "every living creature" lives under the sign of the rainbow (cf. Gen. 9:10).

---

17. Derek Kidner, *Genesis. An Introduction and Commentary. The Tyndale Old Testament Commentaries* (Chicago, 1967), p. 101, concludes that the temporally limited character of the legislation regarding the eating of certain flesh has the effect of temporally limiting the legislation regarding capital punishment. He comments: ". . . one cannot simply transfer verse 6 to the statute book unless one is prepared to include verses 4 and 5a with it."

This inclusion of the totality of the universe in God's redemptive covenant finds vivid recognition in Paul's expression concerning the final expectation of the redeemed:

> For we know that the whole creation groans and suffers the pains of childbirth together until now. And not only this, but also we ourselves, having the first fruits of the Spirit, even we ourselves groan within ourselves, waiting eagerly for our adoption as sons, the redemption of our body (Rom. 8:22f.).

Not only man, but the entire universe shall experience ultimate deliverance from the curse.

This universal character of the covenant with Noah provides the foundation for the world-wide proclamation of the gospel in the present age. God's commitment to maintain faithfully the orderings of creation displays his longsuffering toward the whole of humanity. He desires to make known the testimony of his goodness throughout the universe.

At a subsequent point in the history of redemption, the Psalmist reflects on the regularity of day and night as witness to the universality of God's redemptive program. Day following day utters speech, and night following night shows knowledge. The "voice" of these regulated ordinances goes out through all the earth, and their words to the end of the world (Ps. 19:2–4). Wherever man is found, the witness of God's ordering as determined by the covenant with Noah testifies to the glory of the Creator.

God's commitment to maintain a universal witness to the whole of humanity through the ordering of creation later plays a significant role in the missionary mandate of the apostle Paul. In establishing that the gospel should be proclaimed among all nations, he appeals to the universal witness borne by God through creation (cf. Rom. 10:18 in its reference to Ps. 19:4). The world-wide scope of the testimony of creation provides the foundation for the universal proclamation of the gospel. The God who has commissioned the witness of himself to the ends of the earth through creation also has shown himself to be "Lord of all, abounding in riches for all who call upon him" (Rom. 10:12).

This universal witness of the ordering of creation roots deeply in the covenanting word to Noah. By the provisions of the Noahic covenant God committed himself to a course of universal testimony. Creation's witness of grace toward sinful man still provides the platform from which the universal proclamation of the gospel should be launched.[18]

6. Sixthly, the seal of the covenant with Noah emphasizes the gracious character of this covenant. In a context of threatening judgment symbolized by the bloated rain-clouds, God designates the overarching beauty of the rainbow to depict his grace-in-judgment. Having once destroyed the world, thereby depicting the immutability of his righteous decrees, the Lord God now couples the clouds with his rainbow to manifest his free and unmerited purpose of grace.[19]

---

18. II Pet. 3:3–10 also appears to establish its base for the universal proclamation of the gospel on the covenant with Noah. Sinners may mock the word of new covenant prophecy concerning a consummating judgment (vv. 3, 4). But Noah's flood indicates the certainty of God's ultimate intentions (vv. 5, 6). As "by the word of God" ($\tau\tilde{\omega}\ \tau o\tilde{v}\ \theta\epsilon o\tilde{v}\ \lambda\acute{o}\gamma\omega$) the world first came into being, so "by the same word" ($\tau\tilde{\omega}\ \alpha\dot{v}\tau\tilde{\omega}\ \lambda\acute{o}\gamma\omega$) the present universe is being sustained for the judgment of fire (vv. 5, 7). The reference to the "same word" refers broadly to the word of God which had been manifested so powerfully at creation. But it also appears to refer more specifically to the covenanting word spoken to Noah. On the basis of this post-diluvian word, the earth continues to be maintained to the present.

The longsuffering of God, who does not wish any to perish (v. 9), manifests itself in the context of this covenanting word that God will maintain the whole of creation until the judgment of fire (vv. 7, 10). In the cosmic context of these verses, describing the purposes of God respecting the whole of creation (vv. 6, 7), the "desire" of God that "all" should come to repentance should be interpreted universally. The fact that God may "desire" what he has not explicitly "decreed" simply must be taken as one of those areas of God's purposes that cannot be comprehended by the finite mind. The context would not favor the limitation of this desire to the "elect," despite the possibility that "longsuffering to *you*" could be interpreted as meaning longsuffering to the believing recipients of Peter's letter. The point of the text is not that God is longsuffering toward the elect, not willing that any of the elect should perish. The present delay of judgment on the world indicates his longsuffering to the whole of humanity, despite the fact that ultimately not all shall be saved. Cf. John Murray and N. B. Stonehouse, *The Free Offer of the Gospel* (Phillipsburg, n.d.), pp. 21–26.

19. Von Rad, op. cit., p. 130, notes that the word for "rainbow" in the text is the word normally used for "battle-bow." He suggests that the colorful rainbow indicates that God has laid aside his battle-bow after the flood. Cf. Meredith G. Kline,

It is no accident that the throne of the righteous Judge of heaven and earth is depicted as having "a rainbow round about the throne, like an emerald to look upon" (Rev. 4:3). What a joy it should be to the true sharer of God's covenantal grace in Christ that the sign and seal of God's good purposes arches the place of his final disposition.

In conclusion, some attempt may be made to evaluate the definition of the term "covenant" previously suggested as it related to the covenant with Noah. May the covenant with Noah be described as a "bond-in-blood sovereignly administered"?

In one sense the covenant with Noah offers the greatest tension-point for the suggested definition of the term "covenant." The covenant with Noah is a "bond"; it is a bond "sovereignly administered." But in what sense may the covenant with Noah be described as a "bond-in-blood"? How is pledge-to-death involved in the Noahic covenant?

Two factors in the covenant with Noah indicate the presence of this aspect of the covenant idea. First, notice the alternatives involved in the period anticipating the formal ratification of the covenant with Noah. God will destroy man from the face of the earth; but Noah will find grace in the eyes of the Lord. Life and death indeed are the underlying motifs of the Noahic epoch, as seen in the dramatic representation of God's attitude toward the seed of the woman and the seed of Satan. Secondly, note the solemn provision concerning capital punishment; "whosoever sheddeth man's blood, by man shall his blood be shed" (Gen. 9:6). Undoubtedly life and death are involved in these words. Death shall come to the covenant-breaker who takes the life of man, while preservation will be the result of proper observance of these stipulations.[20]

"Genesis," *New Bible Commentary Revised* (Grand Rapids, 1970), p. 90: *"My bow* translates *qešet,* the usual meaning of which is the weapon. Thus, the recurring rainbow imposed on the retreating storm by the shining again of the sun is God's battle bow laid aside, a token of grace staying the lightning-shafts of wrath."

20. Cf. Delbert R. Hillers, *Covenant: The History of a Biblical Idea* (Baltimore, 1969), p. 102, who suggests the presence of self-malediction in the fact that the "bow" is aimed toward God. He quotes a medieval poem:

To summarize, the covenant with Noah provides the historical framework in which the Immanuel principle may receive its full realization. God has come in judgment; but he also has provided a context of preservation in which the grace of redemption may operate. From the covenant with Noah it becomes quite obvious that God's being "with us" involves not only an outpouring of his grace on his people; it involves also an outpouring of his wrath on the seed of Satan.

> My bow between you and me
> In the firmament shall be,
>
> . . . .
> The string is turned toward you
> And toward me is bent the bow,
> That such weather shall never show,
> And this beheet I thee.

While the suggestion of divine self-malediction is intriguing, the context does not provide adequate support for the idea. It is difficult to see how such an idea would suit subsequent descriptions of God's throne being arched graciously by a bow (cf. Rev. 4:3).

8

Abraham:
The Covenant of Promise

THE sovereign aspect of God's relationship with Abraham was made quite apparent at the time of the patriarch's initial call. God did not suggest meekly that if Abraham would depart from his fatherland, he would be blessed. Instead, the word of God came in terms of a solemn charge: "Get thee out of thy country, and from thy kindred" (Gen. 12:1).

This same tone appeared at the institution of the covenant seal of circumcision. The Lord declared to Abraham: "I am God Almighty; walk before me, and be blameless. And I will establish my covenant between me and you . . ." (Gen. 17:1, 2). Nowhere does any suggestion of "agreement" or "contract" emerge from these narratives. The Lord God sovereignly dictates the terms of his covenant with Abraham.

By far the most significant passage in the patriarchal narrative dealing specifically with the covenant concept is the intriguing description of the formal inauguration of the Abrahamic covenant found in Genesis 15. This narrative clearly indicates the essence of a covenant to be a "bond in blood sovereignly administered."

This particular administration of God's commitment to effect redemption appropriately may be designated "the covenant of promise." God sovereignly confirms the promises of the covenant to Abraham.

THE FORMAL INAUGURATION OF THE ABRAHAMIC COVENANT

A heart-rending question occasions the formal establishment of God's covenant with Abraham. The patriarch asks with concern: "Lord Yahveh, how shall I *know* that I shall inherit (the land you have promised)?" (Gen. 15:8). Abraham believes God's word. But he needs a strengthened assurance.

God had granted magnanimous promises to Abraham. But now the patriarch was aging. His wife remained childless. The culture of Abraham's day sensibly had made provision in the event of barren parents.[1] It was possible to "adopt" into the family a household servant. This adopted "son" would become legal heir.

Was this legal procedure of adoption the way in which the childless Abraham must interpret God's word of promise? Was it inevitable that Eliezer of Damascus would become his heir? (vv. 2, 3).

The Lord declares unequivocally his sovereign intentions. None other than a son born of Abraham's own loins shall possess Abraham's promises (v. 4).

But what assurance can be supplied? Is there some way by which the word of promise can be confirmed?

The Lord graciously assures the patriarch by formal ratification of a covenant-bond. He orders Abraham to present certain animals before him (v. 9).

---

1. Cf. E. A. Speiser, *Genesis* (Garden City, 1964), p. 112; Derek Kidner, *Genesis* (Chicago, 1967), p. 123.

The patriarch needs no further instruction. He knows the procedure well. In accord with the custom of the day, Abraham halves the animals and sets the corresponding pieces over against each other. The birds he slays, but does not divide.[2]

At this point, the narrative indicates that the symbolic meat of the slaughter attracts birds of prey which attempt to devour the flesh which Abraham has prepared. The patriarch finds it necessary to intervene, and to frighten away the wild creatures with their rabid appetites (v. 11).

As Abraham passes into a visionary state, God communicates to him the course of events which must precede the full realization of the promises. Abraham must not despair. He must not become uneasy because of delay in fulfillment. God provides an overview of the course of the history which shall lead eventually to the possession of the land by the seed of Abraham. Having been granted this perspective, the patriarch is encouraged to wait patiently.

For 400 years, Abraham's descendants will endure oppression in a strange land. After this period they shall come out with great possessions. Finally they shall enter the land that has been promised (vv. 13, 14).

Why must such an extended period of deprivation be endured? Why should not Abraham himself possess the land of promise immediately?

Only God's grace to sinful men provides an adequate response to this question. The grace of God's longsuffering expressed toward the current inhabitants of the land explains the delay. Because "the iniquity of the Amorite is not yet full" (v. 16), the descendants of Abraham must endure 400 years of exile from the land of promise.

At the conclusion of these words of prophecy, Abraham witnesses a most amazing phenomenon. A "smoking oven" and a "flaming

---

2. This distinctive treatment of the birds finds codification subsequently in biblical legislation (cf. Lev. 1:14–17). It is not that Mosaic legislation has colored the admittedly ancient narrative of Genesis 15; instead, the more ancient pledge-to-death tradition of covenantal inauguration under Abraham has provided the pattern for animal sacrifice under Moses.

torch" pass between the pieces of torn flesh which had been arranged earlier (v. 17).

What is the meaning of this striking ceremony? Why does a visible manifestation of the godhead "pass between the pieces"?

The immediately succeeding statement of the narrative supplies the needed insight: "On that day the Lord made a covenant with Abram" (v. 18). The dividing of the animals, coupled with the passing between the pieces, results in the "making" (literally "cutting") of a covenant.

By dividing animals and passing between the pieces, participants in a covenant pledged themselves to life and death. These actions established an oath of self-malediction. If they should break the commitment involved in the covenant, they were asking that their own bodies be torn in pieces just as the animals had been divided ceremonially.

Extra-biblical parallels have confirmed the significance of this self-maledictory action involved in the covenant-making ceremony. Several instances of the symbolic slaying of an animal in covenant-making procedures have been uncovered recently. One Syrian text dating into the eighteenth/seventeenth centuries B.C. records an agreement in which a certain Abba-AN donated a city to Yarimlim: "Abba-AN is bound to Yarimlim by oath and he has cut the throat of a sheep." Other texts from Mari dating in the eighteenth century B.C. refer to the killing of an ass at the conclusion of a covenant. Even the term "to kill an ass" appears to be a technical expression for making a covenant.[3]

By the inherent pledge to death of the covenant-inauguration procedure, a "bond in blood" is established. Parties of the covenant

---

3. Cf. D. J. McCarthy, *Treaty and Covenant* (Rome, 1963), pp. 52f., who indicates that the phrase "to cut a covenant" occurs in cuneiform texts from Qatna dating to the fifteenth century B.C. as well as in Hebrew, Aramaic and Phoenecian texts. Cf. also Meredith Kline, *By Oath Consigned* (Grand Rapids, 1968), p. 17; Leon Morris, *The Apostolic Preaching of the Cross* (London, 1956), p. 64. These last two authors both cite an eighth century B.C. Babylonian treaty: "(and just as) this calf is cut to pieces, so may Mati'el be cut to pieces and his nobles be cut to pieces."

commit themselves for life and for death in the covenantal relationship.

In the case of the Abrahamic covenant, God the Creator binds himself to man the creature by a solemn blood-oath. The Almighty chooses to commit himself to the fulfillment of promises spoken to Abraham. By this divine commitment, Abraham's doubts are to be expelled. God has solemnly promised, and has sealed that promise with a self-maledictory oath. The realization of the divine word is assured.

SUBSEQUENT ALLUSIONS TO THE INAUGURATION CEREMONY OF THE ABRAHAMIC COVENANT

God's commitment to Abraham as vivified in the ceremony of covenant inauguration continues to swell with significance throughout redemptive history. The Lord's pledge-to-death made to Abraham casts its distinctive mold on the whole of subsequent Israelite history.

A reference to this same ceremony of covenantal inauguration just before the kingdom of Judah was carried into captivity indicates that the significance of this covenant-making ceremony continued throughout history without being diminished. Fourteen hundred years had transpired. Yet the covenant inaugural ceremony witnessed by Abraham had lost none of its cultural relevance.

The reappearance of a reference to such a concrete method of covenant inauguration after an intervention of 1400 years merits careful analysis. According to the context of Jeremiah 34, Jerusalem was under siege by Babylon (vv. 1, 6, 7). In an apparent effort to recover the lost favor of Israel's God, King Zedekiah assembled all the people for a ceremony of covenant renewal (vv. 8, 9). The people responded to this call to rededication by complying with the elementary stipulations of the original Mosaic covenant regarding the sabbatical release of Israelite slaves (v. 10).

However, the firmness of resolve on the part of the people wavered. No sooner had all Israelite slaves been released than they were reclaimed again by their masters (v. 11). At this point the prophet brought to king and people the word of their slighted covenant God:

> Therefore thus says the Lord, "You have not obeyed Me in proclaiming release each man to his brother, and each man to his neighbor. Behold, I am proclaiming a release to you," declares the Lord, "to the sword, to the pestilence, and to the famine; and I will make you a terror to all the kingdoms of the earth.
>
> "And I will give the men who have transgressed My covenant which they made before Me, when they cut the calf in two and passed between its parts—the officials of Judah, and the officials of Jerusalem, the court officers, and the priests, and all the people of the land, who passed between the parts of the calf—and I will give them into the hand of their enemies and into the hand of those who seek their life. And their dead bodies shall be food for the birds of the sky and the beasts of the earth" (Jer. 34:17–20).

To appreciate fully the potent significance of this passage, several points must be noted:

1. The language of Jeremiah 34 echoes quite distinctly the language of Genesis 15. The double reference to the "passing between the parts of the calf" (Jer. 34:18, 19) and the detailed description of the devouring of the covenantally-cursed bodies by birds of prey (v. 20) reflect unmistakably the language describing the inauguration of God's covenant with Abraham. This allusion to the experience of Abraham is even more remarkable in its specificness because of the confirmed antiquity of Genesis 15.[4] Yet Jeremiah's allusion gives no impression whatsoever of drawing from the dusty

---

4. Note the evaluation of Gerhard von Rad, *Genesis* (Philadelphia, 1961), p. 184: "The narrative about God's making of the covenant (vv. 7–18) is one of the oldest narratives in the tradition about the patriarchs . . . in our narrative about the making of the covenant we have an original segment from the oldest patriarchal tradition." While von Rad would support a critically-oriented documentary analysis of the chapter, he nonetheless asserts: "Verses 7–18 are very ancient tradition from the patriarchal period itself."

pages of antiquity. The prophet has no fear that his particular description of covenant renewal will appear irrelevant or incomprehensible to his audience.

2. Jeremiah's appeal to a covenantal pledge-to-death cannot involve only a literary allusion to Abraham's experience. Instead, it is a very real description of an actual covenant-renewal ceremony just enacted by Zedekiah and his people.[5] Notice again the language of verses 18 and 19: ". . . they cut the calf in twain and passed between the parts thereof; the princes of Judah, and the princes of Jerusalem, the eunuchs, and the priests, and all the people of the land . . . passed between the parts of the calf." In effect, Jeremiah says, "*your* princes, *your* priests, you people yourselves, *you* are the ones who pledged yourself to death by passing between the covenantal pieces." This language is not the language of mere literary allusion to the ancient experience of Abraham. The context of an actual covenant-renewal ceremony argues against this interpretation. Something the people did in Jeremiah's day corresponded to the pledge-to-death involved in the Abrahamic covenant.

3. What did Zedekiah and people do to renew the covenant? The simplest conclusion would suggest that Zedekiah copied rather literally the covenant-making ceremony followed by Abraham as described in Genesis 15. However, other considerations point to a more complex situation than might be imagined at first. Despite the straightforwardness of references to "passing between the pieces," it would appear much more certain that Zedekiah followed the covenant-making ceremony instituted in Moses' day rather than the ceremony of Abraham's day.

The procedure for covenant-making developed in Moses' day provided Zedekiah with his pattern for covenant-renewal. The formal assembly, the reading of the law, the response of the people—these elements belong integrally to the making of a covenant as established by Moses, not by Abraham.[6]

---

5. D. R. Hillers, *Treaty-Curses and the Old Testament Prophets* (Rome, 1964), p. 26, assumes that a calf was slain, and that the people actually paraded between the pieces.

6. This pattern appears at the point of initial institution of the Mosaic covenant

Evidence within the text of Jeremiah 34 indicates that just such a procedure was followed. The pivotal point of the narrative turns about the sabbatical release of Hebrew slaves (cf. vv. 8–12). Quite obviously, Zedekiah was attempting to regain the favor of God in a context of impending doom by this action. But why should he select this single ordinance from all the Old Testament legislation? Why should he begin with the dramatic release of all fellow-Hebrews who had become slaves?

Zedekiah begins by the release of Hebrew slaves because such an action would follow naturally as the outworking of a covenant-renewal ceremony according to the Mosaic pattern. The reading of the law would have been an essential part of this ceremony. The first of the list of specific ordinances in the book of the covenant (Exod. 20–24) concerns the sabbatical release of Hebrew slaves:

> Now these are the ordinances which you are to set before them. If you buy a Hebrew slave, he shall serve for six years; but on the seventh he shall go out as a free man without payment. If he comes alone, he shall go out alone; if he is the husband of a wife, then his wife shall go out with him (Exod. 21:1–3).[7]

It therefore seems clear that the procedure followed by Zedekiah conformed to the pattern of Mosaic covenant renewal ceremonies, involving as a crucial factor the reading of the book of the law.

4. But some explanation must be given for the evident consciousness of the significance of the Abrahamic procedure on the part of Zedekiah and the people. If the ceremony of covenant renewal followed the Mosaic pattern, why does the prophet indicate that the people "passed between the pieces?"

The circumstances of Jeremiah's narrative indicate that something in the reenactment of the Mosaic ceremony corresponded to the

---

(Exod. 24:1–8). Cf. subsequently Josh. 24, II Kings 23, and Neh. 8 for covenant-renewal ceremonies following the Mosaic pattern.

7. This law was especially significant to Israel. They had been redeemed from bondage; they were never to return to bondage. All three law-codes of the Pentateuch record this principle (cf. Exod. 21:1–3; Lev. 25:39–43; Deut. 15:1, 12–18).

pledge-to-death associated with the Abrahamic covenant. The entirety of the people may not have paraded literally between divided animal carcasses. But inherent in the Mosaic ceremony must have been an activity which involved the same commitment.

A ritual which was embedded in the formal inauguration procedures of the Mosaic covenant committed the people to a life-and-death involvement with the Lord of the covenant. Apparently the blood-sprinkling ritual described in Exodus 24:8 substituted for the literal "passing between the pieces" of Genesis 15.

First the law was read. The people responded with a verbal commitment to obedience (Exod. 24:7). Then Moses sprinkled the blood on the people as he declared: "Behold, the blood of the covenant, which the Lord has made with you" (Exod. 24:8). This blood of sprinkling symbolized not only the cleansing of the people. It also consecrated them to keep the covenant on pain of death. The same pledge-to-death which played such a prominent role in the inauguration of the Abrahamic covenant manifested itself in the inauguration of the Mosaic covenant. Sheer statistical considerations may have occasioned the substitution of the blood-sprinkling ritual for the ceremony of passing between the pieces. An entire nation hardly could be paraded between the pieces of slain animals. But an equally significant ceremony of blood-sprinkling could be instituted.

The suggestion that Jeremiah saw in the Mosaic ceremony the same pledge-to-death found in the Abrahamic ritual finds strong support from the repeated appearance of the distinctive curses implied in the Abrahamic covenant throughout Israel's history. In his vision, Abraham drove away the birds of prey which gathered about the ceremonial carcasses (Gen. 15:11). This portion of his vision symbolized the ultimate fate of the covenant-breaker. Not only would his body be slain; it would be devoured by the wild birds of the heavens. Woe to the covenant-breaker who once has pledged himself to death!

The identical woe is spoken over Israel in the context of the curses and blessings involved in the Mosaic covenant. The Lord solemnly warns Israel's potential covenant-breakers: "Your carcasses shall be food to all birds of the sky and to the beasts of the earth, and there shall be no one to frighten them away" (Deut. 28:26).[8]

The subsequent history of Israel displays most vividly the consequences of covenant violation. Israel under Moses had pledged itself to death if it should break the covenant. As a consequence, the prophet Ahijah declared the covenant curse on the house of Jeroboam:

Anyone belonging to Jeroboam who dies in the city the dogs will eat. And he who dies in the field the birds of the heavens will eat; for the Lord has spoken it (I Kings 14:11).

The same curse rests on the house of Baasha:

Anyone of Baasha who dies in the city the dogs shall eat, and anyone of his who dies in the field the birds of the heavens will eat (I Kings 16:4).

Nor does the house of Ahab escape the ultimate curse of covenantal judgment:

The one belonging to Ahab, who dies in the city, the dogs shall eat, and the one who dies in the field the birds of heaven shall eat (I Kings 21:24).

This curse is applied in particular to Jezebel, Ahab's queen:

And the dogs shall eat Jezebel in the territory of Jezreel, and none shall bury her (II Kings 9:10).

This same specific curse permeates the prophecy of Jeremiah himself:

---

8. The close connection of the thought of Jer. 34 to the covenantal curses of Deut. 28 is accented still further by Jeremiah's specific allusion to God's making Israel to be "tossed to and fro among all the kingdoms of the earth" (Jer. 34:17; cf. Deut. 28:25).

And the dead bodies of this people will be food for the birds of the sky, and for the beasts of the earth; and no one will frighten them away (Jer. 7:33).

. . . and their carcasses will become food for the birds of the sky and for the beasts of the earth (Jer. 16:4).

. . . and I shall give over their carcasses as food for the birds of the sky and the beasts of the earth (Jer. 19:7).

A later reference to this curse of the covenant appears in the Psalmist's lament over fallen Jerusalem:

They have given the dead bodies of Thy servants for food to the birds of the heavens, the flesh of Thy godly ones to the beasts of the earth. They have poured out their blood like water round about Jerusalem and there was no one to bury them (Ps. 79:2, 3).

The continuing prophetic application of these curses throughout Israel's history demonstrates the vitality of covenantal self-consciousness throughout the nation. The ultimate judgment of devastation can be understood only in terms of the original pledge to life and death at Sinai, which in turn reflected the covenantal form employed by God in binding himself to Abraham.

This awareness of the threat of covenantal curses also explains the vitality of the Abrahamic covenantal pattern as it appears in Jeremiah 34. No other passage in Scripture reflects the specifics of the Abrahamic covenant-ritual with the vividness of detail found in this text as it describes the termination of Israel's national history.

At first glance, it would appear that a 1400 year gap occurred in Israel's conscious reflection on the covenant-making ritual of Abraham. But if the sprinkling of the nation under Moses had the same effect as "passing between the pieces," no gap at all existed. The ceremony of the Mosaic covenant embodied the substance of the commitment under Abraham, although the form had changed. Israel's subsequent history indicates that no diminishing of consciousness concerning the covenantal pledge ever occurred.

NEW TESTAMENT REFERENCE TO THE INAUGURATION CEREMONY OF THE ABRAHAMIC COVENANT

Reference to the covenantal curses instituted under Abraham does not cease with the prophecy of Jeremiah and of Israel's destruction. Most significantly, the New Testament interprets the new covenant in terms of relief from these same curses.

While promise of future relief from the curses of the covenant may be found in the Old Testament, witness to the actual realization of this promise first occurs in the New Testament. This witness appears particularly in Hebrews 9:15–20 and in the gospel record of the inauguration of the new covenant (Matt. 26:28; Luke 22:20).

Hebrews 9:15–20

Most interestingly, the presentation of deliverance from the curse of covenant-breaking as it occurs in the book of Hebrews appears in a context discussing the inauguration ceremony of the Mosaic covenant. If the blessed relief of the new covenant is to be appreciated fully, it must be considered on the background of the pledge-to-death involved in the inauguration of God's covenant with Israel as mediated through Moses.

The key to understanding the significance of these verses lies in an analysis of the relation of death and a *diatheke*. This single concern unites the entire progress of thought in Hebrews 9:15–20.

The term *diatheke* in Greek may be rendered either as "last will and testament" or as "covenant." While these two concepts may be confused in the mind of twentieth-century readers of the Bible, they maintained quite distinctive significances in the biblical period. The crucial factor for deciding between these possible meanings of the term in Hebrews 9 is the relation of death to *diatheke* throughout the passage.

The connection between death and a "last will and testament" is obvious. This concept registers immediately in the mind of the modern interpreter, since "last will and testament" plays a continuing role in current culture. The death of a testator activates the provisions of his will. By death the testament takes effect.

The relation between death and a "covenant" is not so immediately obvious. Since "covenants" according to the biblical pattern do not play a vital role in modern cultures today, the current reader finds it more difficult to maintain a grasp on the essence of the concept. Particularly, the integral relation of death to a "covenant" escapes the modern reader.

Yet death is as inseparably related to "covenant" as to "testament." If the present study of God's covenant with Abraham establishes anything, it indicates the vital relation of death to covenant. Essential to the inauguration both of the Abrahamic and Mosaic covenants was the symbolic representation of the death of the covenant-maker. The long history of God's terminal judgments on Israel finds prophetic interpretation in the light of God's execution of the death-curse on covenant breakers.

Death and covenant clearly relate. They relate concretely in two ways. First, the death of the covenant-maker receives symbolic representation at the time of the inauguration of the covenant. The covenant-making procedure is not complete without this pledge-to-death aspect. Secondly, the death of the covenant-violator receives historical actualization when covenantal judgment is executed. Once a transgression of covenantal commitment has occurred, death is inevitable.

So both "testament" and "covenant" involve death. Death activates a testament. Death inaugurates and vindicates a covenant.

Clearly the opening verse in this section of Hebrews is concerned with the relation of death to "covenant":

And for this reason He is the mediator of a new *covenant*, in order that since a death has taken place for the redemption of the transgressions that were committed under the first *covenant*, those who have been called may receive the promise of the eternal inheritance (Heb. 9:15, NASB).

A death has taken place for the redemption of transgressions committed under the first *covenant*. The *diatheke* in Hebrews 9:15 is the Mosaic covenant. God did not establish through Moses a "last will and testament." He established instead a "covenant."

This verse speaks of Christ's death as the factor which removes transgressions committed under the first *diatheke*. In no way does the death of a "testator" remove transgressions committed against a last will and testament. The death of a testator is not a vicarious, substitutionary death.

But the death of Christ the maker of the new covenant provided redemption from the curses incurred due to the violation of the old *covenant*. His "blood of the covenant" inaugurated the new covenant while at the same time removing the curses of the old covenant. *Diatheke* in Hebrews 9:15 refers clearly to "covenant," not "testament."[9]

The relation of death to "covenant" is the subject of Hebrews 9:18-20 even more clearly than in verse 15:

> Therefore even the first covenant was not inaugurated without blood. For when every commandment had been spoken by Moses to all the people according to the law, he took the blood of the calves and the goats, with water and scarlet wool and hyssop, and sprinkled both the book itself and all the people, saying "This is the blood of the *covenant* which God commanded you" (Heb. 9:18-20).

---

9. The reference in v. 15 to an "inheritance" should not tempt the interpreter to revert to the "testamentary" concept. For inheritance also played a most vital role in the Old Testament covenantal framework. The inheritance of life equalled the blessing of the covenant. It was the exact opposite of the curse-option. Covenantal inheritance found its typological representation in the possession of the land of Canaan, symbolizing the life of peace and security provided by God for his people. The possession of this "inheritance" was not dependent on death, but on covenantal faithfulness. Death related to inheritance in the covenant not as the necessary prerequisite for claiming the inheritance, but as the diametrical opposite of possessing the inheritance. In Heb. 9:15, Christ is "mediator of a new covenant, in order that . . . those who have been called may receive the promise of the eternal inheritance."

"Blood" and *"diatheke"* in these verses recall the inauguration ceremony of Sinai. By sprinkling the blood, Moses did not institute a last will and testament. God did not die in order to activate a "will" for Israel. Instead, the ceremony at Sinai instituted a covenantal relationship. The sprinkled "blood of the covenant" solemnly consecrated God and Israel to one another for life and death.

The "blood" of Sinai as discussed in Hebrews 9:18–20 represented a covenantal rather than a testamentary arrangement. Death sealed the covenant.

The relation of death and *diatheke* in Hebrews 9:16, 17 arouses greater debate. Sandwiched between verses that clearly relate "death" to a covenantal framework, these verses nonetheless raise again the question of the significance of the term *diatheke*.[10]

Because of the clarity of Hebrews 9:15 and 18–20, it seems appropriate to begin by supposing that the term *diatheke* would possess the same meaning in Hebrews 9:16, 17.[11] From this perspec-

---

10. For a more detailed discussion of the significance of *diatheke* in Heb. 9:16, 17, and notations concerning the relevant bibliography, see the present writer's unpublished dissertation, *A People of the Wilderness: The Concept of the Church in the Epistle to the Hebrews* (Richmond, Va., 1966), pp. 43ff.

11. Other factors in addition to context favor the assumption that *diatheke* in Heb. 9:16, 17 means "covenant" rather than "testament." First, the consistent usage of the term *diatheke* as "covenant" in the Septuagint points· toward the presumption that the same significance would be found in Hebrews. Cf. E. Hatch, *Essays in Biblical Greek* (Oxford, 1889), pp. 47f., who says there can be "little doubt that the word must be invariably taken in the sense of 'covenant' in the N.T., and especially in a book which is so impregnated with the language of the LXX." Cf. also Vos, op. cit., pp. 33f.

Secondly, the consistency in usage of the term by the New Testament itself, both within and outside Hebrews, favors the meaning "covenant." Of the 31 times in which the term occurs outside these two verses, 31 times the word means "covenant" rather than "testament." Only in Gal. 3:15 may a serious case be made for the meaning "testament." This consistent usage reveals the thought-patterns of the New Testament theologians. They worked with the concept of "covenant," not "testament."

Thirdly, the ineffective character of an argument based on a verbal pun argues against the meaning "testament." Certainly some force of persuasion would be lost if the reader were asked to move from the meaning "covenant" to the meaning "testament" and back to the meaning "covenant" within the span of four verses.

tive, the phraseology at the beginning of verse 17 is most striking: "For a covenant is made firm *over dead bodies."*

A testament (singular) is not made firm "over dead bodies" (plural). Only one body is required for the activation of a last will and testament. But a multiple of dead bodies is associated immediately with the inauguration of a covenantal relationship. Many beasts are slain to symbolize the potential of covenantal curse.

With the covenant-inauguration ceremony in mind, the language of verse 16 also should be noted: "For where [there is] a covenant, of necessity the death of the covenant-maker must be brought forward." The language conforms precisely to the procedure by which covenant commitment was vivified in the Old Testament. As the covenantal relationship was sealed, the death of the covenant-maker was "brought forward."[12]

The contextual connection of Hebrews 9:16 with the preceding verse lends support to the assumption that "covenantal" not "testamentary" arrangements provide the framework for understanding the writer's argumentations. Christ died to redeem from the transgressions committed under the first covenant (v. 15). This death was made necessary because "the death of the covenant-maker" was "brought forward" at the point of covenantal inauguration (v. 16). By the grace of God, Christ has substituted himself in the place of covenant-violators. He has died in their stead, taking on himself the curses of the covenant.

---

12. Meredith Kline, *Treaty of the Great King* (Grand Rapids, 1963), p. 41, certainly is correct in searching out the pattern of ancient covenant-making for the key to understanding Hebrews 9:16, 17. But rather than looking to the pledge-to-death which is at the heart of covenant inauguration, he turns to the provisions for dynastic succession in the ancient treaties. In this manner, he seeks a basis for justifying a "testament/covenant" play on *diatheke* in Heb. 9. However, the theme of Heb. 9:15ff. is not that of Christians as dynastic successors of Christ, even though this "succession" be modified to mean "co-regency with the living Testator." Instead, the theme of Hebrews 9:15ff. is covenant inauguration. Rather than developing in a rather novel fashion a secondary aspect of the ancient covenantal pattern, the writer to the Hebrews straightforwardly develops the heart of the covenant-making ceremony.

The last phrase of verse 17 presents the most difficult problem for a consistent translation of *diatheke* as "covenant" throughout the passage. The phrase reads literally: "for [a covenant] is not strong [valid] while the covenant-maker lives."

It is understandable that this phrase has inclined interpreters toward the translation "testament." Clearly a "testament" is not valid while the testament-maker lives. But the opposite would seem true with respect to a "covenant." A covenant is indeed valid while the covenant-maker lives.

However, this last phrase of verse 17 does not occur in isolation from its context. It is a secondary clause, dependent grammatically on what has preceded.

The first part of verse 17 indicates that a covenant is "made firm" over dead bodies. This language harmonizes quite appropriately with the ancient covenant-making procedures. The second part of verse 17 refers to the "making strong" of the covenant. It would appear that the "making firm" ($\beta\epsilon\beta\alpha\iota\alpha$) of the covenant and the "making strong" ($\iota\sigma\chi\acute{\upsilon}\epsilon\iota$) of the covenant allude to the same principle at work in covenantal relations. The secondary portion of the verse should be interpreted in the light of the primary portion.

Furthermore, the strong connective between verses 17 and 18 must be considered. "Wherefore [$\H{o}\theta\epsilon\nu$]," according to verse 18, "the first covenant was not inaugurated without blood." Now the reference clearly is to the blood-shedding procedure associated with *covenant inauguration*. If verse 18 is drawing an inference from verse 17 with respect to the blood-shedding of covenant inauguration, it would appear mandatory to read verse 17 in terms of covenant inauguration rather than in terms of testamentary disposition.

For these reasons, it would seem more appropriate to read the latter portion of verse 17 in terms of covenant inauguration. A covenant does not become strong (valid) "while the covenant-maker lives," because the making of a covenant must include the symbolic death of the covenant-maker. No covenant-making procedure is complete apart from the symbolic representation of the death of the one making the covenant.[13]

The detailed argumentation of the previous discussion must not be allowed to detract from the major point of the passage. The curses incurred because of the transgressions of the old covenant have fallen on Jesus Christ. His death is to be understood in terms of the long history of God's dealing with his people. By bearing the full consequences of covenantal pledge-to-death, Christ delivers from the curse of the covenant. No remission from guilty transgression could be gained without the shedding of blood. Christ therefore presented his body as the sacrificial victim of the covenantal curse.

The Inauguration of the New Covenant (Matt. 26:28; Luke 22:20)

With this perspective in view, it is appropriate to look more closely at the record of the original inauguration of the new covenant by the Lord Jesus Christ as found in the Gospels. Matthew 26:28 may be compared with Luke 22:20 to provide a fuller picture of the event.

In presenting the cup to his disciples, Jesus says: "This is my blood of the covenant, which is poured out for many unto remission of sins" (Matt. 26:28). The "pouring out" (ἐκχέω) of Christ's blood reflects the sacrificial language of the Old Testament, and the process by which the curses of the covenant were heaped on a substitutionary victim.[14] Christ explains his death to be "unto remission of sins."

---

13. The greatest difficulty with this interpretation of v. 17b is that it requires that the reference to the death of the covenant-maker be interpreted as a symbolic rather than an actual death. This problem could be resolved by suggesting that the writer has assumed a violated covenant. Given the situation in which stipulations have been violated, a covenant is not made "strong" so long as the covenant-maker lives. In this case, the death envisioned would be actual rather than symbolical. This line of interpretation contains some commendable features. But the strong contextual emphasis on covenant inauguration points in the direction of symbolic rather than actual death.

14. Note the usage of the term in the Septuagint in relation to Israel's sacrificial system as found in Lev. 4:17, 12, 18, 29, 30, 34; 8:15; 9:9; 17:4, 13.

His death effects deliverance from the covenantal death-curse by the removal of old covenant violations. Jesus offers his blood as the basis for deliverance from the curses of the covenant.

The gospel of Luke adds a further dimension to this procedure by mentioning the "new" covenant being established by Christ: "This cup is the new covenant in my blood, even that which is poured out for you" (Luke 22:20). Not only does Christ's blood remove the curse of the old covenant; simultaneously it introduces the blessed condition of the new covenant.

This dual significance of Christ's blood echoes the dual role of God's words to Adam in the original institution of the covenant of redemption. The infliction of the curses of the covenant of creation was coupled immediately with the announcement of the blessings of the covenant of redemption.[15] While both man and woman experienced curse for sin, at the same time they received promise of blessing through redemption.

Now in Christ this dual role of curse and blessing finds its consummative significance. As Christ takes to himself the curses of the old covenant, he simultaneously inaugurates the blessed condition of the new.

In conclusion, God's covenant with Abraham may be characterized particularly as the covenant of promise. By the solemn ceremony described in Genesis 15, God promised redemption.

The emphasis on divine promise in this covenant is brought out strikingly by one distinctive aspect of the narrative. Contrary to what might be expected, Abraham does not pass between the divided pieces representing the covenantal curse of self-malediction. The Lord of the covenant does not require that his servant take to himself the self-maledictory oath. Only God himself passes between the pieces.

By this action, God promises. The Lord assumes to himself the full responsibility for seeing that every promise of the covenant shall be realized. It is not that Abraham has no obligations in the

---

15. See above, pp. 103–5.

covenant relation. Already he has been required to leave his fatherland (Gen. 12:1ff.). Later he shall be required unequivocally to administer the seal of the covenant to all his male descendants (Gen. 17:1, 14). But as the covenant is instituted formally in Genesis 15, the Lord dramatizes the gracious character of the covenantal relation by having himself alone to pass between the pieces. This covenant shall be fulfilled because God assumes to himself full responsibility in seeing to its realization.[16]

The pleading voice of the patriarch had urged: "How can I *know?* How can I be sure?"

The solemn ceremony of covenantal self-malediction provides the Lord's reply: "I promise. I solemnly commit myself as Almighty God. Death may be necessary. But the promises of the covenant shall be fulfilled."

In Jesus Christ God fulfills his promise. In Him God is with us. He offers his own body and his own blood as victim of the covenantal curses. His flesh is torn that God's word to the patriarch might be fulfilled.

Now he offers himself to you. He says: "Take, eat; this is my body. This is my blood of the covenant shed for many. Drink, all of you, of it."

16. O. Kaiser in "Traditionsgeschichtliche Untersuchung von Gen. 15," *Zeitschrift für die Alttestamentliche Wissenschaft*, 70 (1958): 120, says: "Dieser kühne Anthropomorphismus betont die Unauflöslichkeit der göttlichen Zusage, da sich Gott schlechterdings nicht selbst zerstören kann." ("This bold anthropomorphism emphasizes the indestructibility of the divine promise, since God absolutely cannot destroy himself.")

9

The Seal of the
Abrahamic Covenant

GENESIS 15 describes the formal inauguration of the Abrahamic covenant. God symbolically "passes between the pieces," and solemnizes his promise to the patriarch. Genesis 17 records the institution of the official seal of the Abrahamic covenant. The patriarch and his seed receive in their flesh the sign of the covenant.

Between these two monumental chapters, Scripture records the lapse of Abraham's faith. In spite of the spectacular vision of covenant inauguration experienced by Abraham in Genesis 15, he nonetheless stumbles into a reliance on the flesh in Genesis 16.

Possibly it is because of this failure on the part of the patriarch that a more permanent reminder of God's relationship with him is instituted. Some abiding sign must be given which will last beyond the visionary stage of experience. Circumcision as the seal of the Abrahamic covenant remains permanently with the patriarch to remind of the surety of the promises.

It is interesting to note in this context the permanently abiding character of the seal of the new covenant. The covenant-sealing Holy Spirit abides with the believer until the day of his redemption as a token of his engagement to be the Lord's (cf. Eph. 1:13, 14).

In dealing with the covenant seal of circumcision, three areas in particular will be noted: the original significance of circumcision, circumcision in Old Testament history and theology, and the New Testament fulfillment of the Old Testament seal.

THE ORIGINAL SIGNIFICANCE OF CIRCUMCISION

Exegetical Comments on Genesis 17:9-14

The formal introduction of the covenantal seal of the old covenant begins with an unequivocal injunction addressed to the patriarch. God first recounts his numerous commitments in the covenantal relationship (cf. Gen. 17:6-8). He shall make Abraham exceedingly fruitful. Kings shall come from him. God will establish his covenant as an everlasting covenant, to be a God to Abraham and to his seed. He will give Abraham the land of his sojourning. All of these things God will do for the patriarch.

"And *you*" (v. 9). Now, emphatically, the Lord of the covenant lays responsibility on his creaturely beneficiary. Earlier, God had commanded that Abraham walk before him in obedience with a life-transforming thoroughness (v. 1). But now he announces with emphasis one specific requirement. Abraham and his seed have no choice in the matter. Divine fiat speaks inescapably: "You shall keep my covenant, you and your seed after you."

"This is my covenant . . . every male among you shall be circumcised" (v. 10). The seal of the covenant relates so closely to the covenant itself that the covenant may be identified as the seal. This identification of the covenant by its seal is expressed even more explicitly in verse 13b: "My covenant shall be in your flesh for an everlasting covenant." Far from being an optional aspect of the covenantal bond, the seal *is* the covenant.

"It shall be for a sign of the covenant" (v. 11). A sign gives a witness. It testifies to the reality of the relationship that has been established. Circumcision offers its perpetual witness to the reality of the covenantal bond.

"The son of eight days shall be circumcised among you" (v. 12). Contrary to the general practice of the nations at large, circumcision for Israel is not to be a sign of introduction into manhood, associated with the arrival of puberty.[1] Instead, it involves the eight-day-old infant, and therefore emphasizes the principle of solidarity between parents and children in the covenantal relationship.

"The one who is born in (your) house and the one bought from any stranger which is not of your seed (shall be circumcised)" (v. 12b). From the day of its original institution as a covenant sign, circumcision was open to gentiles. It was not intended exclusively as a racial badge, but more broadly as a covenantal sign.

"The uncircumcised male . . . that soul shall be cut off from his people" (v. 14). A most severe judgment awaits the person who rejects this covenantal sign. He shall be excommunicated from the fellowship of the covenant community.

As this scriptural announcement introduces the seal of the old covenant, the solemnity of God's directive must be noted. God has declared that this sign shall be administered among his people. To treat the sign lightly, or to ignore the stipulations associated with the sign, is to expose oneself to the judgments of the God of the covenant.

The Theological Significance of the Seal as Originally Instituted

It cannot be maintained that the practice of circumcision originated with Israel.[2] Not only among Shemites, but among representatives of practically every other ethnic group, circumcision has been

---

1. Cf. Francis Ashley Montagu, "Circumcision" in *Encyclopedia Britannica* (Chicago, 1963), 5: 799.
2. As indicated by Vos, *Biblical Theology,* p. 103.

practiced in one form or another. The Canaanite contemporaries of Israel stood out quite strikingly as an exception to this rule.

Because of the widespread practice of circumcision among the nations, the unique role of circumcision in the thinking of Israel must be underscored. The following points may be noted with respect to the import of circumcision as originally instituted for Abraham:

1. Circumcision symbolized inclusion in the covenant community established by the initiative of God's grace. It was the sign of the covenant. As such, it brought people into relationship with the God of the covenant and into fellowship with the people of the covenant.

2. Circumcision indicated the need for cleansing. The hygienic act of the removal of the foreskin symbolized the purification necessary for the establishment of a covenant relation between a holy God and an unholy people.

The application of circumcision to the first father of the family line of promise indicated that physical descent alone was "not sufficient to make true Israelites. The uncleanness and disqualification of nature had to be taken away."[3]

This understanding of the theological significance of circumcision stands in blankest contrast with subsequent Jewish misappropriation of the rite. Circumcision should have humbled the people of Israel by pointing to their innate unworthiness to be God's people. Instead, the sign was misunderstood as indicating that they were especially meritorious before God. That which should have been for them a source of humility became to them a source of pride.

3. Circumcision as originally instituted does not suggest merely a need for cleansing. It symbolizes also the actual process of cleansing which is needed. Not only does it indicate that man by nature is impure. It also represents the removal of defilement essential for the achievement of purity.

3. Ibid., p. 105.

It is significant in this connection to note that the heart of the covenantal relationship connects immediately with the circumcision-seal. Because Yahweh will be Israel's God (v. 7), the people must be circumcised. The holiness of the God of Israel requires that Israel also be holy.

This cleansing significance of circumcision is brought out forcefully through an allusion to the old covenant rite by Jesus Christ in John 7:22, 23. In the context of John's Gospel, Jesus' opponents are accusing him for healing a man on the Sabbath. The Lord responds by referring to the ancient practice of circumcision, a rite which had been instituted in the period of the fathers well before the days of Moses. If his adversaries proceed to circumcise a man on the eighth day even though that day should fall on the Sabbath, why should not he proceed to heal a man on the Sabbath? They make part of a man clean on the Sabbath by circumcision; should he not make a "whole man healthy" (ὅλον ἄνθρωπον ὑγιῆ) on the Sabbath by healing?

Circumcision, therefore, which is "from the fathers," partially cleanses. It does not merely communicate the need for cleansing. It actually symbolizes and seals the cleansing necessary for covenantal participation.

4. This cleansing is accomplished by the excision of the foreskin of the male reproductive organ. The "cutting away" of a natural part of the human body as a symbol of religious cleansing suggests the necessity of the execution of judgment as an act essential for purification. By circumcision the sinner undergoes a judgment that purifies.

5. The rite of cleansing as originally instituted had for Abraham special significance with regard to the propagation of the race. Several factors relate the rite of circumcision to the question of the propagation of the race:

(a) Quite explicitly, circumcision is instituted for Abraham's seed as well as for Abraham himself. Before the seed had been born, it was determined that the sign of the covenant was to be applied to them. All subsequent seed, without exception, must receive in their flesh the seal of the covenant.

(b) It is the male reproductive organ that is involved in the rite of circumcision. For that reason, circumcision has special significance with regard to the propagation of the race.

This single rite serves as the seal for the total bond which God has made with Abraham. The promise concerning the seed, the land, and the blessing all are sealed by this single sign. But because it is the male reproductive organ that is involved in circumcision, it would appear that the rite has special significance with regard to the propagation of the race.

(c) In Israel, circumcision is to be applied to infants eight days of age. Because of this application of the covenantal sign to the infant, it would appear that the sign has special significance with respect to the propagation of the race.

What may be concluded from the fact that circumcision has special significance with respect to the propagation of the race? Two points may be suggested.

First, it may be concluded that the rite of circumcision implies that the race is sinful and in need of cleansing. Sin is not merely a matter of the individual, but of the race. From the point of its original institution, circumcision implies the guilt of the race.

Secondly, the close relation of this covenantal seal to the propagation of the race indicates that God intends to deal with families. God in his work of redemption intends to restore the solidarity of the creation order of the family. Instead of setting the natural order of creation against grace, God sets sin over against grace. The promise of the covenant, sealed by the initiating rite of circumcision, addresses itself to the solidarity of the family unit.

CIRCUMCISION IN OLD TESTAMENT HISTORY AND THEOLOGY

Throughout Israel's history, circumcision always is presented as a rite intending to have a God-ward as well as a man-ward dimension.

At its very essence, circumcision is a covenantal sign between Israel and its God.

This fact indicates that circumcision never should be regarded purely as a national badge, symbolizing only a physical relationship among the people of Israel. Indeed, circumcision did have a national significance. It served to introduce people into the externally organized community of Israel. But it also was intended to represent the God-ward relationship that was the essence of the covenant.

This God-ward dimension of the circumcision-seal manifested its presence in every major epoch of Old Testament history. Beginning from the point of its inauguration and extending throughout the history of Israel, circumcision indicated the status of a man in relation to God as well as his status in relation to the nation of Israel.

Already the theological import of the seal of circumcision at the time of its institution has been discussed. This aspect of the rite found reinforcement in the days of Moses. Moses admonished Israel in the plains of Moab to circumcise the foreskin of their heart, and to be hardened against God no more (Deut. 10:16). Elsewhere Moses indicated that God would circumcise the heart of Israel and its descendants, so they would love the Lord with all their heart (Deut. 30:6). The outward sign of cleansing symbolized the inner purification necessary for a life of obedience and love to God.

These texts clearly build on a symbolism of cleansing inherent in the rite of circumcision. By speaking of heart-purification, Moses introduces no novel concept of circumcision which was not present from the moment of its original institution. It is not that circumcision once meant merely attachment outwardly to the nation of Israel, and now is to mean something additional. Instead, Moses simply is making forceful application of the significance of spiritual cleansing that always belonged to the rite of circumcision. The application of the term "circumcision" to a process of heart-cleansing indicates that God's intention from the beginning by the rite of circumcision was to symbolize the inner purification necessary for the establishment of a proper relation between the holy Creator and the unholy creature. By the rite of circumcision men were identified before the world as God's holy people. It was to their shame that their hearts did not conform to the holiness that the sacred rite they had received was intended to depict.

Exodus 12:43–49 presents the requirement that non-Israelites must be circumcised to participate in the passover. The existence of such a requirement should not be interpreted as evidence of a sense of superiority within the Israelite nation. Exactly the opposite implication must be concluded. Any Gentile might participate in the highest privilege of Judaism, if he should indicate a willingness to meet the same requirements laid on the Jew himself.

This absolute openness to the incorporation of Gentiles into the community of Israel has far-reaching significance affecting the interpretation of massive portions of the Old and New Testaments. Many traditions of interpretation build on an implicit assumption that God has a distinctive purpose for the racial descendants of Abraham that sets them apart from Gentiles who respond in faith and obedience to God's program of redemption. This entire herme-neutical superstructure begins to totter when it is realized that "Israel" could include non-Abrahamic Gentiles just as well as ethni-cally related Jews. In elaborating on the significance of the applica-tion of circumcision to the Gentile community, the Jewish commenta-tor Benno Jacob says:

> Circumcision is a national and religious symbol and remains such beyond the people that are descended from Abraham by birth. Every stranger who submits to it receives Abraham as his father and becomes an Israelite.[4]

The circumcised Gentile "becomes an Israelite." Since this is the case, obviously "Israel" cannot be defined simply in terms of racial distinctives. As Jacob further states:

> Indeed, differences of race have never been an obstacle to joining Israel which did not know the concept of purity of blood. . . .

---

4. B. Jacob, *The First Book of the Bible: Genesis. His Commentary Abridged, Edited, and Translated by Ernest I. Jacob and Walter Jacob* (New York, 1974), p. 115.

Circumcision *turned a man of foreign origin into an Israelite* (Exod. 12:48).[5]

This participation in the passover on the part of the circumcised Gentile cannot be reduced merely to involvement in an ethnic or national experience. Enjoyment of the covenantal fellowship meal with the God of the covenant epitomizes the significance of Passover. Those who eat the Passover lamb dwell in comfortable security while the death-angel sent from God "passes over."

Communion with God and his people in so rich a context requires appropriate preparation. The Gentile, like the Jew, must be circumcised in advance of this privilege. He must receive the appropriate cleansing from the defilement of his sinful condition.

Because of the momentous significance of participation in the Passover meal, circumcision cannot be reduced merely to a racial or national badge. The God-ward relation of the participant must be involved as well as the man-ward relation.

Evidence in the books of Joshua-Kings also supports this conclusion. When Israel enters the land of promise, the people arrive in an uncircumcised condition. The unbelieving generation had fallen in the wilderness, and the younger generation had not been circumcised. In a significant act of faithful obedience to God's command, the people undergo the debilitating operation of circumcision despite their location in the midst of a hostile territory.

After their healing, the Lord interprets to Joshua the significance of the event. "This day I have rolled away (גַּלּוֹתִי) the reproach of Egypt from you." As a permanent reminder of this event, the place is memorialized by being called "Gilgal" or "Rolling" (גִּלְגָּל—Josh. 5:9). Apparently the description of the removal of Egypt's reproach in terms of a "rolling" alludes to the process by which the foreskin is removed in circumcision.

Unquestionably the rite of circumcision communicates more than ethnic derivation at this point. By the process of circumcision, a

---

5. Ibid., p. 233, emphasis added.

cleansing has occurred. The reproach of Egypt has been removed. The people no longer abide under the bondage of an oppressor in an alien land. Instead, they have become participating heirs in the covenant made with their fathers. Circumcision in this instance relates specifically to the promise concerning the possession of the land.

To be heirs of that land which is God's holy possession, the people also must be holy. This holiness finds its symbolic accomplishment in the nation's circumcision at Gilgal.

The defiled character of the uncircumcised Philistines appears in sharpest contrast with the holiness of God's circumcised people. Repeatedly the Philistine enemies of Israel are designated as "uncircumcised." Goliath is the "uncircumcised Philistine" (I Sam. 17:26, 36). Saul would rather die than fall into the hands of the uncircumcised (I Sam. 31:4). David dreads the prospect of the news of Saul's death spreading into Philistine territory, for then the daughters of an uncircumcised people would begin to gloat (II Sam. 1:20).

In passages such as these, it is highly unlikely that the term "uncircumcised" refers merely to the non-Israelite character of the persons involved. The term is packed with implications of uncleanness, defilement, and unworthiness.

This same conclusion finds support from the employment of the circumcision-imagery by the later prophets of Israel. The men of Judah are admonished to circumcise themselves before the Lord, and to remove the foreskins of their hearts (Jer. 4:4). Already they are Israelites. Already they possess the "badge" of national membership. But the transformation of life-pattern from unrighteousness to righteousness has not been accomplished. The essence of the purification symbolized by circumcision needs to be realized in their lives.[6]

From this overview of the significance of circumcision in Old Testament history and theology, it should be evident that circum-

---

6. Other passages in the prophets developing the circumcision-theme may be found in Jer. 9:25, 26; Ezek. 28:10; 31:18; 32:19–32.

cision persistently speaks to the question of man's relation to God. Never does the rite shrink to a level of being merely a badge of national membership. At the point of its inception and throughout Israelite history, circumcision functions as the sign of the covenant.

THE NEW TESTAMENT FULFILLMENT
OF THE OLD TESTAMENT SYMBOL

As with all essential elements of Old Testament revelation, the seal of the Abrahamic covenant finds its truth-in-symbol fulfilled in the New Testament. Several passages in the New Testament comment explicitly on the consummating reality of the Old Testament seal. Other portions of New Testament Scripture relate more indirectly to the question of the abiding significance of this seal. In any case, the New Testament does provide an adequate basis for understanding the role of the reality of the circumcision-symbol in the life of the new covenant believer.

Of awesome importance in appreciating the significance of this rite is the fact of the circumcision of Jesus Christ. As the glories of the new covenant are being introduced, the "things of the old covenant are not recklessly cast aside."[7] To redeem men that were under the law, God sent forth his son, born of a woman, born under the law (cf. Gal. 4:4). Jesus was conceived by the Holy Spirit and knew no sin. Yet "to fulfil all righteousness," he underwent the prescribed rites of cleansing (cf. Matt. 3:15). As a sign that he voluntarily was taking on himself the obligations of his people, Jesus submitted first to circumcision and later to the baptism of John.

The fact that Jesus formally received his name in conjunction with the rite of circumcision helps illuminate the significance of the act for Christ. His name is "Jesus," "Jehovah saves" (Luke 2:21). His cleansing is not for his own sake, but for the sake of the sinful people whom he is saving.

---

7. Norval Geldenhuys, *Commentary on the Gospel of Luke, The New International Commentary on the New Testament* (Grand Rapids, 1968), p. 117.

The clear indication of decisive relief from the external process of circumcision under the new covenant appears in the narrative concerning the spread of the Gospel among Gentiles in the book of Acts. The purifying Holy Spirit takes up residence in uncircumcised Gentiles to the astonishment of circumcised Jewish believers (Acts 10:44–48). If the covenantal reality of "I shall be your God" may come to pass apart from the external rite of initiation, how is it possible to continue insisting that Gentiles be circumcised? The reality of the new covenant does not require that Gentiles become Jews before they may become Christians. Instead, it requires that both Jews and Gentiles become new creatures through their oneness with Christ by means of faith alone.

This revolutionary perspective finds formal ratification at the time of the council of Jerusalem. Those who would require that Gentiles be circumcised before they may be received into the fellowship of God's people cannot be sustained (Acts 15:1). They are answered by reference to the fact that "God who knows the heart" bore witness to the acceptability of the gentile believers by making no distinction between circumcised and uncircumcised. He granted the Holy Spirit to uncircumcised Gentiles just as he had done to Jewish believers (Acts 15:8–9).

Once this principle has been acknowledged, it never can be reversed. Never again is the formal rite of circumcision to be imposed upon God's people. As a matter of fact, the "gospel of circumcision" is an "antigospel." Paul could not possibly have expressed himself more pointedly: "If you receive circumcision, Christ will be of no benefit to you" (Gal. 5:2).

This aggressive affirmation concerning the end of the formal rite of circumcision must not be understood in a shortsightedly wooden sense. Paul himself ordered the circumcision of Timothy immediately after receiving the decree of the Jerusalem council (Acts 16:3). By following such a procedure, he demonstrated his freedom in Christ to be made "all things to all men that he might by all means save some" (I Cor. 9:22).

The usurpation of the circumcision-rite goes much more deeply than a formal forbidding of the external practice of circumcision. It speaks to the eschatological character of the present day. Never again may a return be made to the older shadow-forms involved in Israel's ritualistic activities. The reality has had its historical manifestation. To require repetition of the formalities of the shadow is to substitute a man-ordered ritual for a God-ordered reality.

There can be no question that the formal rite of circumcision has come to its end so far as its significance for redemption is concerned. The testimony of the New Testament clearly affirms this fact.

However, the reality symbolized in the formal rite of circumcision certainly has significance for the new covenant believer. Cleansing from impurity and the incorporation into the covenant community sustains a vital significance for the Christian. Several portions of the New Testament Scriptures affirm this fact.

First of all, several passages relate the essence of the new covenant to the circumcision-symbol of the old covenant. As reality replaces shadow, so the essence of cleansing replaces its older symbol.

Romans 4:3, 9–12 read as follows:

3. For what does the Scripture say? "AND ABRAHAM BELIEVED GOD, AND IT WAS RECKONED TO HIM AS RIGHTEOUSNESS."
. . . .
9. Is this blessing then upon the circumcised, or upon the uncircumcised also? For we say, "FAITH WAS RECKONED TO ABRAHAM AS RIGHTEOUSNESS."

10. How then was it reckoned? While he was circumcised, or uncircumcised? Not while circumcised, but while uncircumcised;

11. and he received the sign of circumcision, a seal of the righteousness of the faith which he had while uncircumcised, that he might be the father of all who believe without being circumcised, that righteousness might be reckoned to them,

12. and the father of circumcision to those who not only are of the circumcision, but who also follow in the steps of the faith of our father Abraham which he had while uncircumcised.

Verse 11 particularly is significant. The circumcision-symbol of the old covenant is related to the essence of the old covenant.

Abraham received the sign of circumcision as a seal of the right-eousness of faith. Abraham's true righteousness is associated directly with the outward symbol of circumcision. The intention of circum-cision was to seal the reality of righteousness.

At the same time, the passage develops two "fatherhoods" for Abraham. These "fatherhoods" serve to interpret the consummating reality of the new covenant in terms which indicate a strong line of continuity with the provisions of the old covenant. Abraham is father (1) of all who have faith without being circumcised (i.e., believing Gentiles); he is also the father (2) of circumcised people who, in addition to having experienced the external rite of circum-cision, also walk in the pattern of the faith-steps of Abraham (i.e., believing Jews).

This passage therefore indicates that those related to Abraham by the circumcision-symbol of the old covenant are joined to the Christ by faith, along with those who experience the essence of circum-cision's symbolism without ever experiencing the external rite itself. As a result, the circumcision-symbol of the old finds a significant meeting-point with the essence of the new covenant. The cleansing symbolized in the one corresponds to the reality experienced in the other. Old Testament circumcision relates meaningfully to New Testament purification.

It may be that the emphasis on the "fatherhood" of Abraham in these verses intends to allude to the cleansing ritual of circumcision. Having direct relation to the organ of propagation, the circumcision of the first father of the faithful symbolized a purification appro-priate for his becoming the head of the line of those who would be justified by faith.

Romans 2:25–29 also relates the essence of the new covenant to the circumcision-symbol of the old. The following points in particu-lar may be noted:

1. The circumcision symbol of the old covenant has no value whatsoever unless it be joined with the true righteousness which it represents. According to verse 25, "circumcision is of value, if you practice the law; but if you are a transgressor of the law, your circumcision has become uncircumcision."

2. The man who experiences the essence of righteousness through the new covenant will be regarded as "circumcised" although he actually never has experienced the seal of circumcision (vv. 26, 27).

3. The symbol of circumcision under the old covenant is not the thing which makes a man acceptable to God. Only the true circumcision of the heart by the Spirit accomplishes the cleansing which is sufficient to make a man acceptable to God (vv. 28, 29).

These verses presuppose that circumcision continues to have significance in the new covenant context. It has significance not as an external rite, but as a symbolic representation of the reality of righteousness. Circumcision in the Old Testament symbolizes the righteousness that comes through faith. In the epoch of the new covenant, the external rite of circumcision is not a requirement for God's people. But the essence symbolized by the rite must have its true manifestation in the heart of the believer.

Philippians 3:3 draws the closest possible parallel between the essence of the new covenant and the circumcision symbol of the old. "We *are* the circumcision," affirms the apostle. The one who worships in the Spirit of God personifies the reality of the cleansing rite of the old covenant.

This series of passages relates the circumcision-symbol of the old covenant to the reality of the new. The verses aid the new covenant believer in appreciating the significance for himself of the old covenant seal.

Secondly, the application of the same vocabulary of "sealing" ($\sigma\phi\rho\alpha\gamma\acute{\iota}\zeta\epsilon\sigma\theta\alpha\iota$) to the rite of circumcision and to the possession of the Holy Spirit provides a bridge to connect the two concepts. In Romans 4:11, circumcision is described as "a seal ($\sigma\phi\rho\alpha\gamma\acute{\iota}\varsigma$) of the righteousness of faith." Elsewhere, Paul applies the same term in its verbal form ($\sigma\phi\rho\alpha\gamma\acute{\iota}\zeta\epsilon\sigma\theta\alpha\iota$) to the possession of the Holy Spirit by the New Testament believer:

(God) sealed us and gave us the Holy Spirit in our hearts (II Cor. 1:22).

Having believed, you were sealed in him with the Holy Spirit of promise (Eph. 1:13).

And do not grieve the Holy Spirit of God, by whom you were sealed for the day of redemption (Eph. 4:30).

The application of the same terminology to circumcision and spirit-possession binds the two concepts together. The covenant ritual of sealing finds its fulfillment in the new covenant reality of sealing.

Thirdly, the interconnection between the seal of circumcision and the seal of the Holy Spirit provides the formal basis by which the corresponding purification rites of the old and new covenants relate to one another. Circumcision under the old covenant is replaced by baptism under the new covenant. The cleansing rite of the one covenant is replaced by the cleansing rite of the other. This relationship between circumcision and baptism finds specific development in Colossians 2:11, 12.

According to Colossians 2, the new covenant believer is not to be taken captive through human tradition (v. 8). The most basic reason he is not to be taken captive is that he now is "in Christ," and all sufficiency is to be found in him. Note the repeated emphasis on the "in Christ" theme:

In him (ἐν αὐτῷ) dwells all the fulness of deity bodily (v. 9).
In him (ἐν αὐτῷ) you have been made complete (v. 10).
In him (ἐν ᾧ) also you were circumcised (v. 11).
. . . having been buried with him (αὐτῷ) in baptism; and in him (ἐν ᾧ) you were raised through faith in the work of God (v. 12).[8]

The most significant points for the present discussion center on the reference to union with Christ in circumcision, and the relation of this circumcision to baptism. Verse 11 affirms that participants in the new covenant experience circumcision. In him you were circum-

---

8. The (ἐν ᾧ) of v. 12 might be taken as referring to baptism (ἐν τῷ βαπτισμῷ). In any case, it is in union with Christ (αὐτῷ) that death to sin and life to righteousness become a reality.

cised. Obviously the allusion cannot be to the physical rite required under the old covenant. The Christian experiences the reality of cleansing from defilement symbolized in the rite.

This circumcision is described as being "not made with hands." It does not owe its origin to man's handiwork.[9] Instead, God himself has performed a work of purification within the heart of man.

The old covenant initiating rite of circumcision was peculiarly susceptible to a pure externalism in religion. This fleshly, bloody aspect of the rite communicates well its old covenant shadow-form. In a most definitive sense, it is a rite that is "made with hands."

After affirming that the Christian does experience the reality of circumcision, Paul elaborates on the significance of this point. It involves the "putting away off" of the body of the flesh. By the use of the doubly prefixed $\dot{a}\pi$-$\epsilon\kappa$-$\delta\acute{v}\sigma\epsilon\iota$, the apostle appears to allude specifically to the process of circumcision, in which the foreskin, symbolizing the pollution of the flesh, is "put away off."[10]

In this expression, Paul has provided a profound illumination of the significance intended in the ritual of circumcision. The cutting off of the foreskin of the procreative organ represented the violent removal of the inherently sinful nature of man. This same significance now is being applied to the initiation rite of baptism.

Paul states that this circumcision of the new covenant believer is accomplished "in the circumcision of Christ." This phrase could refer either to the circumcision which Jesus himself experienced, or the circumcision which Jesus instituted. The decision between these two alternatives is difficult.

---

9. According to Edward Lohse, $\chi\epsilon\iota\rho o\pi o\iota\eta\tau os$ always is used in the N.T. to set forth "the antithesis of what is made with men's hands to the work of God" (*Theological Dictionary of the New Testament* [Grand Rapids, 1974], 9: 436).

10. All New Testament occurrences of $\dot{a}\pi\epsilon\kappa\delta\acute{v}\sigma\iota s$ and its verbal forms appear in Colossians. It is found rarely outside the New Testament. Some have suggested that Paul minted the word (cf. James Hope Moulton and George Milligan, *The Vocabulary of the Greek Testament* [London, 1952], p. 56). Possibly Paul may have added $\dot{a}\pi\acute{o}$ to $\dot{\epsilon}\kappa\delta\acute{v}\omega$, "to strip one (of his garment)" to convey the idea of a complete stripping. Certainly the term is appropriate in a discussion of the subject of circumcision.

Paul could be saying that the Christian experienced circumcision at the point in history in which Jesus was circumcised. This "circumcision" of Jesus could refer to the rite which he underwent as an eight-day-old infant, or to his "circumcision," figuratively speaking, at the point of his crucifixion.[11]

On the other hand, Paul could be saying that the Christian experiences "circumcision" by putting away the old man at the point of his baptism into Christ. The "circumcision of Christ" would refer to the circumcision which Christ instituted, in contrast with the circumcision of the old covenant.[12]

While the decision between these two interpretations may be difficult, the weight of the context appears to support the second view. The "circumcision of Christ" is the circumcision which Christ has instituted for the new covenant participant. Aside from the fact that the death of Christ is not developed in Scripture explicitly as a "circumcision," the passage at hand is talking primarily about the application of redemption to the believer rather than its accomplishment for the believer. It may be admitted that the experience of the believer is related immediately to the "union with Christ"

---

11. For this view, see E. K. Simpson and F. F. Bruce, *Commentary on the Epistles to the Ephesians and the Colossians. The New International Commentary on the New Testament* (Grand Rapids, 1957), p. 234; Meredith G. Kline, *By Oath Consigned* (Grand Rapids, 1968), pp. 47, 71. Kline, following with consistency his view that circumcision symbolized oath-curse in the Old Testament, associates circumcision only with death (p. 71), and does not relate it also to resurrection. On p. 47, he does indicate that because of the union of the believer with Christ, circumcision "takes on, alongside the import of condemnation, that of justification." Yet it must be noted that Kline is not presenting this positive side of the rite as central to the rite itself.

12. This view is held by John Calvin, *The Epistles of Paul the Apostle to the Galatians, Ephesians, Philippians and Colossians. Calvin's Commentaries* (Grand Rapids, 1965), p. 184; John Eadie, *Commentary on the Epistle of Paul to the Colossians, Classic Commentary Library* (Grand Rapids, 1957), p. 151; R. C. H. Lenski, *The Interpretation of St. Paul's Epistles to the Colossians, to the Thessalonians, to Timothy, to Titus and to Philemon* (Minneapolis, 1946), p. 105; and William Hendriksen, *Exposition of Colossians and Philemon, New Testament Commentary* (Grand Rapids, 1964), p. 115. For a thorough discussion of the alternatives, see Larry G. Mininger, *The Circumcision of Christ* (unpublished Th.M. thesis at Westminster Theological Seminary, 1971), pp. 40–51.

concept. It is "in Christ" that the believer dies and rises again. Yet the weight of the passage relates specifically to that point in history at which the Christian is initiated experientially into Christ.

A full appreciation of the significance of these verses hinges on an understanding of the relation of the next phrase to its context. Paul says "you were circumcised . . . having been buried with him in baptism."[13]

This phrase could be understood in one of two ways. Paul could be saying: "after having been buried with him in baptism, you were circumcised." In this case, Paul would be thinking of some experience of the Christian subsequent to his baptism which could be categorized as his "circumcision."

However, it is much more likely that the two events being described should be understood as occurring simultaneously.[14] The "circumcision" of the Christian is not to be understood as following his baptism. Instead, the two actions are to be regarded as simultaneous. The rite of cleansing found in the old covenant finds its fulfillment in the rite of cleansing ordered in the new. The thrust of Paul's statement should be represented by coordinating the two actions. The meaning of the passage would be communicated best by a rendering such as "when you were buried with him in baptism, you were circumcised"; or "by being buried with him in baptism you were circumcised."[15]

---

13. The participle employed by the apostle ($\sigma\upsilon\nu\tau\alpha\phi\acute{\epsilon}\nu\tau\epsilon\varsigma$) is in the nominative case, plural in number, and thus modifies the (understood) subject of the verb "ye were circumcised" at the beginning of verse eleven. The word $\sigma\upsilon\nu\theta\acute{\alpha}\pi\tau\omega$ occurs only here and in Romans 6:4 in the New Testament. In both places it refers to the figurative "burial" of baptism.

14. While the aorist participle may denote action prior to the main verb, this notion of relative past time "is not at all necessarily inherent in the aorist participle" (Robert W. Funk, *A Greek Grammar of the New Testament and Other Early Christian Literature* [Chicago, 1961], p. 175). If the temporal force of the aorist participle were to place its action prior to the verb which it modifies, the implication would be that the Christian's "circumcision" followed his baptism.

However, it is not necessary to place the action of an aorist participle temporally prior to the main verb. According to Funk's translation and revision of F. Blass and A. Debrunner's Greek grammar, "the element of past time is absent from the aorist participle especially if its action is identical with that of an aorist finite verb" (ibid., p. 175).

15. It is important to note that the 1978 edition of the *New International Version*

The net result of Paul's statement is to bind together in closest possible fashion the two rites of circumcision and baptism. The apostle simply has laid the one act on top of the other. In the fullest possible sense, baptism under the new covenant accomplishes all that was represented in circumcision under the old. By being baptized, the Christian believer has experienced the equivalent of the cleansing rite of circumcision. As has been said:

> To experience the circumcision of Christ in the putting off of the body of the flesh, is the same as being buried with him and raised with him in baptism through faith. If this be so, the only conclusion we can reach is that the two signs as outward rites symbolize the same inner reality in Paul's thinking. So circumcision may fairly be said to be the Old Testament counterpart of Christian baptism.[16]

---

makes the grammatical structure of the passage clearer than its earlier renderings. The 1973 edition obscured the relation between circumcision and baptism in these verses by rendering verses 11 and 12 as self-contained units, and by referring Paul's "having been buried in baptism" forward so that the participle modified the (understood) subject of "ye were raised" in v. 12. This translation failed to represent the basic meaning of the verses as determined by the grammatical structure of the various clauses, and depended too heavily on the often-faulty traditional verse division. "Having been buried with him in baptism" belongs with verse 11, and verse 12 should begin with "In him also you were raised. . . ."

The ἐν ᾧ with the additional καί of v. 12 grammatically divides between old and new subject matter. Since "having been buried with him in baptism" stands before this structural divider, it is highly unlikely that it would refer across the "in him also" barrier to "ye were raised." Support for this analysis may be seen in the parallel construction of Eph. 1:7–14. Because "having been buried with him in baptism" precedes the ἐν ᾧ καί of Col. 2:12, its immediate referent should be found in "ye were circumcised" of v. 11 rather than in "ye were raised" of v. 12.

16. P. K. Jewett, *Baptism and Confirmation*, pp. 168f. in David Kingdon, *Children of Abraham; a Reformed Baptist View of Baptism, the Covenant, and Children* (Worthing, 1973), p. 29.

10

Moses:
The Covenant of Law

THE covenant with Moses has provoked some of the greatest debates within Christendom's history. Modern as well as ancient Marcionites who reject the authority of the Old Testament Scriptures habitually direct their criticism toward the Mosaic administration of law. The precise relationship of the Mosaic covenant to the promises that preceded it and to the fulfillments that followed has proven to be one of the most persistent problems of biblical interpretation.

THE PLACE OF THE MOSAIC COVENANT IN MODERN BIBLICAL CRITICISM

Before entering into a discussion of the theological emphases of the Mosaic covenant, some introductory remarks should be made concerning the place of the Mosaic covenant in modern biblical criticism. Equally untiring as the debate over the theological significance of the Mosaic administration of law has been the discussion

167

from an historico-critical perspective of the origin and development of the pentateuchal materials.

Since the days of Julius Wellhausen, the Mosaic authorship of the Pentateuch has been denied by the bulk of critical scholarship. However, more recent decades have seen form-critical studies insisting repeatedly that much in the Pentateuch belongs quite appropriately to the days of Moses. In this regard, two particular lines of development need to be recognized.

Pentateuchal Material and Hittite Treaties

First, attention should be paid to the growing number of works giving recognition to the relation of pentateuchal material to the Hittite suzerainty treaties.[1] In the Ancient Near East, an international treaty form developed which apparently was shared among the nations. References to such treaties go back to the third millennium B.C. In recent years, actual treaty texts have been discovered among the archives of the Hittite empire. Most significant among these texts are documents dating into the late Bronze age (c. 1400–1200 B.C.).[2]

---

1. A helpful survey of materials may be found in D. J. McCarthy, "Covenant in the O.T.: The Present State of Inquiry," *Catholic Biblical Quarterly* 27 (1965): 217–40. Cf. also Warren Malcolm Clark: *Covenant in Israel and in the Ancient Near East: A Bibliography Prepared by Dr. Warren Malcolm Clark for the Use of His Students at Princeton Theological Seminary,* 1968–69. Perhaps two of the most significant works would be G. E. Mendenhall's *Law and Covenant in Israel and the Ancient Near East* (Pittsburgh, 1955), and M. G. Kline's *Treaty of the Great King* (Grand Rapids, 1963). Mendenhall's work provided the initial stimulus for current comparisons between Ancient Near Eastern treaties and the pentateuchal material. Kline has drawn out the historico-critical and biblical-theological implications of these studies.

2. Some effort has been made to relate these biblical covenant-forms to documents of the first millennium B.C. rather than the second millennium B.C. For a discussion of the issues involved, and a refutation of the contention that the pentateuchal material should be related to documents of the first millennium, see K. A. Kitchen, *Ancient Orient and the Old Testament* (Chicago, 1966), pp. 90ff. Among other significant points, Kitchen notes the absence of an historical prologue and of blessings corresponding to curses in the first millennium documents, as well as an inconsistency in the order of literary elements.

These particular treaty forms developed a classical pattern which was employed in documents binding the vassals of the Hittite empire to their conquering lord. The most essential elements of the treaty form included:

1. A preambulatory declaration of the lordship of the conquering suzerain.

2. An historical prologue emphasizing past acts of benevolence.

3. An extensive delimiting of stipulations involving both demands for heart-loyalty and requirements for specific action.

4. Provisions for the official depositing of duplicate copies of the treaty documents in the presence of the respective gods of vassal and suzerain.

5. An invocation of witnesses, often involving the summoning of inanimate objects.

6. A statement of potential curses and blessings related to covenant fidelity.

Observing the basic outline of this treaty form, current scholarship has found a remarkable similarity in the pattern of the Mosaic covenant. Both the portion of Exodus dealing with covenant inauguration (Exod. 19–24) and the entire book of Deuteronomy have been studied in this regard.

Perhaps the most significant discovery to date has been the close similarity between the broad outline of the book of Deuteronomy and the classic pattern of the Hittite treaty form. Extensive parallels in detail press strongly for dating the entire book of Deuteronomy in its present form to the period of Moses.[3]

Pentateuchal Material and the "Deuteronomistic Historian"

At the same time, a second strand of current studies has attempted to date the book of Deuteronomy in its final form almost a millen-

3. Note in particular the well-argued claim of M. G. Kline, *Treaty of the Great King* (Grand Rapids, 1963), pp. 27ff.

nium later. Martin Noth in particular views Deuteronomy as a theological introduction to the work of a "deuteronomistic historian" which must be separated from the first four books of the Pentateuch. Noth links the entire section of Scripture from Deuteronomy through II Kings as a unit, whose final form appeared only in the days of Israel's exile.[4]

It will be most interesting to see which school of thought will triumph in this scholarly tug-of-war. It would be too much to hope that modern critical scholarship would acknowledge a date for the final form of Deuteronomy in the age of Moses, in accord with the similarity of Deuteronomy's form to the classic Hittite treaties, while at the same time recognizing the remarkable oneness of the biblical message as displayed by the connection of Joshua–II Kings to the theology of Deuteronomy. Whatever the case, the discovery of the classic Hittite covenantal form should continue to be one of the significant factors in contemporary biblical studies.

THEOLOGICAL SIGNIFICANCE OF THE MOSAIC COVENANT

This summary treatment of the possible relationship of portions of the Pentateuch to the Hittite covenantal treaties provides a natural basis for a discussion of the theological import of the Mosaic covenant. The Mosaic dispensation rests squarely on a covenantal rather than a legal relationship. While law plays an extremely significant role both in the international treaty forms and in the Mosaic era, covenant always supersedes law.

Essential to the Hittite treaty form was the recognition of the historical context in which legal stipulations functioned. The historical

---

4. Martin Noth, *Überlieferungsgeschichtliche Studien* (Darmstadt, 1943), pp. 12ff.; 87ff. Note interactions with this viewpoint in John Bright, *The Interpreter's Bible: Joshua* (New York, 1953), pp. 541ff.; K. A. Kitchen, "Ancient Orient, 'Deuteronism,' and the Old Testament," in *New Perspectives on the Old Testament* (Waco, 1970), pp. 1ff.

prologue of the documents set the current relation of conquering lord and conquered vassal in the light of past interchanges.[5]

Nothing could be more basic to a proper understanding of the Mosaic era. It is not law that is preeminent, but covenant. Whatever concept of law may be advanced, it must remain at all times subservient to the broader concept of the covenant.

This point is made most obvious by a recognition of the historical context in which the covenant of law was revealed. Historically, the nation of Israel already was in a covenantal relationship with the Lord through Abraham. The Exodus narrative begins when God hears the groaning of Israel, and "remembers his covenant with Abraham, with Isaac, and with Jacob" (Exod. 2:24). After God has established himself as Israel's Lord through the historical fact of the deliverance from Egypt, the law-covenant of Sinai is administered. The Decalogue's "I am the Lord your God which brought you out of the land of Egypt, out of the house of bondage," provides the essential historical framework in which the Sinaitic law-covenant may be understood. As has been stated:

> The laws have their place in the doctrine of the covenant. Yahweh has chosen Israel as His people, and Israel has acknowledged Yahweh as its God. This fundamental O.T. principle is the direct basis of these laws.[6]

Covenant, therefore, is the larger concept, always taking precedence over law. Covenant binds persons; externalized legal stipulations represent one mode of administration of the covenantal bond.

---

5. The suggestion of Gerhard von Rad and Martin Noth that the Sinai-tradition of Israel must be separated from the exodus-conquest narratives finds a strong opponent in studies which compare the Hittite treaty form with the Decalogue. In each instance, law finds its meaning in the larger context of the historical framework of the covenant. For a treatment of the subject, and an answer to the contentions of von Rad and Noth, see John Bright, *A History of Israel* (Philadelphia, 1959), p. 115; Artur Weiser, *The Old Testament: Its Formation and Development* (New York, 1961), pp. 82–90.

6. W. Gutbrod, "νόμος," *Theological Dictionary of the New Testament* (Grand Rapids, 1967), 4: 1036.

God renews an ancient commitment to his people by the covenant of Moses. The law serves only as a single mode of administering the covenant of redemption. Originally established under Adam, confirmed under Noah and Abraham, the covenantal relationship renewed under Moses cannot disturb God's ongoing commitment by its emphasis on the legal dimension of the covenant relationship.

The Distinctiveness of the Mosaic Covenant

If the Mosaic covenant stands in a basic relation of unity with God's earlier covenantal administration, what then is its distinctiveness? What particularly characterizes this covenantal administration? How does it stand apart from God's other ways of dealing with his people?

The Mosaic covenant manifests its distinctiveness as an externalized summation of the will of God. The patriarchs certainly were aware of God's will in general terms. On occasion, they received direct revelation concerning specific aspects of the will of God. Under Moses, however, a full summary of God's will was made explicit through the physical inscripturation of the law. This external-to-man, formally ordered summation of God's will constitutes the distinctiveness of the Mosaic covenant.

The emphasis in the Pentateuch on the "ten words" (עֲשֶׂרֶת הַדְּבָרִים) and the explicit identification of these words with the covenant itself clearly indicate that the distinctiveness of the Mosaic covenant resides in this externalized summation of God's law. Note in particular the language of the following verses:

> . . . And he [Moses] wrote on the tablets the words of the covenant, the ten words (Exod. 34:28).

> So He declared to you His covenant which He commanded you to perform, that is, the ten words; and He wrote them on two tablets of stone (Deut. 4:13).

> When I went up to the mountain to receive the tablets of stone, the tablets of the covenant which the Lord had made with you. . . .

And . . . at the end of forty days and nights . . . the Lord gave
me the two tablets of stone, the tablets of the covenant (Deut.
9:9, 11).

These verses indicate the closeness of identification between the
Mosaic covenant and the "ten words." These words summarize the
essence of the Mosaic covenant.

The same verses emphasize also the externalized character of the
Mosaic law-administration. The stone-engraven character of the
Mosaic covenant does not reflect simply the manner by which
covenantal documents were preserved in the days of Moses. This
stark, cold, externalized form in which the covenant stipulations
appeared manifests eloquently a most distinctive characteristic of
the Mosaic covenant. A law has been written, a will has been
decreed; but this law stands outside man, demanding conformity.
"Law" as it is used in relation to the Mosaic covenant should not be
defined simply as a revelation of the will of God. More specifically,
law denotes an externalized summation of God's will.

In the case of the Mosaic covenant, the prominence of this
external form of God's will provides ample justification for the
characterization of the Mosaic covenant as the covenant of law. This
characterization has the full support of the New Testament Scriptures. "The law was given through Moses," says the apostle John
(John 1:17). In his letter to the Galatians, Paul clearly characterizes
the Mosaic period as the epoch of "law" (Gal. 3:17).

This phrase "covenant of law" must not be confused with the
traditional terminology which speaks of a "covenant of works." The
phrase "covenant of works" customarily refers to the situation at
creation in which man was required to obey God perfectly in order to
enter into a state of eternal blessedness. Contrary to this relation
established with man in innocence, the Mosaic covenant of law
clearly addresses itself to man in sin. This latter covenant never
intended to suggest that man by perfect moral obedience could enter
into a state of guaranteed covenantal blessedness. The integral role
of a substitutionary sacrificial system within the legal provisions of
the Mosaic covenant clearly indicates a sober awareness of the

distinction between God's dealings with man in innocence and with man in sin.

As already has been indicated, God's covenantal commitment to redeem from the state of sin a people to himself was in effect prior to the giving of the law at Sinai. Israel assembled at Sinai only because God had redeemed them from Egypt. For the covenant of law to function as a principle of salvation by works, the covenant of promise first would have to be suspended.

The concrete externalization of covenantal stipulations written on tables of stone never was intended to detract from the gracious promise of the Abrahamic covenant, as Paul argues so aptly. The covenant of law, coming 400 years after promise, could not possibly disannul the previous covenant (Gal. 3:17).

Not only did the covenant of law not disannul the covenant of promise; more specifically, it did not offer a temporary alternative to the covenant of promise. This particular perspective is often overlooked. It is sometimes assumed that the covenant of law temporarily replaced the covenant of promise, or somehow ran alongside it as an alternative method of man's salvation. The covenant of law often has been considered as a self-contained unit which served as another basis for determining the relation of Israel to God in the period between the Abrahamic covenant and the coming of Christ. In this scheme, the covenant of promise is treated as though it had been set aside or made secondary for a period, although not "disannulled."

However, the covenant of promise made with Abraham always has been in effect from the day of its inauguration until the present. The coming of law did not suspend the Abrahamic covenant. The principle enunciated in Genesis 15:6 concerning the justification of Abraham by faith never has experienced interruption. Throughout the Mosaic period of law-covenant, God considered as righteous everyone who believed in him.[7]

---

7. The language of Meredith Kline is misleading on this point. His desire to maintain the distinctive emphasis of the law-covenant may be appreciated. But his statements too easily could be understood in a legalistic fashion. He interprets Paul as saying that the Sinaitic covenant "made inheritance to be by law, not by promise—not by faith, but by works" (*By Oath Consigned,* p. 23).
The distinctiveness of the Mosaic covenant resides in its externalized form of

For this reason, the covenant of law as revealed at Sinai would best be divorced from "covenant of works" terminology. The "covenant of works" refers to legal requirements laid on man at the time of his innocency in creation. The "covenant of law" refers to a new stage in the process of God's unfolding the richness of the covenant of redemption. As such, the law which came through Moses did not in any way disannul or suspend the covenant of promise.

The Place of the Covenant of Law in the History of Redemption

Three aspects of the Mosaic covenant may be stressed in an effort to place this distinctive covenant in its proper biblical-theological setting: the covenant of law is related organically to the totality of God's redemptive purposes; the covenant of law is related progressively to the totality of God's redemptive purposes; the covenant of law finds its consummation in Jesus Christ.

First, the covenant of law is related organically to the totality of God's redemptive purposes. To speak of an organic relationship is to suggest a living, vital inter-connection as over against an isolationistic compartmentalization. The clear enunciation of the will of God at the time of Moses did not appear as something novel in the history of redemption. At the same time, law did not disappear after Moses. Law functioned significantly in the period preceding Moses, and law functions significantly in the period succeeding Moses. While the summation of law in an externalized form may remain as the distinctive property of the Mosaic era, the presence of law throughout the history of redemption must be recognized.

---

law-administration. But the law under Moses cannot be understood as opening a new way of attaining salvation for God's people. Israel must maintain the law, not in order to enter the favored condition of the covenant of redemption, but in order to continue in the blessings of the covenantal relationship after having been empowered to do so through their covenantal oneness-with-God experienced by grace through faith alone. Under both the Mosaic and the Abrahamic covenants man experienced redemption by grace through faith in the work of the Christ who was to live and die in the place of sinners.

1. Law is significant in all administrations prior to Moses.

References to the will of God and to the necessity of obedience to that will may be noted in each of the biblical covenants. Adam, while receiving gratuitously the promise of a saving seed, must work in the sweat of his face to sustain life until the seed should come (Gen. 3:19). Noah receives as an integral part of his mercy-filled covenant the decree of God's will concerning the disposition of man-slayers: "Whoso sheddeth man's blood, by man shall his blood be shed" (Gen. 9:6).

Even more comprehensively, the Abrahamic covenant of promise builds on the responsibility of God's people with reference to the revealed will of God. The total allegiance to his Lord demanded of Abraham involves the whole of his life (cf. Gen. 12:1; 17:1). The patriarch must leave his father's house and walk before the Lord in whole-hearted obedience.[8]

Subsequent happenings under the administration of the Abrahamic covenant further indicate the presence of covenantal law, especially with regard to the sealing ordinance of circumcision. According to Genesis 17:14, "the uncircumcised male . . . who is not circumcised in the flesh of his foreskin, that soul shall be cut off from his people; he hath broken my covenant." Quite a hair-raising incident in this very connection is recorded subsequently in connection with the life of Moses. After having received his commission to deliver Israel in fulfillment of the promise of the Abrahamic covenant, Moses begins the return trip to Egypt with his family:

Now it came about at the lodging-place on the way that the Lord met him and sought to put him to death.

Then Zipporah took a flint and cut off her son's foreskin and threw it at Moses' feet, and she said, 'You are indeed a bridegroom of blood to me.

8. G. E. Mendenhall, "Covenant Forms in Israelite Tradition," *The Biblical Archaeologist*, XVII (1954) 3: 62, suggests that the uniqueness of the biblical covenant with Abraham resides in its absence of stipulations. He is answered effectively by Meredith Kline, *Treaty of the Great King* (Grand Rapids, 1963), p. 23.

So He let him alone. At that time she said, 'You are a bridegroom of blood'—because of the circumcision (Exod. 4:24-26).

Under the provisions of the Abrahamic covenant of promise, God almost slays Moses for failing to observe its stipulations.[9] Obviously law plays a vital role in this covenantal relationship.

The presence of stipulations in the covenants prior to Moses does not detract from the uniqueness of the legal codification under Moses. No other covenant could be characterized convincingly as "the covenant of law." No more fitting designation could be applied to the Mosaic covenant. Yet the continuing presence of covenantal stipulations in every earlier administration relates the covenant of Moses organically with that which precedes. Law simply becomes predominant under Moses.

2. Law is significant in all administrations subsequent to Moses.

Both the Davidic covenant and the new covenant continue to recognize the significance of divine law in redemptive history. At the conclusion of the Mosaic epoch, Israel's history immediately begins the movement "toward a kingship." The establishment of a permanent monarchy in Israel ultimately finds realization by the institution of the Davidic covenant. The provisional dimension of God's covenant with David is expressed rather pointedly at the time of covenant inauguration. Concerning the line of descendency from David, God says: "When he commits iniquity, I will correct him with the rod of men. . . ." The framework in which this potential punishment of iniquity is to be understood is spelled out quite pointedly in David's subsequent death-bed charge to Solomon his son and successor:

> As David's time to die drew near, he charged Solomon his son, saying, "I am going the way of all the earth. Be strong, therefore, and show yourself a man. And keep the charge of the Lord your God, to walk in His ways, to keep His statutes, His commandments, His ordinances,

---

9. This passage is filled with enigmatic statements. Although some question still remains, it seems that Moses is the person attacked by the Lord. Cf. the discussion in Brevard S. Childs, *The Book of Exodus* (Philadelphia, 1974), pp. 95-104.

and His testimonies, *according to what is written in the law of Moses*, that you may succeed in all that you do and wherever you turn, so that the Lord may carry out His promise when he spoke concerning me, saying, 'If your sons are careful of their way, to walk before Me in truth with all their heart and with all their soul, you shall not lack a man on the throne of Israel' " (I Kings 2:1-4).

The law of Moses is thus seen to have an integral role in the Davidic covenant. The entire historical narrative concerning the kings of Israel may be regarded as one magnificent verification of the promise to David, together with its accompanying threat of punishment based on the provisions of the Mosaic covenant of law.

Both the psalm-singers and the prophets of Israel sing and prophesy of the law of God. "Oh how love I thy law; it is my meditation all the day," sings the Psalmist (Ps. 119:97). "I wrote for him the ten thousand things of my law; but they are accounted as a strange thing," complains the prophet (Hos. 8:12). Quite obviously, the law functions significantly in the period of Israel's history embraced by the Davidic covenant. The Davidic covenant cannot be regarded as functioning as an entity to itself, isolated from the decrees of Sinai. The "ten words" continue to possess a primary significance for God's people.

It is with respect to the new covenant that the greatest problems arise concerning the continuing role of law. Is the covenant of law still significant for participants in the new covenant? Do legal prescriptions apply to Christians today? This difficult question shall be treated first by noting some general considerations that need to be kept in mind. Then positive evidence from the New Testament confirming the role of law in the life of the Christian will be noted.

Confusion and debate on this particular issue arise in part from efforts to understand the seemingly contradictory statements of the New Testament itself. On the one hand, a variety of new covenant Scriptures plainly assert:

Sin shall not be master over you, for you are not under law, but under grace (Rom. 6:14).

But now we have been released from the law, having died to that by which we were bound, so that we serve in newness of the Spirit and not in oldness of the letter (Rom. 7:6).

But before faith came, we were kept in custody under the law, being shut up to the faith which was later to be revealed.

Therefore the Law has become our tutor to lead us to Christ, that we may be justified by faith.

But now that faith has come, we are no longer under a tutor (Gal. 3:23–25).

On the other hand, Scripture equally asserts:

Do not think that I came to abolish the Law or the Prophets; I did not come to abolish, but to fulfill.

For truly I say to you, until heaven and earth pass away, not the smallest letter or stroke shall pass away from the Law, until all is accomplished.

Whoever then annuls one of the least of these commandments, and so teaches others, shall be called least in the kingdom of heaven; but whoever keeps and teaches them, he shall be called great in the kingdom of heaven (Matt. 5:17–19).

Do we then nullify the Law through faith? May it never be! On the contrary, I would not have come to know sin except through the Law; for I would not have known about coveting if the Law had not said, "YOU SHALL NOT COVET."

. . . So then, the Law is holy, and the commandment is holy and righteous and good (Rom. 7:7, 12).

What then is the Christian's status? Does he have obligations relating to the Mosaic covenant of law? Or is he freed altogether from law-covenant?

One complicating factor in this whole matter relates to the varied ways in which the term νόμος is used in the New Testament. In the course of a few verses, the apostle Paul may use the same term in three or four different ways. According to Romans 3:21, the righteousness of faith has been witnessed by "the law and the prophets." The term "law" in this phrase refers to the Pentateuch as a literary unit. But the first half of this same verse declares that the righteousness of God has appeared "apart from law." The precise meaning of the term "law" in this phrase is difficult to determine. Most likely it represents a "shorthand abbreviation" for the "works of the law" in terms of man's capacity to please God by his own deeds of righteousness (cf. v. 20, which immediately precedes). But in any case, the meaning of "law" in the first half of Romans 3:21 is quite distinct from the meaning of the same term in the second half of the same verse.

Reading a little further in the apostle's argument, a third use of the term νόμος appears. In Romans 3:27, Paul poses a question. By what "law" is boasting excluded from the justified?

Now Paul uses the term "law" to refer to a general principle. It is by the "principle" of faith-justification that boasting over righteousness is excluded.

Earlier Paul appears to use the term in still a fourth sense (cf. Rom. 2:21–23). First he cites three commandments of the Decalogue. Then he accosts his readers: "You who boast in the law, through your breaking the law, do you dishonor God?" Paul now appears to use "law" to refer more narrowly to the Ten Commandments. It is the "ten words" that his contemporaries have broken.

At other points, context seems to demand that the term "law" be understood as referring specifically to law-keeping as a means of justification. In these cases, the term "law" becomes the equivalent of the Judaizers' misapprehension of the proper role of the law in the history of redemption.

In Galatians 4:21, Paul addresses himself to those who want to be "under law." He speaks to those who would attempt to achieve righteousness before God by personal law-keeping. The apostle spells out a "formula of equivalencies" spanning the history of redemption.

Two antithetical alternatives for realizing acceptance by God face the Galatians. The first alternative traces its lineage back to

Abraham's slave-son Ishmael, who was born out of the patriarch's efforts to assure the fulfillment of God's promises on the basis of his own resources. This alternative for "justification" manifests itself again in the law-covenant of Sinai, which corresponds to the "present Jerusalem."

It is essential to understand Paul's reference to Sinai in the context of the equivalencies which he has developed. The covenant of "law" corresponds to the "present Jerusalem," the Jerusalem of the Judaizers. It is the legalistic misapprehension of the Sinaitic law-covenant that is in the mind of the apostle. Slavery inevitably will result from resorting to natural human resources as a means of pleasing God. Ishmael, the current Judaizers, and unbelieving Israel conjointly find themselves to be slaves.

As this "formula of equivalencies" is considered, it must be stressed that the understanding of Mosaic law with which Paul is contending cannot be viewed as the divinely intended purpose of the giving of the law at Sinai. Even though the middle member of this first triad (Hagar-Sinai-Present Jerusalem) is identified as "Mount Sinai" (v. 25), it does not represent the true purpose of Sinaitic law-giving.

This assertion rests on the clear purpose of law-giving as explicated by Paul in Galatians 3:24. The purpose of the law was to lead to Christ, not to lead away from Christ. The effect of the law on the current Judaizers was not in accord with God's purpose in the giving of the law. By reading the law in terms of an alternative way of salvation, current Judaism blinded itself to the true intention of God in the giving of the law.

The true purpose of God's law-giving at Sinai did not find its proper manifestation in the Judaizers of the first century. Their pride compelled them to pervert God's purpose in law-giving. Instead of serving to convict them of the absolute impossibility of pleasing God by law-keeping, the law fostered in them a deeply entrenched determination to depend on personal resources in order to please God. Thus the law did not serve the purposes of grace in leading the Judaizers to Christ. Instead, it closed them off from Christ. "Law" and "Sinai" in this context must refer to legalistic misapprehension of God's purpose in law-giving rather than the proper apprehension of God's revelation of law.

The contrary "formula of equivalencies" runs from the free-woman Sarah through the covenant of promise to the "above Jerusalem." God's sovereign and gracious intervention in the life of sinful man invariably produces children that are free.

It may be acknowledged that something in the form of law-administration lent itself to an easy misapprehension of its proper purpose in man's redemption. The externalized, codified form of law readily came to be understood as offering a way of life other than the faith-principle crystallized under Abraham. It was possible to understand law properly as a schoolmaster that would lead to Christ by increasing awareness of sin. Or it was possible to misunderstand law as a taskmaster that led away from Christ by diverting concentration from faith-righteousness to works-righteousness. It is this latter perspective that the apostle has in mind when he addresses himself to those who wish to be "under law." "Law" in this context points to the misapprehension of the law's purpose as reflected in Abraham's misdirected efforts to provide a son for himself and in the Judaizer's efforts to provide righteousness for themselves.

To this point, several different uses of "law" in Paul have been noted. Other more refined significances may be involved. Clearly it is necessary to exercise extreme care in evaluating biblical statements about the role of the "law" in the life of the Christian. When the New Testament affirms bluntly "you are not under law but under grace" (Rom. 6:14), clearly it does not mean "you are not under the Pentateuch." It does not mean "you are not under the Ten Commandments." Most probably in the context of Romans 6, it means "you are not under the Mosaic covenant as a principle which would make righteousness depend on the individual's personal resources as law-keeper."

One positive step toward solving the difficult question of the Christian's relation to the law may be taken by noting once more the distinctiveness of law-administration emphasized under Moses. Under the Mosaic covenant, law appeared as an externalized summation of the will of God. The Christian does not live under an externalized ministration of law engraved in stone tablets. Instead, he lives with the law written in his heart. While the Christian always stands obligated to reflect the holiness and righteousness required in God's law, he no longer relates to that law as an impersonal code standing outside himself. Instead, the Spirit of God constantly ministers the law within the heart of the believer.

This understanding of the question gives recognition to the fading form of law-administration under the Mosaic covenant, while also treating seriously the continuing significance of the essence of that same law. While this explanation may not satisfy all the problems arising from the Christian's relation to the law, it does provide one fruitful area for reflection.

In addition to these general considerations, it is important to present positive evidence from the New Testament which affirms the continuing significance of the Mosaic covenant of law:

First of all, presumptive evidence favors the continuing significance of the essence if not the form of the Mosaic law-covenant into the present day. It is obvious from Scripture that men today continue under the provisions of other administrations of the covenant of redemption. Romans 16:20 refers to the ultimate bruising of the head of the serpent under the Christian's feet. The language clearly indicates the continuing significance of God's covenant with Adam. II Peter 3:5-7 notes the significance of God's judgment on the wicked in Noah's day, and appeals to the covenanting word spoken to Noah which currently preserves the earth.

The designation of Abraham as "the father of us all" (Rom. 4:16, 17) indicates the significance today of the covenantal promise concerning an innumerable seed. Even today, the "root of Jesse" rules as the hope of the Gentiles, in accord with the covenant with David (Rom. 15:22). These references to the continuing significance of the covenants with Adam, Noah, Abraham, and David into the present could be expanded greatly.

Are we to conclude that all the various covenantal administrations of the Old Testament find continuing significance for believers today with the single exception of the Mosaic covenant? Are we to presume that the covenant of law alone among the divinely-initiated covenants has lost its binding significance?

To the contrary, presumption would favor the continuing significance of the Mosaic covenant for the believer today. These other covenants play a vital role in the life of believers. Is the Mosaic law-covenant so materially different that it would not also continue to play a significant role in the life of the new covenant believer? While an argument of this sort cannot be conclusive in itself, it does have some bearing. Presumption would favor the continuing significance of the Mosaic covenant of law.

Several other considerations establish more concretely the continuing significance of the provisions of the covenant of law for the Christian. While the externalized form of the Mosaic covenant may be superseded by the inner realities of the new covenant, the central essence of the covenant of law enters vitally into the life of the believer today. In particular, note the following considerations:

(a) Christians are told repeatedly that their fullest state of blessedness derives from their keeping God's law. Numerous exhortations in the letters of Paul presuppose the necessity of keeping God's commandments. Even the promise of long life associated with the fifth commandment is held out as a promise of God to the children of the new covenant. If they should fulfil the command to honor father and mother, they will receive God's distinctive blessing (Eph. 6:1–3). This same attitude is reflected quite emphatically by Christ as he completes the sermon on the mount. Not the hearer, but the doer of Christ's words will be blessed by firmness of foundation (Matt. 7:24–27). No reader can misunderstand the exhortation of James: "Be ye doers of the word, and not hearers only, deluding your own selves" (James 1:22).

Under the new covenant, the Holy Spirit works in a most vital way to bring Christians into conformity with the will of God. But the believer is responsible actively to make use of the means of grace available to him. If he does not obey God's law, he will not live in the fullest state of God's blessing.

(b) Christians who live in unrighteousness are chastened by the Lord. The writer to the Hebrews applies an Old Testament admonition directly to New Testament believers: "Whom the Lord loves he disciplines, and he scourges every son whom he receives" (Heb. 12:6).

Paul shocks the Corinthian Christians, cavorting about the Lord's table. Many of them are weak and sickly, while others have been judged by death for their sin (I Cor. 11:30–32).

Such references to the chastening activity of the Lord would not be conceivable apart from the continuing significance of law for God's people. The reality of a chastening activity among Christians today serves as indisputable proof that believers live under an abiding obligation to do the will of God.

(c) Christians shall be judged according to the deeds they have done. Scripture is quite consistent on this point.[10] While salvation comes by faith in the work of Christ alone, judgment will be dispensed according to a man's own deeds, whether they be good or evil. Since the "ten words" of the Mosaic covenant provide a basic summation of the will of God, their abiding significance in the life of the believer is assured.

The Mosaic covenant of law relates organically to the totality of God's redemptive purposes. It is never to be regarded as an appendix to the unfolding of redemptive revelation. To the contrary, law plays a significant role in every phase of redemptive history.

Secondly, the covenant of law is related progressively to the totality of God's redemptive purposes. A second major aspect of the Mosaic covenant must be noted if this distinctive administration of God's grace in salvation is to be accorded its proper biblical-theological setting. The covenant of law not only relates organically, it also relates *progressively* to the totality of God's redemptive purposes.

The characterization of the revelation of God's law as fitting into a progressive unfolding of God's will does not by any means intend to suggest that the revelation was deficient at any point. To the contrary, the progressiveness of the biblical revelation gives appropriate recognition to the fuller manifestation of the truth of God in each successive epoch.

To prove the progressive relation of the covenant of law to the

---

10. Cf. Leon Morris, *The Biblical Doctrine of Judgment* (Grand Rapids, 1960), pp. 66f.

totality of the revelation of God, two points must be established. First, it must be shown that the Mosaic covenant represents an advancement beyond all of God's earlier dealings with his people. Secondly, it must be established that the era of Mosaic legislation represents a less mature stage of the manifestation of God's purposes in redemption than the developments that follow.

1. The Mosaic covenant is an advancement beyond all that precedes.

First, then, the Mosaic covenant represents an advancement beyond all of God's earlier dealings with his people. This advancement does not relate to some incidental aspect of the Mosaic covenant. An advancement is not made merely at the periphery of this covenant, affecting only its frills. Instead, the advancement relates to the very heart and core of the distinctive element of Mosaism. By presenting an externalized summation of the will of God, the Mosaic covenant advances positively the revelation of God's purposes in redemption.

Often the suggestion is made that the people of God were in a better condition under the Abrahamic covenant of promise than under the Mosaic covenant of law. Rather than rashly accepting the conditional covenant mediated through Moses, Israel should have pled humbly for a "continued relationship of grace" at Sinai.[11] Such suggestions clearly imply that Israel was better off under the terms of the Abrahamic covenant rather than under the terms of the Mosaic covenant.

The concept of a continued progression in the unfolding of God's redemptive truth cannot allow for such a movement of retrogression. Several points may be noted in particular which display the revelation of law under Moses to be an obvious advancement over previous covenantal administrations:

(a) In its nationalizing of the people

The covenant of law represents an advancement in its nationalizing of the covenant people. To this point, God's dealing had been

---

11. C. I. Scofield, *Rightly Dividing the Word of Truth* (New York, 1923), p. 22.

with a family. Now he covenants with a nation. Such a national covenant would be impossible without externally codified law.

The immediate context of the covenant-ratification ceremony of Moses emphasizes this formation of Israel into a nation to be God's own. Seventy representative elders are chosen from among the people (Exod. 24:1). Twelve pillars are erected as representative of the 12 tribes of Israel (Exod. 24:4). The effect of this formal ceremony already had been solemnized by God's earlier words addressed to Israel through Moses:

> Now then, if you will indeed obey My voice and keep My covenant, then you shall be My own possession among all the peoples, for all the earth is Mine; and you shall be to Me a kingdom of priests and a holy nation (Exod. 19:5, 6).

Essential to the national solidifying of this people to be God's own was the definitive revelation of the will of God for the conduct of his people.

(b) In comprehensiveness

The covenant of law represents an advancement in the comprehensiveness of the revelation of God's will. The "ten words" contain a complete summation of the will of God. By receiving this fuller revelation, Israel stands in a much better relation to the God of the covenant.

Some forms of perfectionism may delight in a deliverance from "all known sin." No more dangerous state may be imagined. Sin always will be present in the life of God's people until the consummation. It is far better for the people of God to be fully aware of the precise nature of their particular sin rather than continuing to sin in ignorance. God's law serves as an essential tool in making his people understand the nature of their sin.

For this reason, the fuller revelation of the will of God in the Mosaic covenant should be regarded as a great boon. The Christian should not look askance at the ancient Jew who regarded the law as the great ray of light amidst the darkness of heathendom. Perhaps from at least one perspective the ancient saying stemming from the school of Hillel has merit: "Where much flesh is, are many worms; where much treasure is, many cares; where many women are, great superstition; and where much law is, there is much living."[12]

(c) In humbling ability

The covenant of law represents an advancement over that which preceded in its humbling of men, thereby preparing them for the riches of Christ's grace. The apostle Paul has emphasized soundly this significant role of the law, which may be regarded as something of a "blessing-in-reverse." Paul notes that the law was added "because of transgressions, until the seed should come . . ." (Gal. 3:19). As a revealer of sin, the law supplied a vital service to the Abrahamic covenant of promise. By exposing fully men's inadequacy to establish righteousness by law-keeping, the Mosaic covenant has contributed to the cause of redemptive grace.

(d) In typological significance

The covenant of law represents an advancement in its typological significance. The precepts of law offered the outline for the type of life expected for God's holy people. While Israel never achieved the full potentialities of this holiness-type, the law nonetheless served to sketch the pattern of life desired for God's people. They are to be characterized by a life that reflects the holiness of the God of the covenant.

It may be concluded, therefore, that the Mosaic covenant of law was an advancement over the Abrahamic covenant of promise. That which was the very essence of the Mosaic covenant represented a step of progress in God's redemptive purposes.

Most serious consequences will develop inevitably from a denial that God's revelation consistently progresses throughout redemptive history. It may be admitted quite readily that the arrival of the full delineation of God's will brought with it problems which had not previously existed. Ask any distraught parent of a modern teenager if he regards the state of teenage as an advancement over infancy.

---

12. Quoted in H. N. Ribberbos, *When the Time Had Fully Come* (Grand Rapids, 1957), p. 63.

The parent may hesitate to respond immediately as he recalls the multiplication of problems involved in the abrupt arrival of teenaged years. But in the end it cannot be denied that the gangly youth stands much closer to the full realization of manhood than does the infant.

In just such a manner, the childlike trust of Abraham may appear to have definite advantages over the sometimes rowdy adventures of Israel under law. Yet the patient student of Scripture will detect a definite progress toward the goal of Christ.

Is that not basically the substance of the example employed by Paul in Galatians 3:23–26? The law is a schoolmaster, an externalized disciplinarian, to bring us to Christ. As teenagers under a tutor, so was Israel under the law. Yet their condition under law was a vital step of advancement over the infancy that had preceded.

2. The Mosaic covenant is less than all that succeeds.

Secondly, the Mosaic covenant represents a less mature stage of the manifestation of God's purposes in redemption than all that follows. It unveils less of the truth of God than the Davidic or the new covenant.

God's covenant with David clearly embodies an advancement over Moses in the revelation of law. Particularly, the permanent establishment of a representative king over Israel indicates an advancement in law-administration. Moses himself may have embodied features of a kingly representative of the God of the covenant. But no abiding principle for succession-maintenance was included in Mosaic legislation. At the end of Joshua's period of leadership, Israel disintegrated into the tumultuous period of the judges. Not until God's covenanting word concerning the house of David was there established some assurance of a maintained stability within the theocracy. With the anointing of David, law began to be administered in Israel by the "man after God's own heart."

The localization of God's throne in the Zion/Jerusalem complex also represents an advancement beyond preceding revelations of God's law in Israel. The mobile sanctuary of Moses was replaced by a more stabilized situation. Under David, God's rule of righteousness was established in permanency.

Even more pointedly, it should be underscored that the covenant of Moses is less than the new covenant in its manifestation of the role of God's law in the life of God's covenant people. Stress in Scripture emphasizes the new mode by which God's law is administered under the new covenant. Under the old covenant, law came through tables of stone. But now, the covenant is administered in a dramatically new fashion.

The description of the new covenant in the book of Jeremiah focuses on the distinctiveness of this new mode of ministry of God's law:

> "But this is the covenant which I will make with the house of Israel after those days," declares the Lord, "I will put My law within them, and on their heart I will write it; and I will be their God, and they shall be My people."
>
> "And they shall not teach again, each man his neighbor and each man his brother, saying, 'Know the Lord,' for they shall all know Me, from the least of them to the greatest of them," declares the Lord, "for I will forgive their iniquity, and their sin I will remember no more" (Jer. 31:33–34).

The distinctiveness of the ministry of law under the new covenant resides in its inward character. Rather than being administered externally, the law shall be administered from within the heart. The consequence, according to Jeremiah, will be that no need will remain for an externalized propounding of God's law. All shall know him and all shall conform naturally to his will. Quite obviously, the Mosaic covenant's writing on tables of stone cannot compare with the glories of this new covenant.

Several problems arise with respect to the apprehension of the full significance of this prophetic word of Jeremiah. How is this statement to be related to other passages associating the inward writing of the law with the ministry of the Mosaic covenant itself?[13]

---

13. Cf. Deut. 6:6; 30:14; Ps. 37:31; 40:8; 119:11.

How does Jeremiah's assertion concerning the absence of the need of a teaching ministry relate to the actual state of believers today under the new covenant?

Such questions emphasize the need for maintaining a balance between the harmonizing unity of the single covenant of redemption and its historical diversity.

The life-experience of the believer under any epoch always will have a direct relationship to the revelation that has been made available to that point. The self-revelation of God throughout the ages may be regarded as the "raw material" used by the Holy Spirit to apply the benefits of redemption to the life-experience of the believer. For this reason, advancement in revelation involves advancement in life-experience. The believer under the old covenant may have experienced in essence the same realities of redemption experienced by believers under the new covenant. But heightened revelation also involves a deeper and richer experience of deliverance from sin and its consequences.

Questions associated with the reality of the newness of the new covenant must be considered in this framework. Because the Christ now has come in incarnate fashion, the degree of revelational intensity has swollen far beyond the circumstances prevalent in earlier historical epochs. The new covenant Scriptures now make available to the church in permanent form a God-inspired interpretation of the magnificent benefits made available by the coming of Christ. The fuller revelation available today brings with it a richer experience of redemption's grace.

A passage of equal significance to the classic statement of Jeremiah showing the superiority of the new covenant over the Mosaic administration of law may be found in II Corinthians 3. In this portion of Scripture Paul clearly indicates that the Mosaic covenant of law is less than the new covenant which has succeeded it.

In this chapter, Paul exposits for the New Testament believer three symbols which appeared in connection with the institution of the Mosaic covenant. Each of these symbols embodies a primary truth concerning the old covenant, and at the same time provides a basis of comparison with the new covenant. These three symbols are: (a) the symbol of the glory of Moses' face; (b) the symbol of the fading of the glory of Moses' face; and (c) the symbol of the veil which covered Moses' face.

(a) The symbol of the glory of Moses' face

Paul refers to the symbol of the glory of Moses' face in II Corinthians 3:7ff.:

> But if the ministry of death, in letters engraved on stones, came with glory, so that the sons of Israel could not look intently at the face of Moses because of the glory of his face, fading as it was, how shall the ministry of the Spirit fail to be even more with glory? For if the ministry of condemnation has glory, much more does the ministry of righteousness abound in glory (II Cor. 3:7-9).

The fact that Moses' face radiated the glory of God at the time of the giving of the law clearly symbolized the greatness of the old covenant. Never does Paul treat the old covenant in a disparaging manner. Much to the contrary, he attributes full honor to the Mosaic covenant as a dispensation instituted by God.

Paul, however, does not stop with the recognition of the glory of the Mosaic covenant. He proceeds to point out that the glory of the new covenant exceeds the glory of the old covenant. In fact, the old covenant's glory must be recognized as having been paled into insignificance by the surpassing glory of the new covenant:

> For indeed what had glory, in this case has no glory on account of the glory that surpasses it (II Cor. 3:10).

Although the old covenant had its glory, it could not compare with the greater glory of the new covenant.

The comparative "glories" of these two epochs relate to that which each covenant administers. Although a revelation from God that came in glory, the old covenant ministered "death" and "condemnation." Because of the law's effectiveness in revealing sin, it subjected man to curse.

In sharpest contrast, the new covenant may be characterized as a "ministry of the Spirit," a "ministry of righteousness." Instead of bringing in its wake condemnation and death, the new covenant effects righteousness and life. The superiority of this consummative covenant resides not merely in its having some material characteristic of greater glory. Instead, that which the new covenant accomplishes declares to the world its greater glory.

(b) The symbol of the fading of the glory of Moses' face

Paul secondly comments on the symbol of the fading of the glory of Moses' face. In II Corinthians 3:7, 13, Paul notes that the glory of Moses' face faded. His interpretation of the significance of this fading appears in verse 11, where the same term used to describe the declining of the glory of Moses' face (καταργέω) is applied to the entire Mosaic covenant of law: "For if that which passes away [i.e., the ministration under Moses] was with glory, much more that which remains [i.e., the ministration of the new covenant] is in glory." Not only was the glory of the old covenant symbolically represented at the time of the giving of the law; the provisional and transitory character of the old covenant also received symbolic representation. Moses' radiance faded, symbolically depicting the fading of the ministration of law.

This fading character of the Mosaic administration contrasts with the permanence of the new covenant. The new covenant excels the old covenant not only in the greatness of its glory; it excels also in the permanence of that glory. The new covenant is "that which remains" (v. 11).

(c) The symbol of the veiling of Moses' face

The third symbol present at the giving of the law relates to the veiling of Moses' face:

> Having therefore such a hope, we are using great boldness, and are not as Moses, who was (repeatedly) putting a veil on his face, so that the sons of Israel might not gaze to the end of that which was passing away.
>
> But their minds were hardened. For until this very day the same veil remains at the reading of the old covenant, it not being revealed that

it is done away in Christ. But until this day whenever Moses is read a veil remains over their heart (II Cor. 3:12-15).

Paul does not stop simply at recognizing pragmatically the presence of a veil in the law-giving sequel. He offers a most profound interpretation of the symbolic value of the veil employed by Moses. Even further, Paul asserts the continuing presence of this symbolic veil in the midst of current Judaism.

Notice carefully verse 14: "for until this very day the same veil remains at the reading of the old covenant, it not being revealed that it is done away in Christ." Notice that it is the "same" veil (αὐτός) that appeared in Moses' day which continues to the present. Paul does not intend to suggest that some 1500 year old relic still exists. Nor does he intend to conjure up some allegorical interpretation of Moses' veil. Instead, he desires only to exposit the original significance of the "same" veil.

What is the effect of a veil? Generally a veil keeps something from being revealed.

What does the symbolic veil of Moses keep from being revealed to Israel even today? Paul answers this question explicitly in verse 14: "The same veil remains, it not being revealed . . . that it (i.e., the old administration of law) is done away in Christ."[14] The tragic thing about Judaism in Paul's day was that it did not comprehend the transitory character of the Mosaic dispensation. Judaism rightly understood the glory of the old covenant. But it did not grasp the fading character of that glory. The veil therefore symbolized the blindness of Israel to the transitoriness and fading character of the Mosaic covenant. They could not see the end of the law as it was to be realized in Christ.

Generally, it is supposed that the function of Moses' veil was to shield Israel from the excessiveness of the glory of Moses' face. This interpretation appears to conform to the statement in II Corinthians

---

14. It would be sheer doubletalk to equate the subject of "it is done away" with the veil, since the veil is the subject of "it remains" in the immediately preceding clause. Paul would then be saying that the veil of their blindness still remains, since the veil of their blindness has been taken away.

3:7. In this verse, Paul reminds the Corinthians that the old covenant came with glory, "so that the sons of Israel were not able to gaze at the face of Moses because of the glory of his face [which glory was] fading."

However, several considerations point in another direction for analyzing the significance of Moses' veil in the Sinai narrative:

First, the structure of this verse places emphasis on the *fading* character of glory of Moses' face.[15] Moses' face was radiant indeed; but it was a *fading* radiance that marked his countenance.

Secondly, no mention whatsoever is made of Moses' veil and its function in this verse. Subsequently in his discussion, Paul indicates the function of the veil. Moses put a veil on his face, "that the sons of Israel might not gaze to the end of that which was passing away" (v. 13). Although the significance of this phrase has been disputed vigorously, the most convincing position seems to be that Paul is saying that Moses donned his veil that the sons of Israel might not stare at Moses' face while the glory was *fading*.

Thirdly, a closer look at Exodus 34:29–35 strongly supports the view which understands the veil as concealing the *fading* character of Moses' glory rather than the excessive character of his glory.

According to Exodus 34, the radiant Moses first appeared before the people, who fled from him (vv. 29, 30).[16] This fear on the part of the people would not necessarily imply a glory so excessive that it could not be endured. The very fact that rays of light eminated from Moses' face would have provided adequate basis for arousing terror in their hearts. As a matter of fact, the people returned to Moses when he summoned them, and they stood in his unveiled presence while he delivered to them the law (vv. 31, 32).

The text explicitly indicates that Moses completed giving the law

---

15. The separation of the adjectival characterization of Moses' glory from the noun which it modifies emphasizes the fading character of the glory. Cf. F. Blass and A. Debrunner, *A Greek Grammar of the New Testament* (Chicago, 1961), #473.

16. The text actually says that the skin of Moses' face "horned." The use of the term קָרַן in Hebrew, reflected in the Latin Vulgate, apparently provided the source of later artistic representations of Moses with horns protruding from his head.

to the people before he donned his veil. Only after Moses had finished speaking with them did he put the veil on his face (v. 33).[17]

The narrative proceeds to indicate the pattern by which Moses delivered the law to the people in its various installments (vv. 34, 35). Moses would return to the Lord's presence, remove his veil, and receive an additional portion of the law's revelation. The text is quite explicit that the people (habitually) would see the skin of Moses' face that it shone (v. 35). After delivering his message, Moses would replace the veil on his face (v. 34).[18]

In his exposition of this passage, Paul pointedly indicates that the glory of Moses' face was fading in character. How did he determine this fact? Nothing in the narrative of Exodus 34 explicitly mentions that the glory of Moses' face ever faded.[19]

Apparently Paul deduced the fact of the fading character of the glory of Moses' face from the function of the veil in the narrative. Moses was repeatedly donning his veil, says Paul, so that Israel might not gaze to the end of that which was fading (II Cor. 3:13).

The degree to which Israel perceived the significance of the symbol of Moses' veil is difficult to determine.[20] Paul interprets the symbolism of the veil in terms of Israel's blindness to the transitory character of Mosaic law (v. 14).

---

17. For a full discussion of the significance of the Hebrew construction as indicating that Moses completed his communication of the law before donning his veil, see Umberto Cassuto, *A Commentary on the Book of Exodus* (Jerusalem, 1967), p. 450, and his extended discussion of the force of "and he finished" (וַיְכַל) in *A Commentary on the Book of Genesis,* Part I (Jerusalem, 1961), pp. 61f.

The LXX is quite pointed: καὶ ἐπειδὴ κατέπαυσε λαλῶν πρὸς αὐτούς, ἐπέθηκεν ἐπὶ τὸ πρόσωπον αὐτοῦ κάλυμμα.

18. Note the corresponding emphasis of Paul concerning the habitual character of Moses' donning his veil. Moses "was putting" (ἐτίθει) a veil on his face, so that the sons of Israel might not look to the end of that which was fading (II Cor. 3:13).

19. The rabbis actually concluded that the glory of Moses' face never faded, but remained with him until death, and even after death in his tomb. Cf. Hermann L. Strack and Paul Billerbeck, *Kommentar Zum Neuen Testament Aus Talmud und Midrasch* (München, 1926), 3: 515.

20. Philip Edgcumbe Hughes, *Paul's Second Epistle to the Corinthians* (Grand Rapids, 1962), p. 109, suggests that a veiling of the fading of Moses' glory would involve subterfuge, which would be unworthy of the apostle.

However, it is possible to understand the veiling of the fading glory as having a

The very fact that the veil symbolized "blindness" infers that Israel was in a state of nonperceptibility with respect to the significance of the veil. If Israel had apprehended the full significance of the veil, then their apprehension would constitute a contradiction of the truth which the veil was intended to symbolize.

Yet it is doubtful that Israel had no awareness whatsoever of the fading character of the glory of Moses' face. It would not be essential for the veil to conceal completely Moses' fading glory in order to function in a symbolic manner. Still further, Israel must have seen Moses' face at a later time without the "horning" phenomenon, unless it is to be posited that Moses wandered in the wilderness for the entire 40 years with his face veiled.

But the heart of Israel was blind to the symbolic significance of the veil. Their own blindness was displayed openly in a symbolic manner before them. Yet even this self-portrayal could not awaken them to the transitoriness of the Mosaic covenant.

Even today, this same veil remains. Whenever Moses is read, Israel is blind to the transitoriness of the law (II Cor. 3:15). They are so impressed with the glories of the revelation of God's law that they have become blinded to the temporary character of the Mosaic administration of law.

Paul, however, does not despair over Israel. For no veil covers the ministry of the new covenant. Its glory does not fade. With "unveiled face" (v. 18) every new covenant believer stands in the immediate

---

symbolic significance rather than representing subterfuge. It is not necessary to posit that the Israelites had no awareness whatever of the fading character of Moses' glory. They saw Moses in his glory. They saw him without his glory (unless with the rabbis, it is held that Moses' glory never faded). What they did not see was the transitional fading-process. It was the veil that kept the Israelites from seeing this fading, and this fact could have been deduced by Moses' contemporaries. They saw his unveiled glory for long stretches of time as he delivered the various installments of the law. Why then should Moses don his veil? Not because the Israelites were sinners whose vision of Moses' glory had to be interrupted because of their unworthiness. Instead, Moses donned his veil so that the Israelites might not look to the termination of the glory of his face. This donning symbolized their blindness to the transitory character of Mosaic legislation.

presence of the Lord. He shares in the uniquely privileged position of Moses, rather than simply receiving from Moses the report concerning God's revelation. Beholding constantly as in a mirror the glory of the Lord, he is "metamorphosized" from glory to glory.

Moses passed from glory to fading glory. Only temporarily, after immediate confrontation with the Lord, did his face radiate God's glory.

But the participant in the new covenant passes from glory to glory. Because the Lord, who is the Spirit, lives within the believer, his glory never fades. By the Lord, the Spirit, he is changed into the likeness of God's own son.

The old covenant may have come with glory. But its fading glory hardly compares with the abiding glory of the new covenant. In every way, the new covenant excels that which preceded it.

The Mosaic covenant was glorious. But the new covenant is more glorious. The Mosaic covenant never was intended to be the end of God's covenantal dealings with his people. Instead, at the very time of its institution, the Mosaic covenant was represented as being progressively related to the totality of God's purposes. While containing a clearer manifestation of redemptive truth than that which preceded, it also contained much less truth than the consummation of the covenant which was to follow.

The covenant of law consummates in Jesus Christ. According to Matthew 5:17, Christ indicated that he did not come to destroy the law but to fulfill it. By his coming, he consummated all of God's purposes in the giving of the law.

In the sermon on the mount, Jesus manifested himself as the new lawgiver. His "I say unto you" (Matt. 5:22 etc.) displayed his role in relation to the law as superior to that of Moses. Rather than reporting a revelation which he had received, Christ propounded the law of the new covenant as its author himself.

On the mount of transfiguration, Jesus appeared in a glory greater than Moses. The brilliance of the sun radiated from him as he manifested his true inner glory. Rather than merely reflecting the rays of God's brilliance, he himself originated his own transfiguring glory (Matt. 17:2). Although Moses and Elijah appeared with him, in no wise were they equal to him. Ultimately, the disciples saw "Jesus only," and heard the divine voice declare "This is my beloved son . . . hear him" (Matt. 17:5, NASB).

Moses the law-mediator ministered as a servant in God's house. But Christ the law-originator rules as Son over God's house (Heb. 3:5, 6).

Paul the apostle indicates that Christ is the end of the law to all who believe (Rom. 12:4). The convicting, condemning power of the law exhausts its accusations in Christ.

In order to be that end, Christ fulfilled all righteousness. He kept the whole law perfectly, while at the same time bearing in himself the curses of the law. From every perspective, the covenant of law consummates in Jesus Christ.

11

Excursus

Which Structures Scripture— Covenants or Dispensations?

GOD'S initiatives in the establishment of covenantal relationships structure redemptive history. His sovereign interventions provide the essential framework for understanding the great biblical epochs. This perspective has characterized the present treatment of the biblical materials throughout.

A major alternative for analyzing the structure of biblical history is offered by a school of evangelical thought more popularly known as "dispensationalism."[1] Dispensationalism has set itself over against covenant theology as a means for grasping the architectonic structure of biblical revelation.

As the dispensational perspective is being evaluated, it should not be forgotten that covenant theologians and dispensationalists stand

---

1. For an historical survey of the movement, see Clarence B. Bass: *Backgrounds to Dispensationalism* (Grand Rapids: Wm. B. Eerdmans, 1960), pp. 64ff.

side by side in affirming the essentials of the Christian faith. Very often these two groups within Christendom stand alone in opposition to the inroads of modernism, neo-evangelicalism, and emotionalism. Covenant theologians and dispensationalists should hold in highest regard the scholarly and evangelical productivity of one another. It may be hoped that continuing interchange may be based on love and respect.

More recently, dispensationalism has tended to minimize the significance of the "dispensations" as characterizing its distinctive system. Dispensationalists note that "covenant" theologians also make use of "dispensational" terminology.[2]

Yet the use of similar terminology does not involve inevitably agreement in principle. As a matter of fact, the concept of the dispensations held by the "dispensationalists" sets their perspective on biblical history over against the viewpoint maintained by the covenant theologian.

Interestingly, the difference of approach in dispensational and covenantal history-structuring manifests itself in two different systems appearing within dispensationalism itself. If covenant theologians make use of the term "dispensation," so also do dispensationalists make frequent use of the term "covenant." As a matter of fact, two alternative systems for structuring redemptive history function within dispensational thinking itself. One of these systems is "covenantal," and the other "dispensational."

As interpretive remarks by dispensationalists regarding covenants and dispensations are compared, a significant tension emerges. It is as though the history of redemption had two structurings. At points these two structurings interrelate closely with one another. At other times, they vie for prominence. It is not easy to determine which of these systems actually should be understood in the mind of the dispensationalist himself as the key to understanding the progress

---

2. See the discussion of Charles Caldwell Ryrie, *Dispensationalism Today* (Chicago: Moody Press, 1965), pp. 43f. Ryrie indicates that neither the recognition of dispensations in Scripture nor an agreement respecting a specific number of dispensations provides the essential hallmark of "dispensationalism."

of redemptive history. The question presses forward: Which structures Scripture—covenants or dispensations?

The present investigation will move through the various epochs of redemptive history by noting the optional perspectives afforded in covenantal theology and in dispensationalism. Because of the developing nature of dispensational thinking, more than one description of some epochs will have to be noted. Dispensational theologians have been quite active during the past few decades in refining their system of biblical analysis. Certainly it would not be fair to treat the dispensationalist today as though his modes of expression were identical to those which characterize the "old" Scofield Bible as it first appeared in 1909. Yet at the same time, these early foundations cannot be ignored altogether. For the earlier dispensational theology continues to provide the basic mode of approach for dispensationalism today.

As this "journey" through the various structurings of the history of redemption progresses, three matters should become evident. First, it should become clear that some significant refinements have developed in more recent expressions of the dispensational perspective. Second, it should become clear that a significant point of tension exists within dispensationalism itself as it views the covenants and the dispensations as two options for structuring redemptive history.[3] Third, it should become clear that a basic difference of perspective exists between the structure of redemptive history as understood by the covenantal theologian and by the dispensationalist.

---

3. At this point, one potential misunderstanding should be dispelled which might arise as a result of the arrangement of materials in the present synopsis of opinions. It should not be supposed that the "old" Scofield Bible (1909) contained only a series of notes dealing with the dispensations, and had nothing to say with respect to the covenants. Neither should it be supposed that the "new" Scofield Bible (1967) contained only notes about the covenants, and had nothing to say concerning the dispensations. It is only because of a desire to contrast the treatment of dispensations and covenants in dispensational theology while at the same time indicating something of the progression of thought in dispensationalism that comments have been limited primarily to notes about the "dispensations" in the "old" Scofield Bible, and to notes about the "covenants" in the "new" Scofield Bible.

THE COVENANT OF CREATION

Covenant theology understands God's relationship to man at creation from a covenantal perspective. Man's responsibility as created in God's image to form a culture glorifying to the Lord indicates something of the breadth of human responsibility established by creation. The whole of the universe was to be brought into subjection to the glory of God. The ordinance of marriage and the institution of the Sabbath implied that man's obligation to his Maker extended to every area of human activity. At the same time, a special test of probation with respect to the noneating of the tree of the knowledge of good and evil focused attention on man's specific responsibility to obey the word of the Lord simply because it was the Lord's word. By the establishment of this all-encompassing relationship, God bound Himself to man the creature. This relationship established by creation serves as the foundational basis for understanding the whole of human history as it develops from this point.

The epoch that corresponds to the covenant of creation according to the "old" Scofield Bible is called the dispensation of "innocency." This dispensation is described as "an absolutely simple test" which ended in the judgment of the expulsion.[4] This particular dispensation receives very little elaboration in the old Scofield Bible. No explanation is given concerning the broader responsibilities of man created in God's image. Only the reference to the "simple test" describes the actual character of this relationship. Such an abbreviated perspective on man's responsibilities as created eventually must have a most significant effect on the overall view of the meaning of Christianity.

More recent dispensational thinking on the dispensation of "innocency" may be found in C. C. Ryrie's *Dispensationalism Today.*[5]

---

4. C. I. Scofield, ed., *The Scofield Reference Bible: The Holy Bible* (New York: Oxford University Press, 1909), p. 5, n. 5. This work hereinafter shall be referred to as the "old" Scofield Bible.

5. Ryrie, op. cit., pp. 57f.

Ryrie indicates that Adam's responsibilities involved maintaining the garden and not eating the fruit of the tree of the knowledge of good and evil. He notes man's broader responsibility with respect to the garden, although he does not elaborate on the significance of this obligation. He also introduces into the discussion a significant feature at this early stage that characterizes his treatment of the dispensations. He attempts to provide scriptural limitations which bracket the particular epoch under discussion. In this case he sets the limits of the dispensation of innocency as Genesis 1:28–3:6. As shall be seen subsequently, this effort to provide the points at which each dispensation begins and ends creates some troublesome problems for dispensational interpretation.

A much fuller perspective on God's relationship to man at creation is found in the notes of the Scofield Reference Bible with respect to the "covenant" God established with man at creation. The "new" Scofield Bible capsules the substance of God's original covenant with man:

> The first or Edenic covenant required the following responsibilities of Adam: (1) to propogate the race; (2) to subdue the earth for man; (3) to have dominion over the animal creation; (4) to care for the garden and eat its fruits and herbs; and (5) to abstain from eating of one tree, the tree of the knowledge of good and evil, on penalty of death for disobedience.[6]

Except for failing to mention the role of the Sabbath in God's creation ordinances, this description of man's original relationship to his Creator has much to commend it. It deals quite adequately with man's broader responsibilities, while at the same time indicating the specific test under which man was placed at creation.

In comparing the dispensational treatment of the first of the "dispensations" with the first of the "covenants," it cannot be said that these two perspectives actually conflict with one another.

---

6. C. I. Scofield, ed., *The New Scofield Reference Bible: The Holy Bible* (New York: Oxford University Press, 1967), p. 5, n. 2. This work hereinafter shall be referred to as the "new" Scofield Bible.

However, man's original relationship to God finds a much fuller treatment under the dispensational analysis of the "Edenic covenant" than under the dispensational analysis of the "dispensation of innocency."

THE COVENANT OF REDEMPTION

Adam: The Covenant of Commencement

Covenant theology understands the whole of history after man's fall into sin as unifying under the provisions of the covenant of redemption (or more traditionally, the covenant of grace). Beginning with the first promise to Adam-in-sin and continuing throughout history to the consummation of the ages, God orders all things in view of his singular purpose of redeeming a people to himself. Indeed, significant sub-structures within this great expanse of time must be noted. The distinction between old covenant and new covenant marks a major structural division within the history of redemption. Yet even these two great epochs relate integrally to one another as promise and fulfillment, as shadow and reality.

God's initial words to Adam after his fall into sin appropriately may be considered in terms of the commencing of this covenantal history. In his words to the serpent, to the woman, and to the man the Lord decrees the nature of the struggle which shall ensue in the cause of bringing man to salvation. In the sweat of man's face, through the pain of childbirth, by the provision of a singular Champion, God shall achieve for man a thorough-going redemption. This entire program aims toward the restoration of man to the situation of blessing in which he was created originally. Covenantal history thus displays the unifying purposes of God in the world.

The Scofield Bible characterizes the period which immediately follows man's fall into sin as the "dispensation of conscience." According to the "old" Scofield Bible, man under this dispensation "was responsible to do all known good, to abstain from all known evil, and to approach God through sacrifice."[7]

Perhaps the most obvious problematic associated with this description of the state of man immediately after his fall into sin is the failure to center on God's promise concerning the provision of a Redeemer as described in Genesis 3:15. It is not man's conscience that comes to the fore in Scripture immediately after the fall. Instead, it is God's grace that promises to enter the conflict against Satan on behalf of his fallen creature that characterizes the age.

Although not nearly radical enough in its revisions, the "new" Scofield Bible shows appropriate sensitivity to this problem. The revised description of the "dispensation of conscience" introduces a reference to the first promise of redemption. It elaborates on the responsibility of man, as described in the "old" Scofield Bible, to approach God through blood sacrifice by noting that this responsibility is "here instituted in prospect of the finished work of Christ."[8] The note also alters the description of the final result of the "second testing of man." According to the "old" Scofield Bible, the testing of man by his conscience resulted in the absolute depravity of man as described in Genesis 6:5. According to the "new" Scofield Bible, the "result" of this second dispensation is to be found in the promise of redemption as described in Genesis 3:15. Still further, the "new" Scofield Bible modifies this particular dispensation by revising the perspective on the "end" of this period of testing. The "old" Scofield Bible had declared that this "dispensation of conscience" came to an end in the judgment of the flood. But the "new" Scofield Bible affirms that man continued in his moral responsibility as dictated by conscience throughout succeeding ages.

Ryrie's treatment of the "dispensation of conscience" accentuates the problems associated with the "ending" and "beginning" of the various dispensations. As noted earlier, Ryrie indicated that the scriptural limits for the dispensation of innocency ran from Genesis 1:28 to Genesis 3:6. He begins the following dispensation, the

---

7. "Old" Scofield Bible, p. 10, n. 2.
8. "New" Scofield Bible, p. 7, n. 1.

dispensation of conscience, with Genesis 4:1. It is actually quite amazing to note the manner in which the first promise of the Redeemer as found in Genesis 3:15 is omitted from its central place as characterizing the state of man in relation to God after his fall in sin. It would seem quite evident that this omission indicates that the promise of redemption really is not integral to Ryrie's structuring of history. As a matter of fact, Ryrie elsewhere states that the dispensations "are not stages in the revelation of the covenant of grace, but are distinguishingly different administrations of God directing the affairs of the world."[9] In his determination to set the dispensational perspective over against covenantal theology, Ryrie has moved the promise of redemption to fallen man away from its proper center-stage position.

The tension inherent in the dispensational structuring of history is seen at this point by comparing these notations concerning the "dispensation of conscience" with notations from the "old" and the "new" Scofield Bibles with respect to the second or "Adamic covenant." Both reference Bibles describe the Adamic covenant as containing the divine initiative, which conditions the life of fallen man until the kingdom age. The elements of this covenant include the curse of Satan, the first promise of a Redeemer, the changed state of the woman, the burdensome character of labor, and the sorrow and brevity of human life.

The characterization of the state of man after the fall as presented in the dispensational treatment of the "Adamic covenant" possesses a much stronger biblical basis than the description of the same epoch under the rubric of the "dispensation of conscience." The emphasis of the "covenantal" approach centers squarely on an exegetical treatment of Genesis 3:15ff., the very passage passed over by Ryrie. Instead of characterizing the period immediately after the fall as a time in which man was responsible "to do all known good" and "to abstain from all known evil," a responsible analysis of the epoch-making words of God respecting his covenantal commitment to redeem men from their sin appears. It is rather difficult to

---

9. Ryrie, op. cit., p. 16.

understand why the dispensationalist would quarrel with the covenant theologian in his desire to see a single "covenant of redemption" overarching history from God's first promise to Adam to the consummation of the ages if he himself affirms that the conditions established under the "Adamic covenant" were to prevail until the arrival of the kingdom age.

Noah: The Covenant of Preservation

Covenantal theology emphasizes the integral relation of the covenant of Noah with God's original covenant of creation. Man's responsibility under the covenant of Noah to multiply and to replenish the earth can be understood in no other way than a renewal of original creation mandates. Still further, covenantal theology emphasizes that God's covenant with Noah must be understood in the context of God's commitment to redeem a people to himself. If the primary commitment of the Lord in the covenant with Noah is to preserve the earth, this preservation has as its goal a sustaining of the world until redemption may be achieved. God's grace sovereignly centers on a single family. He saves them from the destructive judgment of the flood. He seals his gracious relationship to them by the sign of the rainbow. He enters into a bond with the whole of the created universe, pointing toward the universal offer of the gospel of salvation.

Corresponding to the "covenant with Noah" is the third "dispensation," called the dispensation of "human government." The "old" Scofield Bible indicates that man "utterly failed" under conscience, and that the judgment of the flood marked "the end of the second dispensation and the beginning of the third."[10] The "new" Scofield Bible omits this particular sentence. Instead, it affirms that although this time-era ended with the flood, "man continued in his moral responsibility as God added further revelation concerning Himself and His will in succeeding ages."[11]

---

10. "Old" Scofield Bible, p. 16, n. 1.
11. "New" Scofield Bible, p. 7, n. 1.

Under this dispensation of "human government," man failed to rule righteously, but his responsibility for government did not cease. Instead, this responsibility will continue "until Christ sets up His kingdom."[12] The primary emphasis in both the "old" and the "new" Scofield Bibles is on the failure of Jewish and Gentile governments to perform as God had desired. No particular effort is made to relate the ordinances of this epoch either to creation or to God's ongoing program of redemption.

The treatment of the "covenant" with Noah in dispensational thinking may be characterized as secularistic rather than redemptive-historical. Capital punishment is not put in a perspective that sees it as preserving the earth so that God's purposes of redemption may be accomplished. The eating of animal flesh, the development of government, science and art primarily under the sponsorship of the Japhetic line, and the confirmation of the order of nature are not tied in with God's on-going program of redemption. Even the prophetic declaration concerning the servitude of the descendants of Canaan is presented without any effort to explain its redemptive-historical significance. The only note sounded with some redemptive over-tones relates to Shem's peculiar relation to the Lord. All divine revelation is to come through Shem, and Christ is to be born a Shemite. But this isolated note hardly has the effect of integrating adequately the various aspects of the Noahic covenant into the mainstream of redemptive history. This treatment of the Noahic covenant manifests a secularistic, non-redemptive dimension which characterizes much of the history of dispensational interpretation of prophecy.

Abraham: The Covenant of Promise

Several difficult problems emerge from an analysis of the treatment of the "dispensation of promise" as found in the "old" Scofield Bible. On the one hand, this epoch is described as "wholly gracious

---

12. Ibid., p. 13, n. 3.

and unconditional." But the immediately following sentence indicates that "the descendants of Abraham had but to abide in their own land to inherit every blessing."[13] In successive sentences, the covenant is declared to be unconditional while at the same time conditioned on remaining in the land of Palestine. This concentration on the land of Palestine becomes characteristic of the dispensational treatment of the promises made to Abraham.

It is particularly difficult to appreciate the introduction of a condition that Israel remain in the land in this particular covenant. As the covenant itself is being made, God declares that because the iniquity of the Canaanites is not yet full, Israel will have to sojourn in the land of Egypt for 400 years (Gen. 15:13, 16). Furthermore, at the point at which Jacob reluctantly consents to descend into Egypt, the Lord himself appears and reassures him that his course is right. He is not to fear to go down into Egypt, for God will go down with him and will surely bring him up again (Gen. 46:3, 4).

Another point of tension in the treatment of the "dispensation of promise" by the "old" Scofield Bible has to do with the relation of this dispensation to the period of law that follows. Scofield says that "the dispensation of promise was ended when Israel rashly accepted the law," and that "at Sinai they exchanged grace for a law."[14] Such an analysis of the events of Sinai hardly does justice to the sovereign character of God's covenantal relationships. It is not that Israel "rashly accepted" the law at Sinai; it is that God in His ordering of the progress of redemption's history instituted a new covenantal relationship.

The "old" Scofield Bible also reveals a tension between the "dispensation of promise" and the "covenant of promise." This effort to distinguish between a promise-dispensation and a promise-covenant emphasizes the basic problem in the dual structuring of redemptive history by dispensationalism. The Abrahamic covenant is described as being everlasting because unconditional, while the Abrahamic dispensation is described as ending at the giving of the law.

---

13. "Old" Scofield Bible, p. 20, n. 1.
14. Ibid.

The "new" Scofield Bible has eliminated many of these problematic modes of expression as found in the "old" Scofield Bible. But Ryrie's treatment of this same dispensation manifests the older problems inherent in the "old" Scofield Bible. He says: "The promised land was theirs and the blessing was theirs as long as they remained in the land."[15] Now the false condition of "remaining in the land" is brought forward again as the basis for blessing in the Abrahamic dispensation.

The dispensational treatment of the covenant with Abraham manifests the inherent problematic of a basic dualism involved in their total approach to the interpretation of Scripture. Instead of seeing a single purpose of God that unites his activity throughout the ages, dispensationalism strongly advocates a dual purpose in divine activity. One purpose relates to the nation of Israel, while the other purpose relates to the church of the New Testament age.

According to the "new" Scofield Bible, "the Abrahamic covenant reveals the sovereign purposes of God to fulfill through Abraham his program for Israel, and to provide in Christ the Saviour for all who believe."[16] Rather than seeing this covenant as having a unified goal in bringing salvation ultimately both to Jew and Gentile, the dispensationalist insists that a distinction be made between God's purpose for Israel as established in the Abrahamic covenant, and God's purpose for the nations as established in that same covenant. In expounding the particulars of the provisions of the Abrahamic covenant, the effort is made to interpret particular items either to one or to both sides of God's "dual" purpose. God's promise to make of Abraham a great nation has primary reference to Israel. The promise that Abraham is to be a blessing finds its fulfillment preeminently in Christ. The indicator that those who curse Abraham will be cursed themselves serves as a warning against anti-semitism, while the promise that all the families of the earth will be blessed in Abraham is the great evangelical promise which is fulfilled in Christ.

This distinction between two purposes of God through history

---

15. Ryrie, op. cit., p. 61.
16. "New" Scofield Bible, pp. 19f., n. 3.

may be regarded as the distinctive hallmark of dispensational teaching. Rather than seeing a unity of purpose in God's plan to redeem a people to be his own, dispensationalism maintains that two distinctive purposes for God's activity in the world must be distinguished. One of these purposes relates to ethnic Israel, and the other purpose relates to the Christian church. Ryrie quotes with approval the summarization of dispensational distinctiveness as expressed by Lewis Sperry Chafer:

> The dispensationalist believes that throughout the ages God is pursuing two distinct purposes: one related to the earth with earthly people and earthly objectives involved which is Judaism; while the other is related to heaven with heavenly people and heavenly objectives involved, which is Christianity.[17]

Dispensationalism would assert vigorously that such a conclusion derives from a consistent literalism in biblical interpretation. But it would appear that a much more fundamental principle is at work. Actually, the dispensational distinction between the two purposes of God in history arises from a metaphysical rather than a hermeneutical presupposition. Notice in the quotation from Chafer just cited that one purpose of God has to do with an earthly people and earthly objectives, while the other purpose is related to heaven involving heavenly people and heavenly objectives. Inherent in this distinction is not a "more biblical" consistency of interpretation. Instead, basic to this distinction is a metaphysical or philosophical dichotomy between the material and the spiritual realms. It is this distinction that actually lies at the root of the difference between dispensationalism and covenant theology. Covenant theology does not see redemption as related to a more "spiritual" realm than the realm in which the promises of Abraham operated. Because covenant theology sees redemption from the perspective of creation, no dichotomy exists ultimately between redemption in the spiritual realm and redemption in the physical realm. The activity of Christ in renewing a people for himself does not stop with the restoration

---

17. Cited in Ryrie, op. cit., p. 45.

of "spiritual" relationships. From the very beginning, Christ's goal is the restoration of the total man in his total creational environment. Nothing less than bodily resurrection in the context of a new heavens and a new earth where the entire curse of the fall has been removed can satisfy the biblical concept of redemption. Dispensationalism, however, emphasizes God's activity of setting apart a people for himself physically as it relates to Israel and spiritually as it relates to the New Testament people of God. The distinction is indeed one of metaphysics. A form of Platonism actually permeates the hermeneutical roots of dispensationalism.

God's covenant with Abraham cannot be partitioned so that parts of the covenant relate to ethnic Israel while other parts relate to God's new covenant people. Instead, partitioning must be done on a temporal rather than a metaphysical plane. Without question, God did deal distinctively with ethnic Israel under the Abrahamic covenant during the entire period preceding the coming of Christ. As in the case of all God's institutions under the old covenant, a shadowy promise anticipated the reality of fulfillment. This shadow-form of God's treatment of Israel partook of the same limitations of all other Old Testament institutions. As prophetic type of the anticipated reality, God's dealing with Israel as his elect people could only approximate the meaning of God's real purposes for those who were to be redeemed in Christ.

It must be insisted that the basic distinction involved in God's treatment of his elect people is a temporal rather than a metaphysical one. The redemption of the church in the present age cannot be spiritualized. Christ's bodily resurrection anticipates the intention that God has had all along in redemption. Nothing less than the renewal of the whole of creation, which now waits in anticipation for the resurrection of the sons of God, satisfies the Scripture's expectations of redemption.

Dispensationalism partitions the purposes of God, making one purpose relate to the physical, earthly realm, and another purpose relate to the heavenly, spiritual realm. The whole of the Christian faith cries out against such a distinction. Man cannot be partitioned in such a manner because he was not created in such a dualistic fashion. Man was created as a physical/spiritual complex. The only meaningful redemption man can experience is in terms of the renewal of his total being in the context of his total environment.

For pedagogical purposes, God under the old covenant did indeed foreshadow the ultimate goal of Abraham's "salvation" in terms of the possession of Palestine. But Scripture itself explicitly indicates that this hope of the patriarch found its consummate realization only by his firm faith in the resurrection of the body (Heb. 11:17–19). The old covenant patriarch, as the father of all who believe, is characterized by Scripture as looking for a "better" country, which is "heavenly," although not thereby nonphysical (Heb. 11:14–16).

Moses: The Covenant of Law

From the perspective of covenantal theology, God's dealings with his people under the Mosaic covenant must be understood as contributing significantly to the advancement of the purposes of redemption. As the law formed Israel into a covenant people, it brought God's design for redemption to a new stage of realization. Instead of continuing as a nomadic tribal confederacy, Israel solidified as a distinctive nation, consecrated as God's own priests. Rather than representing in any sense a step of retrogression, the manifestation of law to God's people must be interpreted in terms of a significant step in the advancement of redemptive revelation. Although drastically less in its glory when compared to the brilliance of the new covenant, the Mosaic covenant of law definitely served to advance the purposes of redemption.

Apparently it was felt by dispensationalists that the rather unguarded statements of the "old" Scofield Bible concerning the "dispensation of law" could not stand. The "new" Scofield Bible no longer states that Israel rashly accepted the law, and at Sinai exchanged grace for law. Instead, the note on the "dispensation of law" is designed specifically to counterbalance the common misunderstanding of dispensationalism that accuses their theology of proposing more than one way of salvation for men. It is stressed that the law "was not given as a way of life . . . but as a rule of living for people already in the covenant of Abraham and covered by blood sacrifice."[18] The law is presented as teaching "the marvel of God's grace in providing the way of approach to Himself through typical blood sacrifice."[19] In a further note concerning the giving of the law at Sinai, the "new" Scofield Bible stresses that it is "exceedingly important" to observe that the "law is not here proposed as a means of salvation but as a means by which Israel, already redeemed as a nation, might through obedience fulfill her proper destiny."[20]

All these comments indeed are salutary. The concern on the part of the editors of the "new" Scofield Bible to make it plain that there is only one way of salvation for men must be commended.

Yet it is not apparent that a fully consistent picture emerges even in the more recent dispensational treatment of the subject of the Mosaic law. In two successive notes under Exodus 19:5, the following comments appear:

> What under law was conditional is, under grace, freely given to every believer. The "if" of v. 5 is the essence of law as a method of divine dealing and the fundamental reason why "the law made nothing perfect" (Heb. 7:18–19; cp. Rom. 8:3). To Abraham the promise preceded the requirement; at Sinai the requirement preceded the promise. In the new covenant the Abrahamic order is followed.[21]
>
> The Christian is not under the conditional Mosaic Covenant of works, the law, but under the unconditional New Covenant of grace.[22]

Obviously it is true that there is a sense in which the new covenant believer is not "under the law." The external-to-life, temporary mode of administration of the law has been superseded by the new covenant manifestation of the law written on the heart. But · it is not true that an element of conditionality existed under "law"

---

18. "New" Scofield Bible, p. 94, n. 1.
19. Ibid.
20. Ibid., p. 94, n. 2.
21. Ibid., p. 95, n. 1.
22. Ibid., p. 95, n. 2.

which is not present under "grace." The same "ifs" so apparent under the Mosaic administration as they applied to Israel in the wilderness manifest themselves with even greater portent of judgment in the event of failure under the new covenant (cf. Heb. 3:7, 14, 15; 4:1, 2, 11; 6:4–6).

The problem of the dispensational understanding of the revelation of law in Scripture surfaces rather obviously when their treatment of the "covenant" of law in distinction from the "dispensation" of law is considered. As a matter of fact, both the Old and the New Scofield Bibles present two covenants associated with the revelation of law to Moses. These two covenants are radically different in their substance. One of these "covenants" administered through Moses is conditional in its very essence, and the other is absolutely unconditional, according to dispensationalism.

The "Mosaic covenant" discussed under Exodus 19:5 in the "new" Scofield Bible is said to have been added to the Abrahamic covenant for a limited time only. The Christian is "not under the conditional Mosaic Covenant of works, the law, but under the unconditional New Covenant of grace."[23]

But the revelation given to Israel through Moses is presented elsewhere in the Scofield Bibles as establishing a completely different covenant on a completely different basis. Both the "old" and the "new" Scofield Bibles include treatments of what is designated as the "Palestinian Covenant." The essence of this covenant is interpreted by dispensationalism as centering about God's promise to return Israel to their land. Although the threat of dispersion in the event of disobedience appears in this covenant, the certain conclusion of God's dealing with Israel must be a full restoration to the land of Palestine. This covenant "secures the final restoration and conversion of Israel."[24]

A basic misreading of the text of Scripture apparently has led to the introduction of this additional covenant in contradistinction from the Mosaic covenant established at Sinai. The Scofield Bible

---

23. Ibid.
24. Ibid., p. 1318, n. 2.

uses Deuteronomy 30:3 as the passage of Scripture for introducing this particular covenant. Its provisions are presented as though they were quite distinctive from the provisions made under the Mosaic covenant of law. The emphasis of this "Palestinian covenant," according to dispensationalism, is on the gracious promises of the Lord, comparable to the unconditional promises of the Abrahamic covenant. The final possession of the land of Palestine by Israel is assured by this covenant. Jesus Christ is yet to perform "its gracious promises."[25]

Yet the setting of Deuteronomy 30 requires that it be understood as reporting nothing other than a renewal of the Mosaic covenant of law. The entire book of Deuteronomy presents itself in covenantal form as a renewal of the bond which God established originally with Israel at Sinai. Moses assembles Israel in the plains of Moab prior to his departure from them and renews their covenantal obligations. This covenant-renewal document includes the most terrifying description of the results that would fall on covenant-breakers (Deut. 28:15–68). The fact that gracious provisions concerning the restoration of Israel to Palestine are found to be the core of this portion of Scripture apart from any recognition of potential threats by dispensationalism indicates the basic fallacy in the dispensational distinction between the Abrahamic covenant of promise and the Mosaic covenant of law. Rather than standing in tension with one another, these two epochs of biblical revelation complement one another. As grace clearly may be found in the Mosaic covenant of law, so law clearly may be found in the Abrahamic covenant of promise.

David: The Covenant of the Kingdom

From a covenantal perspective, the establishment of the Davidic covenant in the Old Testament represented a supreme consummation-point in the history of redemption prior to the actual appearance of Christ himself. David's throne definitely introduced a new epoch in

_____

25. Ibid.

Old Testament history, while at the same time typically anticipating the messianic reign of Christ. The localization of God's throne in Jerusalem, and the virtual identification of the Davidic dynasty with the manifestation of God's lordship in the earth, climaxed Old Testament typical representations of the movement toward the establishment of a messianic kingdom.

It is rather remarkable that dispensational theology has no "dispensation of the kingdom" corresponding to the reign of the Davidic line. Because of this absence, it is difficult to determine precisely the relation of the Old Testament version of the messianic kingdom to the progress of redemption in dispensational thinking.

Could it be that no recognition is given in dispensational thinking to the literal, earthly reign of God in Palestine *via* the Davidic kingdom because all such notions have been projected into the future, to be realized only in the millennium? Under David and Solomon, the land was possessed, the kingdom of God existed on earth, God's throne was centered in Palestine, and a literal earthly reign of God came into being. In one sense, the essence of that which has been projected by dispensationalism into a future millennial kingdom already found its realization under the monarchy of Israel in the Old Testament. This fact should make one pause as he defines the future hope of Israel in very similar terms.

Although there is no dispensational kingdom-age in the Old Testament period, the Scofield Bible does speak of a "Davidic covenant." This covenant is described as the basis on which the future kingdom of Christ is to be founded. This domain, which is yet to be given to him, should be understood as a "literal earthly kingdom."[26]

No quarrel may be entered against the insistence that the promises of the Davidic covenant are to be fulfilled in a "literal" and "earthly" fashion. But the current fulfillment of this promise in the present age indicates that Christ's kingdom cannot be restricted merely to an earthly domain. All power in heaven and in earth has been given to Jesus Christ, the Son of David. He reigns in the heavenly Mt. Zion, as well as among the hosts of earth. When he manifests his ultimate

he still acknowledge a kingdom to come yet not restricted to it

---

26. Ibid., pp. 365f., n. 2.

victory over the last great enemy, which is death, his bodily-resurrected citizens shall inhabit "literally" the new heavens and the new earth in which righteousness shall dwell. "Literal" and "earthly" categories do not provide the proper framework for crystallizing the distinction between dispensational and covenantal perspectives on the question of the messianic kingdom promised to David.

Instead, the focal point of disagreement with dispensationalism concerns the question as to whether Christ now has entered his regal office as descendant of David. Has the kingdom of Christ, the anointed Messiah, been postponed? Or has the first stage of its actual realization begun?

A reading of the early chapters of the book of Acts indicates that Jesus Christ does indeed now reign in fulfillment of the promises spoken to David. According to the apostle Peter, it was because David was a prophet and knew that God had sworn to him with an oath to seat one of his descendants on his throne that he looked ahead and spoke of the resurrection of the anointed king who would succeed him (cf. Acts 2:30f.). As fulfillment of this prophecy concerning the seating of one of David's descendants on David's throne, Peter immediately points to Jesus' resurrection and exaltation to the right hand of God. The culminating evidence that this prophecy concerning David's descendant has reached its fulfillment, according to Peter, is found in the outpouring of the Holy Spirit on the day of Pentecost, the very day on which the apostle currently was preaching. The "anointed one" already must have been enthroned prior to the day of Pentecost. The "Christ," whose title indicates that his distinctiveness resides in his being "anointed" by God's Holy Spirit, must have received his regal "anointment" by the day of Pentecost, since he was empowered by this date to pour forth the same Holy Spirit by which he himself was anointed (cf. Acts 2:32f.). In concluding his remarks, the apostle Peter declares that in fulfillment of David's prophecy concerning a greater-than-David who was to be seated permanently at the right hand of God, Jesus Christ has ascended to the right hand of the Father as the anointed king who reigns over the messianic kingdom. As a result of this exaltation, all the house of Israel should know for certain that God has made Jesus both Lord and Messiah (Acts 2:34–36).

It is difficult to imagine any way in which Peter could have expressed more pointedly that Jesus Christ's current exaltation fulfilled God's promise to David that his descendant was to reign as the anointed one of Israel. The question cannot be relegated to one of "literal" or "nonliteral" interpretation. Jesus Christ "literally" is the descendant of David. He sits "literally" on David's throne, since from both the Old Testament and the New Testament perspectives the "throne of David" is to be identified with the throne of God. As the figures of David's throne and God's throne merged in the theocracy of the old covenant, so God's throne and Jesus' position as heir to David's throne seated at God's right hand merge in the new covenant. Today Jesus reigns "literally" in Jerusalem because the "Jerusalem" of the old covenant represented the place of God's enthronement, just as the "Jerusalem" of the new covenant represents the place of God's throne today. Quite obviously, the circumstances of the new covenant excel the circumstances of the old covenant in every way. David, his throne and his city have achieved a greater significance through the fulfillment realized by the coming of Christ. But when viewed from a biblical perspective, the "literal" character of this fulfillment meets and excels every old covenant figuration.

If it is insisted that Christ's throne today actually is in heaven rather than in Palestine, two considerations must be kept in mind. First of all, David's regal power was not derived from the situation of his throne in a topographical area called "Palestine." David drew his authority from the interconnection of his throne with the heavenly throne of God. His locality in Jerusalem simply represented the earthly embodiment of the heavenly rule. Secondly, Christ's present reign at the right hand of the Father does not limit in any respect his involvement in the land of Palestine or in any other material, topographical area of the world. As the resurrected Christ clearly indicated to his disciples, all power has been given to him in heaven and in earth. His present reign cannot be spiritualized into a heavenly realm that does not touch earthly material borders. To the contrary, his heavenly reign manifests itself in earthly concreteness. Christ's throne "literally" fulfills the promises made to David while at the same time stretching beyond the proportions which David himself experienced, in a manner appropriate to the consummative character of the new covenant when compared to the shadowy form of the old.

The New Covenant: The Covenant of Consummation

The great divide in the history of redemption for covenant theologians distinguishes the old covenant with its prophecies and shadows from the new covenant with its fulfillments and realities. Each of the successive covenants made with Adam, Noah, Abraham, Moses, and David finds its fulfillment in the new covenant. The Lord's Supper represents the point of formal inauguration of this new covenant. At this consecrative meal, Christ officially institutes the new age. Indeed, the provisions of the new covenant shall receive a fuller realization in the age to come. At present the believer lives in a tension between the promises of God as already having been fulfilled and the same promises as having yet a richer realization. But it is true nonetheless that the "end of the ages" now has arrived.

The tension inherent in the twofold manner of structuring history within dispensationalism manifests itself once more when its description of the "new covenant" is compared with its description of the "dispensation of grace." The "dispensation of grace" stands out quite distinctly as an epoch with a concrete beginning and ending. It begins with the rejection of Christ by the Jewish nation and ends with the establishment of the millennial kingdom. But the "new covenant" as treated by dispensationalism has the peculiar characteristic of embracing both the church age of the present time and the distinctively Jewish millennial kingdom of the future. The new covenant, according to the "new" Scofield Bible, "secures the personal revelation of the Lord to every believer" (in the church age). At the same time it "secures the perpetuity, future conversion, and blessing of a repentant Israel, with whom the New Covenant will yet be ratified."[27]

---

27. Ibid., pp. 1317f., nn. 1, 2.

It is difficult to justify such a neat distinction of application within the provisions of the new covenant. The writer to the Hebrews, when applying new covenant terminology to the circumstances of the present age, does not eliminate the designations "house of Israel" and "house of Judah" from his quotation of Jeremiah's prophecy (cf. Heb. 8:8).[28] According to the inspired author, the Holy Spirit witnesses "to us" who live today on the basis of our involvement in the "new covenant" (Heb. 10:15ff.).

The "old" Scofield Bible is particularly problematic in its formulation regarding the "dispensation of grace." Possibly for this reason the description of this era receives a rather extensive revision in the "new" Scofield Bible. However, it is important to be aware of the original formulation of this epoch as found in the "old" Scofield Bible.

The description in the "old" Scofield Bible concerning the "dispensation of grace" declares: "The point of testing is no longer legal obedience as condition of salvation, but acceptance or rejection of Christ, with good works as a fruit of salvation."[29] But when at any time in the history of redemption has the point of testing been legal obedience as the condition of salvation? Never has there been a time since the fall of man into sin in which God proposed legal obedience as the way of salvation. Always the acceptance or rejection of Christ by faith alone has been the way of man's deliverance.

In discussing the "dispensation of the church" which corresponds to the "old" Scofield Bible's dispensation of grace, the "new" Scofield Bible omits any statement which suggests that salvation at one time was dependent on perfect obedience by sinful men. Instead, the emphasis lies on the distinctive role of the church in this particular

---

28. The distinction often made in dispensational hermeneutics between the "application" and the "interpretation" of a passage of Scripture must be rejected outright. "Application" *is* "interpretation," and "interpretation" *is* "application." Unless the original meaning of Scripture involves an intended application for a particular situation, it is erroneous exegesis to make such an application. The "meaning" of a portion of Scripture involves both "what is to be understood" by the passage and "what is the purpose" of the passage.

29. "Old" Scofield Bible, p. 1115, n. 1.

period. According to the "new" Scofield Bible the church is to be "carefully distinguished from both Jews and Gentiles as such," although drawing its constituency from both.[30] This careful separation of Jew and Gentile as such from the church provides the basis in dispensationalism for the postponement of the Jewish messianic kingdom until the end of the present age. The rejection of Christ by the Jewish leadership marks the point at which the kingdom promised to the Jews was postponed. A new day began from the dispensational perspective with this postponement of the kingdom. The present era, called the "dispensation of grace" or the "dispensation of the Church," shall continue until the coming millennial age.

No quarrel may be entered against the suggestion that a distinct epoch runs from the time of the Jewish rejection of Christ to the time of his second coming. But there is a vast distinction between understanding Christ as postponing his kingdom due to the Jewish rejection of his offer to them, and Christ as establishing his kingdom even in his suffering at the hands of the Jews. Jesus never merely offered to the Jews the possibility that he should become king among them. Instead, he declared that he was as a matter of fact king among the Jews. It was not that Israel rejected an offer on the part of Jesus that he become their King. It was that the Jews rejected their King!

In his rejection, Jesus manifested the true nature of his kingdom. His power would not be exercised through political or military pressures. In this sense his kingdom was not of this world. Instead, Jesus the King manifested his power through suffering at the hands of sinners. It was this aspect of his kingship that the Jews of his own day could not comprehend. Even his disciples could not understand a king who would suffer.

This is precisely the dimension of the kingship of Christ which dispensationalists have failed to comprehend. Their insistence upon a Jewish millennial kingdom in which Christ subdues the nations by the exercise of political and military authority hinders them from

---

30. "New" Scofield Bible, p. 162, n. 1.

perceiving the presence of God's kingdom today. Reference to a "mystery form of the kingdom" only diverts attention from the oneness of Christ's messianic reign.

The last era according to dispensationalism is the "dispensation of the fullness of times" or, in the "new" Scofield Bible, the "dispensation of the kingdom." Ryrie calls this period the "dispensation of the millennium." This epoch is described as being identical with the kingdom covenanted to David. During this time, "overt disobedience will be quickly punished."[31]

Rather surprisingly, dispensationalism has no dispensation of the eternal state. Ryrie explains this omission by noting that dispensational economies are related to the affairs of this world. Since this world will come to an end with the millennium, there is no need for another dispensation.[32] Rather than having history climax in eternity, Ryrie indicates that God's entire program culminates not in eternity but in the millennial kingdom. This millennial culmination "is the climax of history and the great goal of God's program for the ages."[33]

The dispensational satisfaction with pointing toward the millennial kingdom as the culmination of the ages emphasizes once more the basic tension in their system. Dispensationalism has built its entire approach to biblical interpretation on a metaphysical dichotomy between the material and the spiritual realms. While the church age centers on a supposed heavenly, spiritual realm, the millennium culminates the purposes of God in the material realm.

Such an approach clearly limits a person's concept of the manifestation of the kingdom of God in the present age. Under such a construction, it would be impossible to appropriate the meaning of the reign of Christ in the material realm today. At the same time, the "spiritualizing" of the eternal state has the effect of minimizing the cosmic character of Christ's resurrection as the first fruits of all believers. Obviously, the dispensationalist does not deny the bodily

---

31. Ryrie, *Dispensationalism Today,* p. 63.
32. Ibid., p. 53.
33. Ibid., p. 104.

resurrection of Jesus Christ as a tenant of the Christian faith. But it does appear that there has been an inadequate apprehension of the significance of that resurrection in terms of its potential for the renewal of the totality of the universe in the present and in the future. Christ's resurrection is not merely a detached hope for the future; it is a reality in the present which establishes his physical as well as his spiritual reign over the entirety of the universe.

In conclusion, the following problematics may be indicated as inherent in the dispensational understanding of the structure of redemptive history:

First of all, the dispensational system of biblical interpretation builds on a dichotomy of the purposes of God. God is presented as having one purpose that is earthly and physical and another that is heavenly and spiritual. Says Ryrie: "If the dispensational emphasis on the distinctiveness of the Church seems to result in a 'dichotomy,' let it stand as long as it is a result of literal interpretation."[34] This dichotomy in the purposes of God is metaphysical rather than biblical in origin. The purposes of God are one. That one purpose is the redemption in body and spirit of those who are united with Christ.

The concept of the postponement of the kingdom of Christ until the millennium by dispensational thinking could explain the reason that much American fundamentalistic thinking has not comprehended adequately the implications of the gospel for carrying forward the righteousness of God into every realm of life. If God's kingdom of righteousness has been postponed until some future date, then the obligation of Christians to manifest the righteousness of the kingdom in the present age has been weakened considerably.

Secondly, dispensationalism involves a dual structuring of history. Both the covenantal and the dispensational models are employed to describe the purpose of God throughout the ages. These two structurings quite frequently conflict with one another. The analysis of

---

34. Ibid., pp. 154f.

the "dispensation of innocency" is quite different from the analysis of the "Edenic covenant," even though these two epochs coincide. The "dispensation of conscience" does not manifest the same characters as the "Adamic covenant." Yet these two time periods coincide. Certain "dispensations" receive a rather secularized treatment, while the "covenants" generally reflect the purposes of God along redemptive lines. The dispensations of "conscience" and "moral government" do not relate naturally to God's ongoing program of redemption, although the corresponding covenantal perspective appropriately encourages man's hope of a coming Redeemer.

Thirdly, the dispensational exclusion of the present reign of Christ from the perspective of the Old Testament promise concerning the Davidic Messiah simply does not conform to the New Testament analysis of the present age. Christ's resurrection and ascension to the right hand of the Father provides the basis for understanding the whole of Old Testament prophecy as it consummates in the suffering and exalted king of Israel. The present age is not a "parenthesis" unforeseen by the prophets of old. Instead, men today enjoy the great privilege of tasting now the realities of Christ's eternal kingdom.

The question may be asked once more: Which structures Scripture—covenants or dispensations? The dispensationalist himself ultimately must choose between these two alternatives, since both of them are presented in his own system in ways that conflict with one another. It should be remembered that the covenants are explicit scriptural indicators of divine initiatives that structure redemptive history. The dispensations instead represent arbitrary impositions on the biblical order. In the end it is not human design but divine initiative that structures Scripture.

12

David:
The Covenant of the Kingdom

IN the Davidic covenant God's purposes to redeem a people to himself reach their climactic stage of realization so far as the Old Testament is concerned. Under David the kingdom arrives. God formally establishes the manner by which he shall rule among his people.

Prior to this point, God certainly had manifested himself as the Lord of the covenant. But now God openly situates his throne in a single locality. Rather than ruling from a mobile sanctuary, God reigns from Mt. Zion in Jerusalem. In a climactic sense, it may be said that under David the kingdom has come.

Not only has the kingdom come. The king has come. The ark is brought triumphantly to Jerusalem. God himself associates his kingship with the throne of David. Rejecting the tribe of Ephraim, God delights in designating the tribe of Judah and the house of David as his chosen instrument for sovereignty (cf. Ps. 78:60–72).

God's covenant with David centers on the coming of the kingdom.

The covenant serves as the formalizing bond by which God's kingdom comes among his people.

In considering the Davidic covenant, it is appropriate to begin with some introductory comments based on II Samuel 7. This particular chapter formally establishes God's covenant commitment to David.

INTRODUCTORY COMMENTS BASED ON II SAMUEL 7

The Historical Occasion

The occasion for the formal establishment of the Davidic covenant has great significance. Already God had anointed David as king over all Israel. But the formal inauguration of the *covenant of the kingdom* had to await certain other developments.[1]

First, David took Jerusalem from the Jebusites and established the permanent locality of his throne (II Sam. 5). He had ruled for over seven years from Hebron, a city strategically located in the midst of territory belonging to David's own tribe of Judah. But now he moves to capture a city not yet taken by Israel and more centralized with respect to the whole of the nation.

Secondly, David brought the ark of God to Jerusalem (II Sam. 6). In so doing, he publicly displayed his desire to see his own rule in Israel related immediately to the throne of God. In this manner, the concept of the theocracy found its fullest expression.

Thirdly, God gave David rest from all his enemies (II Sam. 7:1). In other words, he secured the throne in Israel to a degree that never had been experienced previously. Instead of being threatened constantly by marauding armies, Israel became secure as a national

---

1. As noted earlier, the term *berith* is not used in II Sam. 7. Yet there can be no doubt that a covenant actually was established at this particular juncture in Israelite history. Later Scripture speaks expressly of the "covenant" God made with David (cf. II Sam. 23:5; Ps. 89:3; 132:11, 12).

entity. Indeed, not all Israel's foes had been annihilated. But God had "given rest" from their oppressors.[2]

Now the context is prepared for the formal inauguration of the Davidic covenant. The interconnection between David's throne and God's throne, between David's son and God's son finds an appropriate framework in this historical context. A situation of rest from oppressing enemies anticipates appropriately the eschatological kingdom of peace.

The Essence of the Covenant Concept

II Samuel 7 places particular stress on the essence of the covenant concept. Uniquely the passage describes the manner in which God had continued to identify himself with his people: "I have not dwelt in a house since the day I brought up the sons of Israel from Egypt, even to this day; but I have been moving about in a tent, even in a tabernacle" (II Sam. 7:6). All during the days of Israel's sojourn, God sojourned with them. His glory housed itself in a tent, even as Israel lived in tents.

The parallel account in Chronicles is even more specific: "I have not dwelt in a house since the day that I brought up Israel to this day, but I have gone from tent to tent and from one dwelling place to another" (I Chron. 17:5). While the people of the covenant lived a vagabond life, travelling from one temporary dwelling to another, the God of the covenant displayed his readiness to identify with his people by also travelling with them.

More particularly, the essence of the covenant is manifested in God's relation to David. Although wrong in his initial conclusion, Nathan the prophet certainly is correct with respect to his basic premise when he declares: "Go, do all that is in your mind, for the

---

2. Cf. D. J. McCarthy, "II Samuel 7 and the Structure of the Deuteronomic History," *Journal of Biblical Literature*, 84 (1965): 131, who regards this phrase as "practically a technical term in the deuteronomic writings for Yahweh's ultimate blessing on Israel."

Lord is with you" (II Sam. 7:3). The Lord himself reinforces the correctness of this perspective when he says, "I have been with you wherever you have gone" (II Sam. 7:9). At the heart of the Davidic covenant is the Immanuel principle.

Interconnection Between Dynasty and Dwelling-place

One of the most striking aspects structurally of II Samuel 7 is the inversion of phrases as a mode of emphasis. This particular manner of expression brings into closest relationship the concept of "dynasty" and "dwelling-place."

First, God responds with emphasis to David's proposal: "Shall you [אַתָּה] build a house [בַּיִת] for me?" (v. 5). Shall you, a mortal man, determine the permanent dwelling-place for the Almighty?

Then God inverts the pattern of thought: "Yahveh makes known to you that he, the Lord himself,[3] will make for you a house [בַּיִת]" (v. 11). Obviously the house which the Lord shall build for David is not a royal palace, since David already lived in a "house of cedar" (v. 2). David understands God's reference to the "house" to be to his posterity: "You have spoken concerning your servant's house for a great while to come" (v. 19).

David shall not build God's "house," but God shall build David's "house." The inversion of phrases interchanges "dwelling-place" with "dynasty." In both cases, perpetuity is the point of emphasis. David wishes to establish for God a permanent dwelling-place in Israel. God declares that he shall establish the perpetual dynasty of David.

In his gracious words to David, God indicates that these two "permanencies" shall be linked together. He shall establish David's dynasty, and David's dynasty shall establish his permanent dwelling-place. But the order of grace must be maintained. First, the Lord

---

3. The divine name is repeated a second time, apparently for emphasis, and thus paralleling the emphasis on "you" (i.e., David) in v. 5.

sovereignly establishes David's dynasty; then the dynasty of David shall establish the Lord's dwelling-place (v. 13).

The net effect of this close interchange on the basis of the "house" figure is to bind David's rule to God's rule, and *vice versa*. God shall maintain his permanent dwelling-place as king in Israel through the kingship of the Davidic line.

David's Son/God's Son

This chapter also stresses the connection between David's son and God's son. David and his seed are being established in their regal capacity by this covenant. God affirms that the descendants of David shall sit on Israel's throne forever.

At the same time, the Davidic king of Israel shall maintain a special relation to God. God shall be his father, and he shall be God's son (v. 14).

The king's position as son of God finds a pointed development subsequently in Scripture. David himself declares in poetic fashion God's decree concerning the position of honor attributed to Israel's messiah:

> I shall declare the decree of Yahveh
> He said to me,
>> You are my son
>> This day I have begotten you (Ps. 2:7).

The relation established between "son of David" and "son of God" at the inauguration of the Davidic covenant finds consummation at the coming of Messiah. Jesus Christ appears as ultimate fulfillment of these two sonships. As son of David he also is Son of God. Jesus was

> . . . born of the seed of David according to the flesh, who was declared with power to be the son of God by the resurrection from the dead . . . (Rom. 1:3, 4).

The writer to the Hebrews founds a significant aspect of his theological perspective on the fact of Messiah's sonship to God. The superiority of Messiah over every other covenant messenger arises from his unique position as Son of God. This perspective the author of Hebrews establishes by conjoining the messianic sonship-decree of Psalm 2 with the messianic sonship-promise of II Samuel 7 (cf. Heb. 1:5).

The prospect of a chastening of this "son of God" (II Sam. 7:14b) spoils any effort to find the "divine kingship" concept of the Ancient Near East manifested in Israel's understanding of its monarchy.[4] The lordly figure in Israel always was subject to the chastening activity of the one true God, as the history of the monarchy adequately shows.

Yet at the same time, the declaration of II Samuel 7:14 that David's son also is God's Son provides adequate basis for later developments which point toward a "divine Messiah." Isaiah speaks quite clearly of a child born to sit on the throne of David who shall be called "mighty God" (Isa. 9:6). The psalmist addresses pointedly Israel's king: "Thy throne, O God, is forever and ever" (Ps. 45:7). Eventually the history of redemption proves that in a unique sense David's son is God's Son.

DISTINCTIVE QUESTIONS RELATING TO THE DAVIDIC COVENANT

Having noted some introductory points of interest from II Samuel 7, a few distinctive questions relating to the Davidic covenant may be considered.

---

4. Cf. the treatment of the theories of the myth and ritual school by M. Noth in "God, King and Nation in the Old Testament," in *The Laws in the Pentateuch and Other Studies* (Edinburgh, 1966). He indicates that Israel "regards all kings as mortals bound to obey their God" (p. 165).

The king of Israel maintains a unique role in relation to the covenant. To be king in Israel is to be in covenant relation to Yahveh. The two positions are related inseparably.

Still further, the king in his position as national head mediates the covenant to the people. By virtue of his office, he functions as mediator of the covenant.[5]

This distinctive role of the king as covenant mediator is made apparent at the time of David's coronation at Hebron. According to II Samuel 5:3, "King David made a covenant with them before the Lord at Hebron, and they anointed David king over Israel." Integral to David's establishment as king in Israel was his role as covenant mediator for the people.

The reform instituted by Josiah emphasizes the role of king as covenant mediator. When the neglected book of the covenant is discovered in the temple, Josiah takes the initiative in behalf of the people. He calls the assembly. He reads the law. He makes the covenant (II Kings 23:1–3).

Zedekiah also functions as covenant mediator in the crisis of Nebuchadnezzar's invasion. The king makes a covenant with all the people in Jerusalem, specifying obedience to the legislation of Moses (Jer. 34:8). By virtue of his office as king, he possesses authority to bind the people in covenant obligation.

In his office as covenant mediator, the king not only represents God in his authority as covenant Lord to the people. He also represents the people to God. As head of the people, he embodies them and their cause before the Lord. In him "the national form of the covenant-idea assumes . . . the personal form. . . ."[6]

---

5. For the concept of king as covenant mediator, see G. Widengren, "King and Covenant," *Journal of Semitic Studies,* 2 (1957): 21.

6. James Oscar Boyd, "Monarchy in Israel: The Ideal and the Actual," *Princeton Theological Review,* 26 (1928): 53.

The dual responsibility of covenant mediator relates particularly to the king's position as son to God. As son he shares the throne with God his Father. As son he possesses the privileges of perpetual access to the father. By virtue of his sonship, he serves as covenantal mediator.

This role of son of God as covenantal mediator actually serves as the foundational basis for a significant portion of the argumentation of the Epistle to the Hebrews. First, the writer establishes Jesus' unique role as Son, in contrast with angelic mediators of the old covenant (Heb. 1:1–14).[7] At the same time, he elaborates on the twofold function of Jesus as Son of God. Because he is Son, he is king and heir (Heb. 1:2). Because he is Son, he is Priest and mediator (Heb. 5:5, 6).[8]

This role of king as covenant mediator is indeed a significant aspect of the Davidic covenant. Moses and Joshua may have anticipated this role in their capacities as leaders who mediated the covenant.[9] But distinctive to the Davidic covenant is the permanent establishment of one who shall serve in this vital role.

Pivotal Promises in the Davidic Covenant

The provisions of the Davidic covenant center on two promises. One promise concerns the line of David, and one promise concerns the locality of Jerusalem. The purposes of God in redeeming a people to himself center on these two points: David's line and Jerusalem's throne.

The history of the Davidic monarchy as recorded in the books of Kings repeatedly emphasizes these two points. Despite God's severe

---

7. In this section, the writer cites II Sam. 7:14 among other passages.

8. For the development of the two roles of priest and king in relation to sonship in Hebrews, see David G. Dunbar, *The Relationship of Christ's Sonship and Priesthood in the Epistle to the Hebrews,* unpublished Th.M. thesis at Westminster Theological Seminary, Philadelphia, Pa., 1974.

9. Cf. Widengren, op. cit., pp. 14f., 18. Widengren notes the similarities between Josh. 1:7f. and Deut. 17:18f. The king mediates covenant law.

chastening of Israel, he continues to deal graciously with David and with Jerusalem.[10]

The first son of David to sit on his throne learned vividly the meaning of God's chastening activity. God had promised a perpetual preservation of the house of David in contrast with the house of Saul. But he also had given assurance that "if he commits iniquity, I shall chasten him with the rod of men and with the stripes of the sons of men" (II Sam. 7:14).

Because of Solomon's sin, God declared that he would tear the kingdom from him, and give it to his servant (I Kings 11:11). The implication is startling. Someone other than David's descendant shall rule over Solomon's kingdom.

Yet God does not forget his commitment under the Davidic covenant: "However, I will not tear away all the kingdom, but I will give one tribe to your son for the sake of my servant David and for the sake of Jerusalem which I have chosen" (I Kings 11:13).

This identical thought concerning the preservation of the line of David is emphasized in God's message to Jeroboam the Ephraimite. God will tear the kingdom from Solomon: "But he will have one tribe, for the sake of my servant David and for the sake of Jerusalem, the city which I have chosen from all the tribes of Israel" (I Kings 11:32). Twice again in the immediately succeeding verses this point is underlined. God will be merciful and not rend the kingdom from Solomon himself "for the sake of my servant David" (v. 34). To Solomon's son God will give one tribe "that my servant David may have a lamp always before me in Jerusalem, the city which I have chosen for myself to put my name" (v. 36).

Thus the point is made plain. God's chastening activity in the rending of Solomon's kingdom does not terminate the covenant commitment made on behalf of David and Jerusalem.

---

10. M. Noth, "Jerusalem and the Israelite Tradition," in *The Laws in the Pentateuch and Other Studies* (Edinburgh, 1966), p. 125, asserts that the first literary expression of the divine election of David and Jerusalem occurs in the writings of the "Deuteronomist" during the exile. Yet he feels that God's choice of Jerusalem was the official position held at the time of the Davidic and Solomonic monarchies.

As Rehoboam son of Solomon begins his rule, the significance of Jerusalem again is stressed. He reigned in Jerusalem, "the city which the Lord had chosen from all the tribes of Israel to put his name there" (I Kings 14:21). Despite the rending of the kingdom, God maintains his promise.

Subsequently, Rehoboam's son and successor Abijam sins. His kingdom must be judged. But "for David's sake the Lord his God gave him a lamp in Jerusalem, to raise up his son after him and to establish Jerusalem" (I Kings 15:4).[11] Again both David and Jerusalem are linked. God maintains the lineage and the location according to his covenantal promise.

This same emphasis on the preservation of the line of David reappears in connection with the next wicked king of Judah. Nothing explicitly is said of preserving the line of David in the narrative concerning Asa and Jehoshaphat. But in connection with Jehoram, the writer of Kings indicates that though he did evil in the sight of God, "the Lord was not willing to destroy Judah, for the sake of David his servant, since he had promised him to give a lamp to him through his sons always" (II Kings 8:19). Now the destiny of the entirety of Judah depends on God's mercy in behalf of his covenant promises to David.

Still later, as the Assyrian Sennacherib besieges Jerusalem in the days of Hezekiah, the fortunes of the throne and of the city rest on God's promises to David. Isaiah the prophet reassures the troubled Hezekiah. Through his messenger, the Lord announces: "I will defend this city to save it for my own sake and for my servant David's sake" (II Kings 19:34). Again the city of Jerusalem and the throne of David are linked. Both shall be preserved because of the covenanting grace of God.

Hezekiah's prayer for deliverance from death also receives answer in terms of this same dual commitment. God will add 15 years to

---

11. M. Noth argues that the term נִיר should be translated "new break" or "new beginning" rather than "lamp." For David's sake the Lord gave a "new beginning." However, Ps. 132:17 appears to favor interpreting נִיר as "lamp," as Noth himself indicates (ibid., pp. 137; 138, n. 9).

Hezekiah's life: "I will deliver you and this city from the hand of the king of Assyria; and I will defend this city for my own sake and for my servant David's sake" (II Kings 20:6).

As Scripture characterizes the wicked reign of Manasseh, the chosen city of Jerusalem provides the point of reference. The atrocity of the king's sin may be appreciated only as it is realized that it has been done in Jerusalem:

> He built altars in the house of the Lord, of which the Lord had said, "In Jerusalem I will put my name" (II Kings 21:4).
> He set the carved image of Asherah that he had made in the house of which the Lord said to David and to his son Solomon, "In this house and in Jerusalem, which I have chosen from all the tribes of Israel, I will put my name forever" (II Kings 21:7).

These provocations committed by Manasseh set the stage for that which would appear to be inconceivable in the light of all that had preceded. God had maintained his covenantal lovingkindness to David and Jerusalem for all these years. Yet now the doom of Jerusalem must be sealed. Even the vigorous efforts toward reform under Josiah cannot save either the chosen city or the Davidic dynasty. Because of the sins of Manasseh, God declares: "I will remove Judah also from my sight, as I have removed Israel. And I will cast off Jerusalem, the city which I have chosen, and the temple of which I said, 'my name shall be there'" (II Kings 23:26f.).

Prior to this point of devastation, the line of David and the capital of Jerusalem had developed a truly remarkable record. From David's accession somewhere around 1000 B.C. to the fall of Jerusalem, over 400 years had transpired. The average dynasty in Egypt and Mesopotamia during their days of greatest stability was something less than 100 years. David's successors even outlasted the long-lived eighteenth dynasty of Egypt, which endured for about 250 years.

The endurance of David's dynasty contrasts rather vividly with the experience of the kings of Israel to the north. The northern kingdom of Israel managed only two dynasties of any significance, neither of which exceeded 100 years. God clearly was manifesting his unique faithfulness to David.[12]

The importance of the continuing maintenance of Jerusalem as Judah's capital city comes to expression in many ways. Never in the entire history of the southern kingdom is there a hint of the possibility of relocation. Jerusalem stands without question as God's chosen city. God sits enthroned among the cherubim at Zion, and orders the reign of David's descendants from that vantage-point.

The stability associated with Jerusalem contrasts vividly with the instability of the capital of the northern kingdom. The ancient shrine-city of Shechem served as the place of Jeroboam's accession to the throne (I Kings 12:1). Subsequently he strengthened this locality, apparently that it might serve as his capital (I Kings 12:25). Yet evidence indicates that early in the history of the northern

---

12. James Oscar Boyd, "The Davidic Dynasty," *Princeton Theological Review,* 25 (1927): 220ff., notes several distinctive features concerning the Davidic dynasty. He indicates that the people of Judah consistently looked to the line of David for a legal heir to the throne whenever a vacancy occurred. Remarkably, only the alien Athaliah attempted the otherwise rather common conspiracy of annihilating the seed-royal after accession to the throne. The radicalness of the proposal of the Syro-Ephraimate coalition in the days of Ahaz may be appreciated in this light. Their determination was to terminate the Davidic dynasty and to replace it with the "son of Tabeel" (II Kings 16:5; cf. Isa. 7:6).

Also of interest in the dynastic records of David's descendants are the numerous instances of co-regencies of father and son, indicating perhaps an effective device for assuring continuity. Boyd counts eight of the 13 throne-transferrals as involving co-regencies. At one point, Israel may have had simultaneously three crowned kings (Uzziah, Jotham and Ahaz)—father, son, and grandson.

Just at the point where the Davidic line came closest to annihilation, the narrative shows special concern for dynastic maintenance. Jehosheba, aunt to Joash, defies Athaliah her mother to save her infant nephew (II Kings 11:2). Jehoiada the high priest provides this single surviving prince of the Davidic line with two wives, perhaps showing anxiety over the continuation of the seed (II Chron. 24:3). Boyd (p. 226) reckons that Amaziah, son and successor to Joash, was born when the king was only 14 or 15 years of age.

Also unique to Judah is the record of the mothers of the kings. Scripture records the mothers of Judah's kings with only two exceptions (Joram and Ahaz). Apparently Solomon was the only king of Judah to marry outside Israel. This record may be contrasted with the silence concerning the royal mothers of the northern kingdom. The only mother of northern Israelite royalty mentioned is Jezebel of Sidon.

monarchy Tirzah was established as the place of royal residence (I Kings 14:17; 15:21, 33; 16:6, 8, 9, 15, 23). Later Omri selected Samaria as the new site for his capital (I Kings 16:24), which continued until the captivity of the northern kingdom. Yet during this period of centralized stability, some of Israel's kings preferred Jezreel as a place of residence (I Kings 18:45; 21; II Kings 8:29–10:11).

Further evidence of the absence of a centralized place of rule in the northern kingdom relates to centers of worship. Worship centers never were coordinate with royal residences in the north. Dan and Bethel continued to be the main cities of cultic activity throughout the history of the northern kingdom.[13]

This stability associated with the royal throne in Judah had great significance for the people of God. It stood in starkest contrast with the nomadic condition that had marked the life-style of Israel from the days of Abraham. Now God's people were no longer tent-dwellers, always on the move, pilgrims without a permanent dwelling place. Instead, they were inhabitants of a kingdom, settled and secure. No longer was Israel exclusively looking forward to the coming of the kingdom; in a very real sense, God's kingdom had come.

Indeed, the level to which the kingdom of God was realized in Israel under the line of David had decided limitations. This "kingdom" must be placed in the category of an "anticipative" realization in proper keeping with the entire scope of Old Testament experience. The shadow-kingdom of Israel was real. God was reigning in their midst. But it was nonetheless only a shadow of the reality to come.

The perpetual dynasty of David and the permanent capital of Jerusalem find some parallels in evidence from Ancient Near Eastern treaty forms.[14] The Hittite treaties in particular reflect interests similar to those found in the Davidic covenant as recorded in

---

13. For much of this material, see Boyd, op. cit., pp. 228f.
14. Cf. particularly Philip J. Calderone, *Dynastic Oracle and Suzerainty Treaty: II Samuel 7:8–16* (Manila, 1966); and R. de Vaux, "Le roi d'Israel, vassel de Yahve," *Melanges Eugene Tisserant* 1 (1964): 119–33.

II Samuel 7. Specifically, throne-succession and territorial stability receive significant attention in the treaties.

Philip J. Calderone notes at least four cases in the Hittite treaties in which royal lines of conquered peoples were guaranteed support in maintaining dynastic right to the throne.[15] One text reflecting close parallels to the biblical expressions may be found in the treaty granted by Tudhaliyas IV (or Hattusilis III) to the ruler of Datassa:

> As for you, Ulmi-Tassub, [I have affirmed your possession of Datassa]. After you your son and grandson will hold it, and no one shall take it away from them. [But] if anyone of your line sins [against Hatti], the king of Hatti will have him tried, and if he is condemned he will be sent to the king of Hatti where, if he merits it, he will be executed.[16]

Particularly striking in this passage is the provision for chastening disobedient descendants as well as for maintaining the original line. As in II Samuel 7, the disobedient king shall be punished.

In another treaty, the Hittite king Suppiluliuma promises to receive Mattiwasa as his son:

> I will take you to myself in sonship; I will stand by you with aid; upon the throne of your father I will set you.[17]

The character of the sonship envisioned in this document is difficult to determine. The reference may be to an anticipated son-in-law relationship. But the provision is striking for its parallelism with the biblical account.

In addition to concern over dynastic succession, territorial rights also play a significant role in these treaties. One text reads as follows:

> This Suppiluliuma the Great King, king of Hatti, the hero, has granted by the seal these [frontiers], cities, mountains to Niqmadu

---

15. For references to the documents, see Calderone, op. cit., p. 19, n. 20.
16. Ibid., p. 56.
17. Ibid.

[king of] Ugarit, as well as to his sons and the sons of his sons forever.[18]

In another text from seventeenth century B.C. Syria, a certain Abba-AN bestows the city of Alalakh on Yarimlim, swearing never to take the city back.[19]

These provisions provide interesting parallels to the covenantal guarantee granted to David concerning Jerusalem. But it should be noted that the treaty texts do not parallel the specific commitment found in Scripture toward a particular city as capital of a theocracy. In a unique sense, God himself resides in the city of Jerusalem, and rules from its locality.

In summarizing the evidence of parallels between the Hittite documents and II Samuel 7, Calderone acknowledges that each of the various elements in Nathan's oracle "can probably be paralleled in many other types of legal, historical and religious material."[20] It is rather difficult to establish that a direct influence from the culture of the Ancient Near East actually has affected the form and substance of the biblical materials. Both Calderone and McCarthy reject the hypothesis that the *form* of Nathan's oracle parallels the Hittite treaties,[21] although they do see parallels in substance.

In any case, the continuing investigation of such parallels should be noted with care. It may be that a deeper understanding of covenantal provisions found in Scripture will develop along these lines.

The Davidic Covenant: Conditional or Unconditional?

The third and final question concerning the Davidic covenant has to do with the type covenant involved. Is the Davidic covenant to be

---

18. Ibid., pp. 20f.
19. Ibid., p. 27.
20. Ibid., p. 67.
21. Calderone, op. cit., p. 67; D. J. McCarthy, "Covenant in the O.T.: the Present State of Inquiry," *Catholic Biblical Quarterly*, 27 (1965): 238.

regarded as conditional or unconditional? Are its promises contingent on a certain response in David and his descendants? Or does this covenant guarantee the fulfillment of its gracious provisions unconditionally?

Various perspectives on the question. This question has been viewed from a variety of perspectives. Primarily the problem has been framed in terms of whether the Davidic covenant connects with the Abrahamic or the Mosaic covenant as its predecessor.

R. E. Clements asserts that the type covenant made with David could not possibly have arisen by a process of natural development out of the Mosaic covenant.[22] Instead, David's covenant represents a recollection of the ancient covenant made with Abraham.

Clements suggests even more radical modifications of the biblical picture. From his perspective, the Davidic covenant, although represented in Scripture as having come almost 1000 years after the Abrahamic covenant, actually played a crucial role in the Israelite formulation of the Abrahamic covenant. He is quite sure that "there was a material connection between the tradition of Abraham and the rise of David, and the fortunes of the Davidic house greatly affected in Israel the ancient covenant with Abraham."[23] According to the thesis of Clements, all three major promises associated with the Abrahamic covenant must be seen as arising out of the political situation of the Davidic epoch. The promise concerning the "land" grew out of the expansion of the territorial state of David. The promise of the "seed" developed from the reality of a national entity formed under David. The Abrahamic promise concerning the "blessing" to non-Israelite peoples assumes the existence of nations subject to David.

While for Clements the Abrahamic and Davidic covenants interrelate closely, no such connection between David and Moses is possible. Clements affirms that ". . . the Davidic covenant is

22. R. E. Clements, *Abraham and David: Genesis 15 and Its Meaning for Israelite Tradition* (Naperville, 1967), p. 54.
23. Ibid., p. 56.

formally to be distinguished from the type of law covenant found in the Sinai-Horeb tradition."[24]

Bernard Anderson also chooses to emphasize two types of covenants which set apart the Davidic from the Mosaic covenant.[25] The Mosaic covenant represents for Anderson the type covenant that is founded on stipulated obligations, and ultimately leads to chaos. God's covenant with David, however, creates stability and continuity. By emphasizing promise, it holds in check the unpredictable and disruptive tendencies of undisciplined humanity. The Davidic covenant is for Anderson ". . . a covenant which removes elements of contingency and provides a divine guarantee of order, stability, security."[26] Its promise is absolutely unconditional.

Exactly the opposite opinion concerning the Davidic covenant has been expressed by other scholars. Instead of connecting David's promises with those of Abraham, they relate them instead to the stipulations of the Mosaic covenant.

M. Tsevat suggests that the rise of David to power in Israel cannot relate to the sacral traditions of the tribal confederacy, despite the attempt of II Samuel 7 to make just such a connection.[27] Tsevat concludes that the Davidic covenant must be related to Sinai, since the tribal confederacy had its formation at that point in Israelite history. As a result, an inner contradiction must be seen in the substance of II Samuel 7. The covenant with David rests on the conditional structures of Sinai, and the wholly unconditional assurances found in II Samuel 7:13b-16 are out of place. It therefore must be concluded that these verses represent a later gloss which does not belong to the essence of the Davidic covenant.

Tsevat also proposes that the repeated emphasis on the eternal

---

24. Ibid., p. 54.

25. Bernhard Anderson, *Creation versus Chaos* (New York, 1967), p. 75. For this distinction, Anderson cites G. E. Mendenhall, *Law and Covenant in Israel and the Ancient Near East* (Pittsburgh, 1955), p. 50.

26. Ibid., p. 62.

27. M. Tsevat, "Studies in the Book of Samuel III. The Steadfast House: What Was David Promised in II Samuel 7:11b-16?" *Hebrew Union College Annual*, 34 (1963): 71f.

character of the Davidic covenant must be modified. Only in the context of the intrinsic qualifications of the covenant may this promise be regarded as eternal.[28] So long as faithfulness is maintained the line of David shall be preserved. The covenant is "eternal" only in this qualified sense.

Proposed resolution of the question. The question concerning the conditional character of the Davidic covenant must be viewed from various perspectives. The structurally simple bond of the covenant involves a complexity of relationships.

First of all, some distinction must be made between factors of conditionality within the covenant and certainty of realization with respect to the ultimate goal of the covenant. The covenant which God established with David fitted integrally into God's purpose to redeem a people to himself. This fact assures the ultimate realization of the promises made to David. The Lord of this covenant shall not be thwarted in his intention to bring sinners out of the realm of darkness into his gracious domain.

Is it certain that God's purposes to establish a kingdom for himself among redeemed sinners shall be realized? Nothing could be more certain. Shall covenantal lovingkindness be taken from David as it was taken from Saul? Unquestionably it shall not! The purposes of God to establish a messianic royal line through David never shall be thwarted.

The word of certainty concerning the line of David must be seen as an organic whole with the previous covenantal expressions of God's purpose to redeem a people to himself. In this respect, the question concerning the conditionality of the Davidic covenant comes wrongly framed when it is asked in terms of whether the Abrahamic or the Mosaic covenant served as its immediate predecessor. All the various manifestations of the covenant of redemption in Scripture contain this aspect of certainty of realization.

God himself assumes the total responsibility for the fulfillment of

---

28. Ibid., p. 76.

the covenant with Abraham. Only the theophany passes between the pieces (Gen. 15).

It is unthinkable that God would not have brought his people into Canaan under the ordinances of the Mosaic covenant. His determination to chasten the wicked without partiality is apparent. Even Moses himself receives correction at the Lord's hand.

But it is unthinkable that God would fail to bring his people Israel through the desert into Canaan. His purposes to redeem a people to himself shall be realized. Even at the point of greatest apostasy, the certainty of God's realizing his purposes is guaranteed. God may blot out all Israel; but he shall raise up a new nation—from the Israelite **Moses (see Exod. 32:10)!** The nonobservance of Mosaic stipulations certainly will bring punishment. But it will not bring annihilation.[29]

The certainty of God's consummating his purposes for Israel cannot be attributed merely to the Abrahamic covenant. It must be remembered that it is the Mosaic covenant that receives cultic renewal as the people enter the land. This covenant of national election continues to be in effect as well as God's covenant with the patriarchs.

Now a second question concerning conditionality in the covenant may be asked. What about individual participation in the blessings of the covenant? Under Abraham the uncircumcised male was to be cut off. Under Moses the disobedient would not enter God's rest. Under David, the sinful king was to be beaten with the rod of men. In each case, full participation in the blessings of the covenant had a condition. Only as this condition was fulfilled would blessing be assured.

So it may be affirmed that each of God's covenants has a conditional aspect. The purpose of God to redeem a people to himself makes it certain that these conditions shall be met. But this certainty cannot relieve the individual from his obligation before the stipulations of the covenant.

---

29. See M. Weinfeld, "The Covenant of Grant," *Journal of the American Oriental Society,* 90 (1970): 195.

Still a third factor must be considered. Some distinction must be made between God's chastening of his sons and his destruction of the reprobate. This aspect of the conditional character of the covenant emphasizes both the typological form of the experiences of God's people under the old covenant and the temporary aspect of the life of God's people in the present age. Under the old covenant, the chastening of God's sons often was intermingled with the destruction of the reprobate. It is not always apparent which type judgment was being administered. Under the provisions of the Davidic covenant, Israel experienced both the chastenings under Solomon and his successors as well as the ultimate devastation of the exile in which Israel became "not my people." Yet it is not possible to make a neat distinction between the status before God of various persons experiencing these two forms of judgment, classifying some as sons and others as reprobates.

Even in the present day, the very existence of chastening experiences for the believer in Christ reveals the temporary character of the current situation. The day shall come in which no such disciplinary chastenings will be necessary.

In either the situation prevailing under the old covenant, or the situation prevailing under the new, the certain outcome of God's covenant is not disturbed. The presence of threat of judgment on the condition of disobedience does not imply inherently a collapse of the certainty that God ultimately will succeed in his covenanted intention to redeem a people to himself. The question of "conditional" versus "unconditional" must be considered in this light.

Finally, the role of Jesus Christ as the ultimate seed of David speaks rather decisively to this question of conditionality in the covenant. It may be affirmed as emphatically true that David's covenant hinged conditionally on the responsible fulfillment of covenant obligations by Jesus Christ, the seed of David. He satisfied in himself all the obligations of the covenant. Not only did he maintain perfectly every statute and ordinance of the Mosaic law as required of David. He also bore in himself the chastening judgments deserved by David's seed through their covenant violations.

In Christ, the conditional and the certain aspects of the covenant meet in perfect harmony. In him the Davidic covenant finds assured fulfillment.

The ultimate realization of the promise. Acceptance of the absolute certainty of the realization of the provisions of the Davidic covenant creates something of a problem. In the covenant, assurance was given that the line of David would sit on the throne of Israel forever. Yet unquestionably the descendants of David ceased to occupy the throne of Israel.

The Old Testament history of Davidic succession indeed was impressive. It stretched for a period of over 400 years.

But it did not last "forever." It came to an end.

It is not enough to suggest that perpetuity of throne-occupancy was not a part of the promise.[30] The very essence of an eternal covenant with David's dynasty rests in the unbroken character of the kingly line.

What is the solution to this problem?

The breaking off of Davidic throne-succession in Old Testament history may be evaluated in terms of the anticipative role of Israel's monarchy. David's line anticipated in shadow-form the eternal character of the reign of Jesus Christ.

While God actually was manifesting his lordship through David's line, this human monarchy was serving at the same time as a typological representation of the throne of God itself. David's reign was intended to anticipate in shadow-form the reality of the messianic Redeemer who was to unite with finality the throne of David with the throne of God.

Just as the levitical priesthood anticipated the abiding priesthood of Jesus Christ; just as Moses and the school of the prophets

---

30. John F. Walvoord, "The Fulfillment of the Davidic Covenant," *Bibliotheca Sacra,* 102 (1945): 161 says: "It is not necessary, then, for continuous political government to be in effect, but *it is necessary that the line be not lost."* This explanation simply is inadequate. To use Walvoord's own hermeneutical criterion, it is not a "literal" interpretation of the promise to David. The heart of the promise made to David rested in perpetual and unbroken throne-succession.

anticipated the prophet *par excellence;* so David and his throne anticipated the beneficent reign of the coming Messiah.

It is in this context that the failure of the Davidic line must be understood. Inherent in every Old Testament type was an inadequacy which demanded some more perfect fulfillment.

A fuller perspective on this question may be gained by considering the throne of David and his descendants as presented in the Old Testament itself. The establishment of a monarchy in Israel must not be secularized. To the contrary, the virtual identity of Israel's throne with God's throne must be recognized if a truly biblical insight into this question is to be achieved.

The Chronicler in rather startling fashion gives expression to the notion of God's kingship in Israel which was inherent throughout the nation's entire history. As Solomon was established as David's legitimate heir, the Chronicler offered his analysis of the significance of the event:

> And they made Solomon the son of David king a second time, and they anointed him as ruler for the Lord and Zadok as priest.
>
> Then Solomon *sat on the throne of the Lord as king* instead of David his father (I Chron. 29:22).

Notice that the Chronicler is not content to indicate that Solomon in David's line functions as "ruler for the Lord." This affirmation would have been striking enough in itself.

But the assertion goes even further. Solomon sits "on the throne of Yahveh as king!" The throne of David's descendants is nothing less than the throne of God itself.

This perspective on the significance of the Davidic throne accords with the original designation of David as "son" to God, and thus heir to God's throne. It furthermore corresponds with the continual stress in the historical books, in the prophets and in the psalms concerning the closeness of relation between the throne of God in Zion and the throne of David's descendants in Jerusalem. David rejoices at the bringing of the ark to Jerusalem (II Sam. 6) because now his throne is related immediately with the throne of God. The psalmist merges the cause of the Lord with the anointed king of David's line as the object of opposition by the heathen kings (Ps. 2:1, 2). Zion is God's holy mountain on which he has established his king (v. 6).

The prophetic expansion of the Davidic promise fits into this same pattern. As the kingdom crumbles all about them, these seers anticipate the greater day. A greater occupant of David's throne shall come. He shall sit on the throne of his father David forever. He shall rule the whole world in righteousness. He shall merge God's throne with his own, for he shall be Immanuel, Mighty God, God himself.[31]

The two features central to the Davidic covenant as noted earlier relate Israel's kingship immediately with God's throne. Both the line of David and the location of Jerusalem interrelate with the lordship of God himself.

It is in this context of the Old Testament identification of the throne of David with the throne of God that the position of the modern dispensationalist must be assessed. The dispensationalist asserts that Jesus Christ's session at God's right hand has nothing to do with his occupancy of David's throne. John F. Walvoord asserts: "A search of the New Testament reveals that there is not one reference connecting the present session of Christ with the Davidic throne."[32]

However, if it be understood that from the perspective of the Old Testament itself, David's throne was considered as coordinate with God's throne, this position hardly could be maintained. The fact that "the Christ," the anointed one of Israel, is seated at God's right hand, has everything to do with David's throne. Christ's present reign represents the fulfillment of the Old Testament anticipations in this regard.

---

31. Cf. among other passages in the prophets, Amos 9:11f.; Hos. 1:11; 3:4f.; Mic. 4:1-3; 5:2; Isa. 7:14; 9:6; 11:1-10; Jer. 23:5, 6; 33:15-26; Ezek. 34; 37:24.

32. Walvoord, op. cit., p. 163.

This same perspective is found in New Testament evaluations of the significance of Christ's exaltation. In Acts 2:30–36, Peter indicates specifically that because David knew that God would seat one of his descendants on his throne, he spoke of the resurrection of the Messiah. In accord with the general New Testament approach, Peter binds together Jesus' resurrection-ascension-session at God's right hand as a single act of exaltation. God "raised" him, "exalted him" to his right hand, and "made him Lord and Messiah." It is this unified act of exaltation that established Jesus to be the promised Messiah, the anointed King, the successor to David.

The New Testament usage of the Zion/Jerusalem imagery also requires that the validity of Walvoord's statement be questioned. As has been indicated, the maintaining of the Zion/Jerusalem complex was as significant in God's covenant with David as the maintaining of the Davidic line. According to Hebrews 12:22–24, believers in Christ "are (now) come" to Mount Zion, to the heavenly Jerusalem. According to Paul, the significant "Jerusalem" no longer is the "present" Jerusalem, but the "Jerusalem above" (Gal. 4:25, 26). It is from this "Jerusalem above" that life in God's kingdom begins.

The dispensationalist must be commended for his desire to hold strongly to the full veracity of Scripture in its promises. But the denial of any connection between the "throne of David" and Christ's current enthronement at God's right hand must be taken as an effort to limit the magnificent realities of the new covenant by the shadowy forms of the old.

HISTORICAL OUTWORKING OF THE DAVIDIC COVENANT

Taken as a whole, the books of Kings present quite convincingly a distinctive pattern for understanding the history of the monarchy in Israel. This pattern underscores repeatedly God's covenantal faithfulness. Again and again the historian displays the veracity of God's covenant word. Once God's binding oath has been declared with respect to the kingdom, its decree remains inviolable. The covenant Lord of heaven and earth speaks irrevocably among the sons of men.

This overriding thesis of covenantal faithfulness receives quite elaborate development throughout these books. In addition to foundational passages underscoring the provisions of the Davidic covenant, the books present as many as 20 concrete instances displaying the veracity of God's covenantal word, complete with a distinctive "formula of fulfillment." A major section of the books concludes with a summary statement underlining once more the theme of God's covenantal faithfulness.

Foundational Passages

II Samuel 7. Although lying outside the scope of the books of Kings themselves, II Samuel 7 may be regarded as foundational to the entire movement of the monarchy in Israel. The sovereign Lord of heaven and earth has spoken his covenantal word among the kings of Israel. Several times in the chapter reference is made to King David and his sons as kings (II Sam. 7:2, 12, 13, 16). In contrast to the designation of these men as "kings," numerous titles are ascribed to the sovereign Lord of Israel who has initiated this covenant relationship. He is "Yahveh of hosts" (v. 8); "Lord Yahveh" (vv. 18, 19, 20, 28, 29);[33] "Yahveh Elohim" (vv. 22, 25); "Yahveh of hosts, God of Israel" (v. 27). Near the end of the chapter, a climax is reached: "And now, Lord Yahveh, you are He—the Elohim." You are God, the God, the one and only God. This great God has established his covenantal word among the kings of Israel. His word determines

---

33. Walter C. Kaiser, Jr. "The Blessing of David: The Charter for Humanity," in *The Law and the Prophets. Old Testament Studies Prepared in Honor of Oswald Thompson Allis* (Nutley, 1974), p. 310, notes that this particular title (Adonai Yahveh) appears nowhere else in Samuel. Parallels in Chronicles use only Yahveh, except for one "Yahveh Elohim" (I Chron. 17:16). He cites R. A. Carlson as indicating that Abraham used this name for God when the Lord spoke to him in establishing his covenant in Gen. 15:2, 8 (*David, The Chosen King: A Traditio-Historical Approach to the Second Book of Samuel* [Stockholm, 1964], p. 127).

the basis for the history of the kingship in Israel. He has spoken of David's house "concerning the distant future" (v. 19).

Three other passages within the books of Kings establish the central role played by God's covenantal word to David in the history of the kingship in Israel. These passages are I Kings 2:1–4, I Kings 8, and I Kings 9.

I Kings 2:1–4. David now delivers his deathbed charge to Solomon his son. Solomon is instructed to keep the statutes, the commandments, the judgments and the testimonies of God. This admonition clearly indicates that David did not consider God's covenant with him as supplanting the provisions of the Mosaic covenant.

The reason for David's urgency in his charge to Solomon is "that Yahveh may cause to stand his word which he spoke concerning me" (v. 4). David clearly reflects the provisional character of the covenant which God made with him. Only as his descendants walk faithfully before the Lord will they enjoy the blessings of God's covenant word to David.

I Kings 8. At the dedication of Solomon's temple, the prayer of the king clearly reflects the language of God's covenant with David. Solomon repeatedly refers to the word which God had spoken to his father:

> Blessed be the Lord, the God of Israel, who spoke with His mouth to my father David and has fulfilled it with His hand (v. 15).
>
> Now the Lord has fulfilled His word which He spoke; for I have risen in place of my father David and sit on the throne of Israel, as the Lord promised, and have built the house for the name of the Lord, the God of Israel (v. 20).

In both these verses, the key to the events current in Solomon's day is found in the covenant word to David. God's promise has determined the course of history to this point.

Subsequently in his prayer, Solomon returns to this theme. God has been faithful to the word he spoke to David (v. 24). But interestingly, it is not only his word to David. The covenant word spoken to

Moses also has functioned decisively in the establishment of the Israelite monarchy. Solomon offers his testimony that "not one word" has failed of all that God spoke to his servant Moses (v. 56). Both covenants, the covenant with Moses and the covenant with David, blend together to explain Solomon's presence on the throne of Israel's kingdom.

Appeal to God's covenant word also becomes the hope for future expectations. Solomon twice asks God to confirm in the future the word that he spoke to David (vv. 25, 26).

I Kings 9. God appears to Solomon a second time. The Lord now reminds the king of his responsibility to keep the "statutes and ordinances" which have been given to direct his life. If the king will observe these statutes, then God will establish his throne forever, just as he had spoken to David (v. 5). This passage once more unites the Mosaic and the Davidic covenants.

These foundational passages make it quite plain that the future of the monarchy in Israel depends on the provisions of the covenant word to David. If Solomon remains faithful, God's word to David shall be fulfilled in him.

Concrete Instances Displaying the Veracity of God's Covenant Word to David

Using these four foundational passages as background, the unfolding of the history of the kings of Israel may be appreciated from a proper covenantal perspective. God's covenantal word to David now will be verified through the concreteness of historical events.

Commentators occasionally note a "fulfillment-motif" in the book of Kings in isolated instances. But the thoroughness with which this theme has been pursued throughout Kings often is overlooked.[34] By

---

34. Cf., however, the comments of G. von Rad, *Old Testament Theology* (New York, 1962), I, pp. 342ff. He indicates that the writer of this history practically hammers into his readers the thesis that God's word directs history. The history of

a survey of the primary passages demonstrating this thesis, the full impact of the significance of God's word in the book of Kings may be felt.

In tracing the history of the word of God among the kings of Israel, a clear pattern of presentation may be detected. Although slight variations occur in some of the cases under study, the pattern of presentation is as follows: first, God's word experiences *particularization* so that a specific application of the broader word concerning the Davidic covenant is made evident. Then the particularized word of God finds *verification* in the history of Israel. Finally, the author of Kings pointedly calls attention to the fulfillment of God's word through *formularization*. The prophesied events occur "according to the word of Yahveh which he spoke" (כִּדְבַר יהוה אֲשֶׁר דִּבֶּר), or simply "according to the word of Yahveh" (כִּדְבַר יהוה). While other formulas of fulfillment do occur, this particular phrase saturates the books of Kings.[35]

I Kings 11:9-13; 31, 35 (cf. I Kings 12:13-15). Since Solomon had revolted against the kingship of God, part of his kingdom would revolt against him. Yet because of God's covenant word to David, the rending of the kingdom would occur under Solomon's son rather than under Solomon himself.

This prophetic word concerning the chastisement of Solomon's son finds its fulfillment during the reign of Rehoboam. The young king would not hearken to the wisdom of the older men, "for it was a thing brought about of the Lord." God caused the king not to hearken to the counsel of the wiser men of his kingdom "in order that he might cause to stand his word which he had spoken" (I Kings 12:15). The Hebrew phraseology is striking in its similarity to that used in the foundational passages discussed previously.

I Kings 13:1-10 (cf. II Kings 23:15 and 16). Now that the division

---

the Kings of Israel is a fulfillment of an explicit word of the Lord, "since he sets the whole complex in the shadow of the Nathan prophecy" (ibid., p. 342).

35. Von Rad, op. cit., p. 94, n. 23 indicates several formulas employed by the "Deuteronomist." But he does not note this most pervasive method of indicating prophetic fulfillment.

of the kingdom has become a reality, the great concern of Jeroboam is that the heart of northern Israel be weaned from its loyalty to the central place of worship in Jerusalem. So the king summons all Israel to Bethel for the dedication of a new altar (I Kings 12:32f.).

This event becomes the occasion of one of the most remarkable prophecies found in the entirety of Scripture. An unnamed man of God declares that a child shall be born to the house of David who is to desecrate this unholy altar by burning men's bones on its surface. The prophet even goes so far as to specify the child's name. He shall be called Josiah.

God's word of prophecy does not indicate the time at which this judgment shall take place. In the ordering of God's providential longsuffering, it was approximately 300 years later that Josiah appeared as king in Judah.

Quite naturally, critical scholars do not hesitate to declare the impossibility of such an utterance.[36] Yet it is quite in accord with the book's intention to affirm the lordship of God over history that such a spectacular declaration is made.

In affirming the validity of this prophecy, the crucial character of the historical context should not be forgotten. God now speaks his first word of condemnation regarding the altars and the false worship of the northern tribes. Following this prophetic denunciation, the sin of Jeroboam will be the repeated theme of the books of Kings up to the very point of the captivity of northern Israel. It is quite appropriate that a very stringent and specific prophecy be

---

36. "This is the one extensive section in Kings which may be regarded as wholly unhistorical," says Robert C. Dentan, *The First and Second Books of Kings; The First and Second Books of Chronicles. The Layman's Bible Commentary* (Richmond, 1964), p. 51. Norman H. Snaith, *The Interpreter's Bible* (New York, 1954), 3: 324, regards the record of the fulfillment of this prophecy in II Kings 23:15 and 16 as "a later addition." While C. F. Keil, *The Books of Kings. Biblical Commentary on the Old Testament* (Grand Rapids, 1950), p. 203, asserts correctly the biblical concept of predictive prophecy, he nonetheless seeks to offer an interpretation of the name of "Josiah" as "he whom Jehovah supports," rather than suggesting that the prophet did as a matter of fact name King Josiah 300 years before his birth. Keil compares this prophecy with Isaiah's word concerning Cyrus. He regards the term "Cyrus" as "originally an appelative in the sense of sun."

uttered to startle Israel in the light of the hideousness of their sin on this particular occasion. A son of the house of David shall arise to destroy this altar, says the unknown prophet. The whole plan of Jeroboam is doomed to failure from the beginning. He will be unsuccessful in breaking loose from God's ordained center of worship.

The fulfillment of this prophecy is spelled out explicitly by the author of Kings. Not only did a man named Josiah eventually accede to the throne of Israel. In his program of religious reform, he broke down the altar at Bethel. Even more specifically, Josiah "sent and took the bones from graves, and burned them on the altar and defiled it" (cf. II Kings 23:15, 16).

This passage clearly indicates the fulfillment of the prophecy uttered long before. But the author of Kings does not complete his message without appending the formula of prophetic fulfillment. Josiah desecrated the altar at Bethel "according to the word of Yahveh" which had been proclaimed by the man of God.

I Kings 13:11–32. This same unnamed prophet who had performed so faithfully at Bethel now becomes the victim of the judgment of God himself. Although he rejected the bribery of Jeroboam, he could not resist the pleas of one who pretended to have a word from God. As a result of his disobedience to God's command to return directly to Judah after his prophecy against the altar of Bethel, the man of God himself is told that he will not return to Judah safely. As he journeys, he shall be slain by a lion.

"We may be grateful that there is so little of this kind of thing in the Bible," says one critical scholar.[37] Nevertheless, the entire sequence of events adds strength to the theme of the book of Kings. God vindicates his word without respect of persons. The man of God slain by the lion had just uttered one of the most spectacular prophecies in all of Scripture. Yet this same prophet, because of his personal disobedience to the word of God, suffers an untimely fate. The formula of fulfillment occurs at the end of the narrative. The

---

37. Dentan, op. cit., p. 52.

lion slew the man of God "according to the word of Yahveh which he spoke" (I Kings 13:26).

I Kings 14:10, 11, 14 (cf. I Kings 15:28, 29). Jeroboam's son is ill. The king instructs his wife to go to Ahijah the prophet to inquire concerning the health of his son. Ahijah uses this occasion to prophesy concerning the house of Jeroboam. Not only shall this son of Jeroboam die; the king's entire household shall be destroyed.

This prophecy finds fulfillment at the hands of Baasha, throne successor to Jeroboam. I Kings 15:28, 29 records the total destruction of the house of Jeroboam by Baasha. Again the formula of prophetic fulfillment finds full expression. Baasha destroys Jeroboam "according to the word of Yahveh which he spoke."

I Kings 16:1-4 (cf. I Kings 16:10-12). Though Baasha himself had executed the word of God on the house of Jeroboam, he nonetheless proceeds to commit the identical sins. Jehu the prophet indicates that Baasha's house is to be destroyed even as Jeroboam's.

Did Baasha not perceive that disobedience to the word of God would bring to him the same judgment which it brought to Jeroboam? This word of prophecy finds fulfillment at the hands of Zimri. The formula in its undiluted form recurs again. Zimri destroys Baasha "according to the word of Yahveh which he spoke" (I Kings 16:12).

I Kings 16:34 (cf. Joshua 6:26). Joshua placed a solemn curse on anyone attempting to rebuild Jericho (Josh. 6:26). The man who should attempt to rebuild this city would lay its foundation with the death of his firstborn son, and would complete its gates with the death of his youngest son. In the days of the arrogance of Ahab, Hiel of Bethel initiated the rebuilding of Jericho. The text is not explicit, but most likely Hiel built in blatant defiance of Joshua's prophetic word. Particularly after witnessing the death of his firstborn son as a consequence of laying the new foundation for Jericho, it would seem evident that Hiel would have been reminded of the sure consequences of continuation. Yet Hiel persists until he has raised up the gates of the city. As a consequence, he celebrates the completion of the city with the death of his youngest son.

Assuming Hiel was made aware of Joshua's solemn word of prophecy at one point or another, no more blatant revolt against God's word may be imagined. He suffered the loss of his sons "according to the word of Yahveh which he spoke" (I Kings 16:34).

I Kings 17:13–16. The monarchy of Israel failed to extend the beneficent reign of God throughout the earth. Yet the Lord of the covenant continued to display his gracious power among men of all nations. Though many widows lived in Israel during this period (cf. Luke 4:25, 26), God sent Elijah to a widow at Zarephath in the land of Sidon. To this solitary widow God's word of saving grace came in power. Her bowl of flour would not be exhausted, nor would her jar of oil become empty, until the Lord should send rain. This word of God finds fulfillment "according to the word of Yahveh which he spoke."

I Kings 21:17–24 (cf. I Kings 22:34, 35, 38; II Kings 9:21–26, 30–37; 10:10, 17). Ahab just had taken possession of Naboth's vineyard. The innocent man had been stoned through the connivings of Jezebel. As Ahab first strides proudly onto his most recent acquisition, he is met by the prophet Elijah.

Four distinct prophecies occur in this context, all of which find recorded fulfillment in the books of Kings. First, a prophecy is uttered concerning Ahab: "In the place where the dogs licked up the blood of Naboth the dogs shall lick up your blood, even yours" (I Kings 21:19). The substance of the prophecy is that Ahab will meet violent death. As a further humiliation, his blood shall be shed on the very ground of Naboth to which he now lays claim.

The word of the Lord concerning Ahab's death finds vivid reinforcement in the subsequent narrative of Kings. Ahab and Jehoshaphat have entered into a coalition against Syria. The prophetic word to Ahab concerning the certainty of his death in this conflict is delivered by Micaiah, the Lord's faithful prophet.

The descriptive detail of the narrative enforces the contrast between the earthly kings of Israel and the Lord, the true King of the covenant. Ahab and Jehoshaphat "were sitting each on his throne arrayed in their robes . . . and all the prophets were prophesying before them" (I Kings 22:10). Micaiah contrasts their regal pomp with the glories of the one true living Lord, "sitting on his throne, and all the host of heaven standing by him on his right and on his left" (v. 19).

The outcome of the conflicting prophetic projections concerning the ensuing battle cannot be doubted. Despite elaborate attempts to disguise himself, Ahab dies of an arrow shot at random which strikes him precisely in the joints of his armor. In his humiliation, dogs lick his blood, "according to the word of Yahveh which he spoke" (I Kings 22:37, 38).

However, one aspect of Elijah's earlier prophecy concerning Ahab's death had been modified due to Ahab's repentance, imperfect though it may have been. Ahab is spared the added humiliation of dying on the very plot of ground he had snatched from Naboth. This irony is deferred to his son Joram (I Kings 21:27–29).

The second prophecy of this chapter thus concerns Joram, successor to Ahab. To him now belongs the ironical curse of dying violently on Naboth's vineyard. As a result, Joram dies at the hands of Jehu, who casts his corpse into the field of Naboth the Jezreelite. The "formula of fulfillment" occurs again, this time in abbreviated form. Joram dies "according to the word of Yahveh" (II Kings 9:26).

The third prophecy in I Kings 21 deals with the fate of Ahab's posterity. Even as Jeroboam's house suffered annihilation, even as Baasha's house suffered annihilation, so also Ahab's house shall suffer annihilation (I Kings 21:21f.). Elisha repeats this prophecy to Jehu (II Kings 9:1–9). Its fulfillment is recorded in II Kings 10:17. Again the complete formula of prophetic fulfillment occurs. Ahab's seed is eliminated "according to the word of Yahveh which he spoke."

The fourth and final prophecy of this section deals with the fate of Jezebel. God's prophetic mouthpiece predicts that "the dogs shall eat Jezebel in the district of Jezreel" (I Kings 21:23).

This prophecy also is repeated by Elisha (II Kings 9:10). Its fulfillment is recorded vividly in II Kings 9:30–37. Jezebel is residing in Jezreel when Jehu arrives fresh from the battlefield. The blood of Jezebel's son Joram still drips from his hands. With incalculable insolence, the queen paints her eyes and accosts warring Jehu. The rugged warrior commands that she be cast from the banister. The queen of Israel no sooner has struck the earth than Jehu spurs his horses so that they crush her to death.

After a quiet meal to recover his strength from the exhaustion of battle, Jehu determines that Jezebel deserves proper burial, since to her belongs the dignity of being queen of Israel. His men, however, discover that the dogs of the streets of Jezreel have devoured their queen. It is at this point that Jehu recognizes the fulfillment of the prophetic word: "It is the word of the Lord which he spoke" (II Kings 9:36).

The extensiveness of prophetic fulfillment throughout this narrative, and the faithful repetition of the prophetic formula of fulfillment underlines with awesome solemnity the veracity of God's word. What God has spoken shall be done.[38]

II Kings 1:16, 17. King Ahaziah has fallen through his lattice. He suffers severely. Will he survive?

Elijah the prophet sends his message. Because the king of Israel has sought after the god of Ekron instead of acknowledging the one true God, he shall die.

"According to the word of Yahveh" the king dies. The King of heaven has spoken irrevocably among the kings of earth.

II Kings 2:19-22. God's curse had been placed over the city of Jericho from the days of Joshua (cf. Josh. 6:26). But now the word of the Lord goes forth to heal the cursed land that had been devoted to

---

38. John Gray, *First and Second Kings: A Commentary, The Old Testament Library* (Philadelphia, 1963), p. 393, notes convincingly the indicators of prophetic genuineness throughout I Kings 21. He describes the prediction concerning Jezebel as "certainly a typical short, colorful, and very pithy oracle." From his own standpoint every indicator of style suggests a genuinely prophetic utterance. Yet his presuppositional commitment against the possibility of futuristic prediction leads him to deny the genuineness of this passage. He concludes that the oracle "may be secondary, adapted to the actual fate of Jezebel, i.e., prophecy *post eventum.*"

destruction. It is being claimed anew as a part of God's land of fruitfulness. Elisha scatters salt into the spring (a most unpromising agent for healing bitter waters). He speaks in God's name, and the water is healed "according to the word of Elisha which he spoke." The prophetic formula of fulfillment continues to recur.

II Kings 4:42–44. A famine in the land had brought the children of Israel into dire straits. A godly man from Baal-Shalishah had generously provided according to what he had for Elisha's prophetic school. But the portion was hardly enough to feed 100 men.

The prophet Elisha commands a distribution, and promises the meagre provisions shall prove to be more than adequate for all his men. Beginning with only 20 loaves of barley and fresh ears of grain, he satisfies his 100 followers so that they eat to the full and still have some left over. This miracle occurs "according to the word of Yahveh." Now the abbreviated formula is used.

The parallels with Jesus' feeding of the 5000 are quite extensive. The form of the prophetic command given to the disciples in each case is almost identical: "give . . . that they may eat" (II Kings 4:42; cf. Matt. 14:16). The servants to God's old and new covenant prophets respond in a strikingly similar fashion: "What, shall I set this before a hundred men?" (II Kings 4:43; cf. John 6:9). In each case, the narrative notes that some food remains after the people have satisfied themselves (II Kings 4:44; cf. Matt. 14:20).

But as the points of comparison are scrutinized more closely, the vast superiority of Jesus as the greater prophet becomes more apparent. Elisha fed 100 men; Jesus fed 5000, plus women and children. Elisha began with 20 loaves and ears of corn; Jesus began with five loaves and two small fish. Elisha provided only grain products; Jesus provided bread and meat. Elisha's company had an indefinite "some" left over; Jesus' multitude had 12 baskets full. In every way, Jesus excels as the greater prophet.

II Kings 6:15–18. Syria continually was warring against Israel. During one such period, the Israelites demonstrated an uncanny capability to anticipate Syria's maneuvers.

Finally the word came to the king of Syria. Elisha the prophet had been relaying the secret counsels of the king to their Israelite enemy.

A host of horsemen and charioteers are commissioned to hunt down this troublesome prophet. Elisha is discovered and surrounded in the region of Dothan.

But the host of heaven always are more numerous and more potent than the armies of earth. "According to the word of Elisha," the king's army is struck with blindness (v. 18). Once more God's ultimate lordship over the nations is demonstrated.

II Kings 7:1, 2 (cf. II Kings 7:16–20). In this narrative, the city of Samaria is being beseiged by the armies of Syria. Elisha the prophet promises the impossible. The seige will lift by the following day, and the abundance of grain for the starving populace will be so great that prices will be minimal.

One of the king's captains, overhearing Elisha's prophecy, expresses unrestrained skepticism: "If the Lord should make windows in heaven, could this thing be?"[39]

This servant has dared to mock God's lordship over the nations of the earth. He has failed to acknowledge that Assyrian armies as well as Israelite provisions derive their very existence from the one true living God.

The prophet declares the man's fate. He shall see God's provision with his eyes, but he shall never taste their satisfying refreshment (II Kings 7:2b).

This twofold prophecy finds its fulfillment on the following day. As a result of the hasty disbursement of the Syrian army, a measure of fine meal is sold for a shekel "according to the word of Yahveh" (v. 16). The captain of the gate witnesses this miraculous provision,

---

39. It is possible that the captain may have been mocking the provision of manna as recorded in Exod. 16:4, when God rained bread from heaven. Cf. Ps. 78:23–27, which speaks of God's opening the doors of heaven, raining down manna, and giving the people food to eat. If this were the case, the judgment of God on this captain would have been due in part to his mockery of God's miraculous provision in the past.

but never tastes for himself. He is trodden to death at the gate of the city as the ravenous mob presses toward the abandoned provisions of the Syrians. He dies "according to the word of the man of God which he spoke" (v. 17).

II Kings 8:7–15 (cf. II Kings 10:32, 33; 12:18; 13:3, 7; also Hosea 10:14; 14:1; Amos 1:3–5). Benhadad, king of Syria, has fallen ill. He sends his servant Hazael to Elisha the prophet to learn of his prospects for the future. During the interview, Elisha offers three prophecies: Benhadad the king shall die; Hazael shall reign in his place; and Hazael shall afflict Israel. While no prophetic formula of fulfillment is found regarding these prophecies, the particulars of each fulfillment are described in the passages cited.

II Kings 10:30 (cf. II Kings 15:12). Because of Jehu's faithfulness in executing God's wrath against the house of Ahab, God promises that the descendants of Jehu shall reign on the throne of Israel to the fourth generation. The line of Jehu's dynasty consequently runs through his descendants Jehoahaz, Joash, Jeroboam, and Zechariah, and endures for almost 100 years. No other family sat on the throne of Israel nearly so long. The closest rival to Jehu's dynasty was the dynasty of Omri, which lasted less than 50 years. The long dynasty of Jehu, according to the author of Kings, was in fulfillment of "the word of the Lord which he spoke" (II Kings 15:12).

II Kings 14:25. Under Jeroboam II, Israel's borders enlarged almost to the boundaries previously enjoyed under Solomon. This kind of expansion could occur only because God's word of prophecy bore in itself the power to coordinate the whole complex of events determining the course of Ancient Near Eastern history. Assyria lapsed into a period of weakness, allowing for the rapid expansion of Israel under Jeroboam II, "according to the word of Yahveh the God of Israel which he spoke."

II Kings 24:1, 2. As the history of the southern kingdom moves swiftly towards its close, the formula of fulfillment recurs again. Now, however, it is attached not to a single prophetic utterance, but to a conglomerate of declarations. God sends marauding bands of neighboring nations to chastise Judah for its sin, "according to the word of Yahveh which he spoke through his servants the prophets."

This series of invasions fulfils the words of warning which had been issued throughout the long history of prophetism in Israel.

II Kings 20:12-18 (cf. II Kings 24:10-17). Though he had been healed graciously by the Lord, Hezekiah responded foolishly to the flattering attentions paid him by emissaries from Babylon. He responded by displaying pridefully all the riches of his kingdom.

The prophet Isaiah exposed the king's folly and pronounced the divine judgment. All the wealth in which Hezekiah gloried would be carried away (II Kings 20:17; cf. Isa. 39:6).

This prophecy of judgment finds fulfillment in the days of Jehoiachin. God alone was worthy of glory in Israel. As a part of the removal of "glory" from Israel, the king of Babylon took with him all the treasures of the Lord's house, "just as the Lord had said" (II Kings 24:13). Judgment must come on all those who fail to acknowledge Yahveh to be King of kings and Lord of lords. Even the captivity of his own nation must occur to maintain his distinctive role among all the peoples of the earth.

So the entire history of the monarchy in Israel hinges on the word of the Lord. Having established the basis of his covenant relationship with David, God faithfully demonstrates the veracity of his word. From the first chastisement against Solomon to the ultimate deportation of the nation, God's word of the covenant controls history.

Summary Statement by the Author of Kings

In addition to the foundational passages establishing the veracity of God's covenant word, and the numerous concrete instances of the fulfillment of that word, the author of Kings himself offers a summary statement regarding God's covenant word among the kings of Israel. As the northern kingdom experiences its judgmental end, the author appends a rather full statement of the cause of this calamitous event (see II Kings 17:7-41, particularly vv. 7-18). Because of the failure to keep God's covenant, they must be cast out of the land.

References to the statutes, the commandments, the testimonies, and the covenant saturate the passage (cf. vv. 13, 15, 16, 34, 37). All these phrases reflect the language of the foundational passages discussed earlier (cf. I Kings 2:3, 4; 8:57–58; 9:6, 7). Allusion to the "hardening of the neck" by Israel echoes the covenantal language of Exodus and Deuteronomy (II Kings 17:14; cf. Exod. 32:9; 33:3; Deut. 10–16; 31:27; cf. also Jer. 7:26; Acts 7:51). Israel's stubborn refusal to hear and to heed God's word has sealed their fate. The whole history of the monarchy in Israel presents itself as a solemn verification of God's covenant word.

Conclusion

One cannot but be amazed at the architectonic structure of the books of Kings. It is difficult to conceive of a more elaborate or more convincingly executed demonstration of a thesis. The word of the covenant set the course of history, and the word of the covenant had its verification in history. As a result of this elaborate theme-development, several insights into the ways of God with his people may be noted:

1. Some conclusion may be drawn concerning the nature of prophecy from the biblical perspective. Clearly the Scriptures intend to depict the prophets of Israel as predictors of the future. More precisely, the words of Yahveh spoken through his prophets determine the future. God's messengers are not merely good political prognosticators. Their words determine the course of future events. Yahveh may declare the end from the beginning because he is the Lord of history.

To be sure, this declaring of the future does not occur in a vacuum. Because of commitments in the past by the Lord of the covenant, the course of the future is determined. Predictive prophecy occurs only as it relates organically to the covenantal ordinances established between God and his people. But prophecy clearly does contain a predictive element.

2. Insight into the nature of the biblical concept of the covenant may be derived from the thesis of the books of Kings. Because the

whole of the history is determined by the covenant, a visual model of covenant thought-pattern in Israel has been provided.

Clearly, covenant in Israel does not embrace merely philosophical ideologies about God. Only the concreteness of historical reality may explain the covenant concept.

Clearly, covenant in Israel involves a word-contract. Not merely the undefined vagueness of a deed, but the specificness of a word spoken to Israel establishes the covenant relationship. The foundation of the covenant rests on a verbal commitment by Yahveh to David. The history of the covenant cannot be understood apart from awareness of this verbal form.

Clearly, covenant in Israel emphasizes the wholeness of history from Abraham through Moses to David. The achievement of rest in the land under Solomon derives from the promise to Abraham. The criteria of legal stipulations enforced in Israel derives from the law of Moses. The intermingling of the principle of preservation for David's line in a context of repeated chastisements for David's sons derives from God's covenant word to David.

3. Particularly striking throughout the narrative is the relative consistency of contexts in which the specific word of the Lord comes to Israel. Every instance of the "King's word among the kings" up to the point of the fall of Samaria is addressed to the northern kingdom. The overwhelming majority of these predictive utterances relate to God's judgment on his disobedient nation.[40]

It may be suggested, therefore, that the overarching purpose of the books of Kings concerns the justification of the ways of God with his people. If they are his covenant people, why ultimately does he cast them off? These judgments occur "according to the word of Yahveh which he spoke." First he spoke a word of warning to David. Then he spoke repeatedly to specific circumstances in Israel's history.

4. This long history of judgmental realization on the basis of

---

40. The two instances in which the "formula of fulfillment" is applied to the southern kingdom are found in II Kings 24:1, 2, and II Kings 24:10–17. Both cases occur in judgmental contexts.

God's covenant word must be balanced by focusing equal attention on the faithful maintenance of the Davidic line through the history. While calamity strikes repeatedly among Israel's sons in the northern kingdom, God continues to sustain in unbroken fashion the line of David in the south.

Indeed, the kingdom of Judah also ultimately tastes the righteous judgments of God. But the gentle upsurge of events which closes the books of Kings must not be overlooked (II Kings 25:27–30). The king of Babylon released Jehoiachin from prison,[41] spoke kindly to him and set his throne above the other captive kings in Babylon. Furthermore, Jehoiachin was allowed to remove his prison clothes,[42] to eat his meals in the king's presence all the days of his life, and to receive a regular allowance until his death. Thus the books of Kings conclude.

What is the meaning of this quiet upturn in the narrative as the history concludes? Why should a book so laden with the history of God's judgments end by tantalizing the reader's appreciation of his final message by concluding with a definite note of positive hope?

Is not this final incident intended to reflect the "other side" of God's covenant with David? Indeed, God chastened David's sons according to the provisions of the covenant. But never did he remove his lovingkindness as he did from the house of Saul. Even as the last of David's line languishes in prison, God does not forget his covenant mercies.

So the drama concludes with the stage set for a return of David's son to the throne of Israel. The consummation of God's covenant purposes has not yet been realized. The prophetic projection concerning a greater David builds on the surety of God's covenant, and anticipates the ultimate realization of all God's promises.

---

41. The phrase literally states that the king of Babylon "lifted up the head of Jehoiachin king of Judah." The same phrase describes the favorable treatment of Pharaoh's cup-bearer in the Joseph-narrative (Gen. 40:13).

42. Compare the similar phraseology used to describe Joseph's release from prison and his exaltation in the king's presence (Gen. 44:42).

13

Christ:
The Covenant of Consummation

THE expulsion of the people of God from the land of promise at the time of the exile dramatizes their massive failure under the old covenant. This manifestation of a fatal deficiency in covenantal administration does not relate simply to the Mosaic covenant of law. For the end of the Davidic monarchy and the devastation of Jerusalem fulfilled the covenantal curse associated with the Davidic covenant as well. Still further, expulsion from the land of promise may be understood only as a reversal of the beneficence expressed in the covenant with Abraham. Though circumcised formally, Abraham's descendants now were treated as the uncircumcised, and so were cast out of the land. This enactment of covenantal curse in redemptive history vivifies the necessity for some new form of covenantal administration having a more lasting effectiveness than the form by which the covenant was administered through Abraham, Moses, and David.

The prophets of Israel's later history served their contemporaries well by insisting on the inevitability of God's judgment on covenant-breakers. The false idea of a wholly unconditional covenant relationship was proven to rest on an improper assumption.

But these spokesmen for God also delivered another significant message. As Israel entered into a period in which judgment was inevitable, they declared hope beyond devastation. Although Israel had failed in fulfilling its covenantal responsibilities, the Lord God of Israel would not fail in his purpose to establish a great people and a great nation to glorify his own name. The Lord's intention to redeem a people to himself from among the fallen of humanity would not be thwarted.

This expectation of hope beyond devastation took many forms. The prophets spoke most frequently of a return to the land of promise, of a restoration of acceptable worship, of a renewal of a regal messianic line. Specifically, one unifying motif having to do with these restoration expectations involved the anticipation of a new covenant relationship. Although judgment was inevitable, God would establish a new covenant with his people. By means of this covenant relationship, the Lord would bring to certain fruition his commitment to redeem a people for himself. Since the covenant throughout Israel's history had structured God's relationship to his people, it might have been anticipated that the future age of restoration also would assume covenantal form. By the inauguration of a new covenant relationship, the original purposes of God to redeem a people to himself would find satisfactory realization.

Because of its unique role in gathering together the various strands of covenantal promise throughout history, this last of God's covenants appropriately may be designated as *the covenant of consummation.* This covenant supersedes God's previous covenantal administrations. At the same time, it brings to focal realization the essence of the various covenants experienced by Israel throughout their history. Consummation characterizes the substance of this final covenant throughout.

The heart of this consummative realization consists of a single person. As fulfiller of all the messianic promises, he achieves in himself the essence of the covenantal principle: "I shall be your God and you shall be my people." He therefore may be seen as the Christ who consummates the covenant.

The present exploration of the new covenant in promise and fulfillment shall center on an analysis of Jeremiah's new covenant prophecy as found in Jeremiah 31:31–34 (English verse-enumeration). First the broader as well as the more specific context of the prophecy will be considered. Then exegetical observations focusing on particular points of tension will be offered.

THE BROADER CONTEXT OF THE PROPHECY

Jeremiah's word concerning the establishment of a new covenant must not be treated in isolation from the historical situation in which this prophecy occurred. The prophet Jeremiah had insisted that judgment was inevitable for Israel. The nation must experience the devastation of covenantal curse because of its persistence in unrepentant sin. This judgment for covenantal violation was not to come merely in the form of a removal of particular privileges. Instead, it would involve a complete reversal of God's sovereign election procedures. As God once had called Abraham out of Ur of the Chaldees and given him promise concerning a land, so now the seed of Abraham must be cast out of this land of promise. They must be declared "not my people."

This sober word of covenantal devastation, however, is not the only word spoken by Jeremiah. By his announcement concerning the new covenant, the prophet introduces a hope for Israel even beyond this decree of destruction.

Although this passage in Jeremiah alone in the old covenant Scriptures mentions specifically a "new covenant," the concept of the new covenant cannot be restricted to this single prophecy. A significant complex of ideas surrounds Jeremiah's prediction of the new covenant. These ideas are developed rather extensively in a group of prophecies found in Jeremiah and Ezekiel.[1] It is only in the broader context of these passages related to the new covenant that the message of Jeremiah 31:31–34 may be appreciated fully.

Several major motifs emerge which relate essentially to the new covenant concept in these prophets. These motifs include:

The Return of Exiled Israel to the Land of Promise

In the broader context of the new covenant prophecy of Jeremiah, God declares that he will "bring them back to the land" that he had given to their forefathers (Jer. 30:3).[2] An essential aspect of the "everlasting covenant" as developed by Jeremiah involves gathering Israel out of all the lands to which the Lord had driven them in his anger. He shall bring them back so they may dwell safely in Palestine (Jer. 32:37; cf. Jer. 50:5). Once the Lord has brought judgment on Babylon, he will bring Israel back to its "pasture land" (Jer. 50:6–18; cf. v. 19). The prophet Ezekiel also associates the everlasting covenant, the covenant of peace, with the regathering of Israel to their own land (cf. Ezek. 37:21, 26).[3]

Full Restoration of God's Blessing on the Land of Promise

The curses of the old covenant left the land of God's people scorched and barren. But according to the provisions of the "ever-

---

1. Two passages in Jer. and one in Ezek. most obviously parallel the new covenant prophecy of Jer. 31 (Jer. 32:27–44; 50:4f.; Ezek. 37:15–28). All three of these passages refer to an "everlasting covenant." Isa. 55:1–5 and 61:1–9 also make reference to the everlasting covenant, as does Ezek. 16:60–63. Jer. 3:11–18 and 33:1–26 group together the essential elements associated with the new covenant as it is found in Jer. 31 and other passages. See in addition Ezek. 34:1–31, which develops rather extensively the concept of the "covenant of peace" (v. 25).

2. John Bright, *Jeremiah* (Garden City, N.Y., 1965), p. LVIII, notes that Jer. 30, 31 are a unified collection of prophecies which contain "practically the whole of Jeremiah's message of hope." Jer. 30:1–3 serves to introduce these prophecies.

3. Further associations of the new covenant concept with a return to the land are found in Jer. 3:18; 33:26; Ezek. 34:13.

lasting covenant," fields are to be bought which once were declared a desolation as a result of the Babylonian invasion (Jer. 32:43). The city of Jerusalem shall be rebuilt for the Lord. The whole valley polluted by dead bodies shall become holy to the Lord (Jer. 31:38–40).

The resurrectional activity of the Spirit of God in the valley of dry bones attaches to the provisions of the everlasting covenant according to Ezekiel (cf. Ezek. 37:12, 26). God will open the graves of Israel, cause them to come alive, and so will bring them into their land (Ezek. 37:12). He will put his Spirit within them, making the dead to live.

Both Jeremiah and Ezekiel in the passages cited above relate the restoration of the land to this resurrection motif. Not merely those who happen to be alive at the time of the institution of the new covenant shall experience the blessings of restoration to the land. Instead, the dead shall be brought to life so that they too may participate in the complete renovation accomplished by the new covenant.

Divine Fulfillment of Previous Covenantal Commitments

A third motif associated with the new covenant prophecy of Jeremiah relates this consummating covenant to God's previous covenantal commitments. By the new covenant God shall fulfill all the promises of the covenants established earlier with his people. The obedience to God's law which did not materialize under the Mosaic covenant shall find consummate fulfillment under the provisions of the new covenant (Jer. 31:33). Israel's possession of the land as promised to Abraham shall become a solid and unshakable reality. Ezekiel particularly emphasizes the fulfillment of previous covenantal promises through the new covenant. David shall be king over Israel; the nation shall walk according to the statutes of the Mosaic covenant; the people shall live on the land promised to Jacob (Ezek. 37:24, 25). The blessings associated with the new covenant therefore cannot be regarded as the development of a perspective previously unknown to God's people. Instead, this covenant shall bring to fruition the redemptive intentions of God displayed throughout the ages.

Internal Renewal by the Work of God's Holy Spirit

Unique to the administration of the new covenant according to Jeremiah will be the internalized inscription of the law of God. The heart of flesh belonging to the members of the covenant community shall serve as the tablets on which the torah shall be inscribed (Jer. 31:33). Other passages speak of God's putting his fear in the hearts of his people so that they will not turn away from him (Jer. 32:40); of his putting his Spirit within them (Ezek. 37:14); and of the Lord's cleansing them (Ezek. 37:23). Jeremiah declares that in this coming redemption God's people no more shall walk after the stubbornness of their hearts (Jer. 3:17).

The new covenant therefore boasts a unique feature in its power to transform its participants from within their hearts. This uniqueness sets the new covenant apart from the previous covenantal dealings of God with his people.

The Full Forgiveness of Sins

Closely associated with the renewed heart of covenantal participants is the pardon of all sins. This forgiveness is preserved as a foundational principle in the primary new covenant passage in Jeremiah (cf. Jer. 31:34). The prophet elsewhere declares in connection with the everlasting covenant that search will be made for the iniquity of Israel, but no sin will be found (Jer. 50:20). God will cleanse the people of their iniquities, pardoning them fully (Jer. 33:8).[4]

The uniqueness of this pardon of all iniquity in the new covenant

---

4. Compare also the reference to the "covenant of peace" in Ezek. 16:63, which includes the Lord's forgiveness of Israel's sin.

as it might compare with forgiveness under earlier covenants will be discussed subsequently. Suffice it to say at this point that the forgiveness of sins serves as a central feature in prophetic anticipations of the new covenant.

The Union of Israel and Judah

The new covenant will not be made only with a portion of God's people. Instead, a hallmark of the new covenant will be the merging of the kingdoms of Israel and Judah. Jeremiah specifically relates the promise to both the nations (Jer. 31:31). Israel shall come together with the sons of Judah seeking the Lord (Jer. 50:4). As Ezekiel develops his prophetic vision of the everlasting covenant of peace, he speaks of the reunion of the two "sticks" that have been separated from one another (cf. Ezek. 37:15f.). One shepherd-king of the Davidic line shall rule over the reunited nation (Ezek. 34:23). As the people of God are bound in the new covenant to the God of the covenant, so they are bound inseparably with one another.

The Everlasting Character of the New Covenant

Essential to a full appreciation of the distinctiveness of the new covenant is an awareness of its everlasting character. Indeed, this characteristic had been assigned to previous divine administrations. The Abrahamic covenant is characterized as everlasting (Gen. 17:7; Ps. 105:10), as is the Mosaic (Exod. 40:15; Lev. 16:34; 24:8; Isa. 24:5) and Davidic (II Sam. 7:13, 16; Ps. 89:3, 4; 132:11, 12). But the everlasting character of the new covenant seems to imply an eschatological dimension. It is not only the new covenant; it is the last covenant. Because it shall bring to full fruition that which God intends in redemption, it never shall be superseded by a subsequent covenant. Men shall come to Zion to join themselves to the Lord in an everlasting covenant that will not be forgotten (Jer. 50:5).[5] God's

---

5. Cf. Isa. 61:8 and Ezek. 37:26, which also describe this covenant as everlasting.

previous covenants may be regarded as "everlasting" only insofar as they find their realization in the new covenant.

It is essential to see the new covenant prophecy of Jeremiah in this total biblical-theological setting. Although the term "new covenant" occurs only in Jeremiah 31, the complex of ideas depicting the future expectation of God's people has a very broad base. Essentially it may be said that the future age is characterized by the prophets as having a covenantal structure, corresponding to the whole of the Lord's past dealings with his people. While maintaining a balance of continuity with the past, this new covenant possesses unique features belonging to it alone. By this covenant, the intentions of God to redeem a people to himself shall find consummate fulfillment.[6]

THE SPECIFIC CONTEXT OF JEREMIAH 31

Before considering in detail the teaching of Jeremiah 31:31–34 concerning the new covenant, some attention must be given to questions respecting the literary character and context of this prophecy.

It is not possible to reconstruct absolutely the process by which a passage such as Jeremiah 31:31–34 arrived in its present form and context in the book of Jeremiah. It probably is correct to say that the passage originally was a unit to itself, although the precise framework of the unit is difficult to determine. Presently the new covenant prophecy appears in a collection of declarations based on a common theme having to do with the promise of the Lord for the restoration of Israel beyond its devastation.[7] The theme binding together the

---

6. The broader complex of ideas associated with the new covenant prophecy of Jeremiah is developed helpfully in P. Buis "La nouvelle Alliance," *Vetus Testamentum* 18 (1968): 1ff. Cf. also Gerhard von Rad, *Old Testament Theology* (New York, 1965), 2: 270.

7. See John Bright, "Exercise in Hermeneutics: Jer. 31:31–34," *Interpretation*, 20 (1966): 192.

prophecies of Jeremiah 30 and 31 is indicated plainly in the first 3 verses of chapter 30. The prophet is told to write the words the Lord has spoken to him in a book, for the Lord would restore the fortunes of his people. The two chapters are bound together not only by their common theme, but also by a common introductory phrase: "For behold, days are coming, says Yahveh . . ." (cf. Jer. 30:3; 31:27, 31, 38). These chapters have been called "the grand hymn of Israel's deliverance."[8] These chapters represent one of the high watermarks in biblical prophecies of hope.

The date of this particular prophecy cannot be determined. It is not necessary to assume that the captivity of 587 B.C. already has occurred. If the prophet experienced so much personal anguish at the hands of his fellow Israelites because of his consistent emphasis on the inescapable captivity of Judah, it certainly is not difficult to imagine him also looking beyond the abyss of devastation and offering some word of hope to his people.[9]

EXEGETICAL OBSERVATIONS

Several points of tension have marked the interpretation of the new covenant prophecy in Jeremiah. These debated areas of understanding may help in identifying the most significant aspects of these verses. Three points of tension particularly may be noted: continuity versus newness in the new covenant, corporateness

---

8. E. W. Hengstenberg, *Christology of the Old Testament* (Grand Rapids, 1956), 2: 424.

9. No adequate reason has been cited for questioning the authenticity of Jeremiah's new covenant prophecy. Bright concludes that the authenticity of the passage "ought never to have been questioned" (John Bright, *Jeremiah* [Garden City, N.Y., 1965], p. 287).

However, von Rad states: ". . . Jer. 31:31ff. can hardly be the form of the oracle as it was originally spoken by Jeremiah, for he, like the other prophets, usually gave his oracles a verse form" (op. cit., p. 214). A judgment concerning authenticity on the basis of poetical or nonpoetical form is highly precarious, particularly in a book such as Jeremiah's, which has such a mixture of literary forms. On what grounds may it be suggested that a prophet may speak only poetically?

versus individuality in the new covenant, and internal reality versus external substance in the new covenant.

Continuity versus Newness in the New Covenant

Jeremiah's announcement concerning the expectation of a new covenant (בְּרִית חֲדָשָׁה) in itself anticipates a new dimension in God's redemptive working. Rather than suggesting merely the possibility of covenant renewal some time in the future, Jeremiah expects the certain establishment of a new covenant relationship.

Elsewhere the prophets employ the concept of "newness" to characterize their anticipation concerning God's future dealings with his people. Isaiah declares "new things" (Isa. 42:9). He speaks of God's doing something "new" by making a roadway in the wilderness (Isa. 43:19; cf. also Isa. 48:6; 62:2; 65:17; 66:22). Ezekiel anticipates the day in which God will put a "new spirit" within his people (Ezek. 11:19; 36:24–28).

This concept of newness implies a break with the past. God shall act to redeem his people in a way unfamiliar to them. Jeremiah emphasizes the newness of the new covenant by distinguishing his expectations of a new covenant experience for Israel from the experience of the nation formerly (Jer. 31:32). Interestingly, the prophet does not refer specifically to the formal inauguration of the covenant that occurred at Sinai. Instead, he refers to the covenant established on the day in which the Lord brought Israel out of Egypt.

This lack of preciseness does not mean that Jeremiah did not have the Mosaic covenant itself in mind when he developed this contrast. He speaks too specifically of a law written in the heart, implying a contrast with law written in stone. His allusion to the Mosaic covenant by reference to the exodus from Egypt simply conforms to a repeated pattern found in Scripture with respect to the covenants. Historical events associated intimately with the covenant often precede the formal inauguration of the covenantal relationship.[10] According to E. W. Hengstenberg:

---

10. For further discussion of this point, see p. 30 above.

> The substance of the covenant evidently precedes the outward con-
> clusion of the covenant, and forms the foundation of it. The conclu-
> sion of the covenant does not first form the relation, but is merely a
> solemn acknowledgment of a relation already existing.[11]

Although it may be said rather certainly that Jeremiah intends to
refer to the covenant at Sinai by his reference to the day that God
brought Israel out of Egypt, it also must be recognized that his
peculiar form of reference has the effect of emphasizing the historical unity of the various covenantal relationships. For it was under
the provisions of the covenant with Abraham that God brought
Israel out of Egypt (see Exod. 2:24; 6:4; Hag. 2:5). Jeremiah's
contrast, therefore, is not simply with the Mosaic covenant. He
contrasts instead the new covenant with the totality of God's covenantal dealings with Israel previously. As Jeremiah projects into the
future with respect to the new covenant, he stands historically under
the specific provisions of the Davidic covenant. He contrasts the
new covenant explicitly with the Mosaic, but implicitly also with the
Abrahamic and the Davidic covenants. A "new" covenant shall
replace all of God's previous covenantal dealings.

Yet the newness of the new covenant must not stand in absolute
contradiction to the previous covenants. A factor of continuity must
be recognized. Jeremiah does not condemn the old covenant. He
condemns Israel for breaking the covenant (Jer. 31:32; cf. Jer. 2:5, 13,
20, 32). Because of the radical incapacity of man to keep God's
covenant, no lasting purpose will be served through a future reestablishment of this same covenantal relationship.[12]

More specifically, Jeremiah indicates that as an integral part of the
new covenant God will write his torah on the hearts of his people
(Jer. 31:33). The substance of covenant law will provide a basis for
continuity between old and new covenants. Indeed, God shall write
his will on the fleshly tablets of the heart, in contrast with the older

---

11. Hengstenberg, op. cit., p. 430.
12. Cf. Buis, op. cit., p. 10.

engraving of his law on stone tablets. But it will be essentially the same law of God that will be the substance of this engraving.[13]

A further line of continuity with the old covenant dealings of God with Israel may be seen in the fact that the "old" covenant with which the "new" covenant is being set in contrast was a redemptive covenant. Jeremiah mentions specifically that this covenant was established on the day that God redeemed Israel by bringing them out of Egypt. This old covenant cannot be characterized simplistically as a legalistic works-righteousness covenant. All the tender love of God necessary for the accomplishment of redemption was involved in this old covenant relationship. The Lord functioned as "husband" to Israel under this relationship (Jer. 31:32).[14]

In any case, a clear line of continuity must be seen in the relationship of the old covenant to the new. While the new covenant will be at radical variance with the old covenant with respect to its effectiveness in accomplishing its goal, the substance of the two covenants in terms of their redemptive intention is identical.

A third factor indicating the continuity but also the newness of the new covenant in relation to the old may be seen in Jeremiah's emphasis on the role of the forgiveness of sins as foundational in the establishment of the new covenant. Using the literary form of poetical parallelism, Jeremiah says, "I will forgive their iniquity, and their sin I will remember no more" (Jer. 31:34).

---

13. This torah, which was to be written in the heart under the provisions of the new covenant, embraces rather generally the teachings of the law as propounded in the old covenant Scriptures. The term *torah* occurs 11 times in Jer., and involves broad connotations. In Jer. 2:8, "the priests" who had the responsibility of interpreting the law for God's people stand in parallel construction with "those who handle the torah." In Jer. 6:19, "my law" parallels "my words"; and in Jer. 9:13 (12) and 26:4, 5; 32:23 "torah" parallels "voice." These passages indicate that the torah of the Lord was considered rather broadly, referring essentially to the whole of the Lord's teaching.

14. בָּעַלְתִּי might be translated "I was husband" to them, or "I was master" to them. J. Coppens, "La nouvelle alliance en Jer. 31:31–34," *Catholic Biblical Quarterly*, 25 (1963): 15, suggests that whether this phrase authentically belongs to Jeremiah or not, it ought to be translated in light of the parallel in Jer. 3:14, which would support the idea of "master." However, the effort on the part of Jeremiah in chapter 31 to set the failure of Israel under the old covenant in the darkest possible light would suggest that "husband" may be the more appropriate rendering.

This forgiveness of sins is presented by Jeremiah as providing the basic substructure for the new covenant relationship. "Because" God will forgive their sins and will remember them no more, Israel will have no need of a teacher. Every man will know the Lord.

But how can the prophet make so much of the forgiveness of sins as an integral aspect of the new covenant? Was not elaborate provision made under the Mosaic covenant for the forgiveness of sins? Did not Solomon encourage the people at the time of the dedication of the temple to pray toward the temple that their sins might be forgiven? In what sense may Jeremiah suggest that the unique foundational principle of the new covenant will be the forgiveness of sins?

In response to this very legitimate question, it may be indicated that it is just the elaborateness of the old covenant provision for forgiveness that makes understandable Jeremiah's emphasis on the uniqueness of forgiveness under the new covenant. The constant renewal of sacrifices for sins under the old covenant gave clear indication of the fact that sin actually was not removed, but only was passed over. If the sacrifice of the day of atonement actually had established a person once and for all as righteous in the sight of God, why then was the ceremony repeated annually? The blood of bulls and goats inherently had no power to remove sin in the framework of God's just administration of the world. The provisions of the old covenant, founded on such animal sacrifices, could not effect the actual removal of transgressions.

Jeremiah anticipates the day in which the actual shall replace the typical. Instead of having animal sacrifices merely represent the possibility of a substitutionary death in the place of the sinner, Jeremiah sees the day in which sins actually will be forgiven, never to be remembered again. The continual offering of sacrifice to remove sin not only provided a symbolical representation of the possibility of substitution. It also inevitably functioned as a very real reminder that sins had not yet been forgiven. By saying that sins would be remembered no more, Jeremiah anticipates the end of the sacrificial system of the Old Testament.

The subject of the forgiveness of sins thus provides a significant basis for analyzing features of continuity and newness in the relation of the new covenant to the old. The new factor of forgiveness anticipated in the new covenant is the once-for-all accomplishment of that forgiveness. Continuity is seen in the constant typological representation of the reality of forgiveness under the old covenant.

In conclusion, the radical newness of the new covenant receives special stress by Jeremiah's affirmation that this covenant came into effect because of Israel's "nullification" of the old covenant.[15] The end of the old covenant necessitates the inauguration of the new.

Some obvious difficulty appears when it is suggested that Israel is to be understood as having "annulled" the covenant. How is it possible for a vassal to annul a covenant established by a suzerain?

---

15. The predominant usage of the term פָּרַר in the hif'il implies the concept of "making null and void." The term is used of a vow that is "made null and void" by subsequent action. A wife may commit herself by vow; but the husband may proceed to void the wife's vow (cf. Num. 30:8 (9), 12 (13), 13 (14), 15 (16). The husband does not "break" the vow, since only the wife could perform that action. Instead, he "nullifies" the oath his wife has made.

In other passages, the verb is used in a context referring to counsel offered or to purposes determined. The point of these passages is not so much that the counsel offered is "broken," but that it is "frustrated" or "voided" because its promised success is not realized (cf. II Sam. 17:14; Ezra 4:5; Prov. 15:22; Neh. 4:15 (9); Job 40:8; Isa. 44:25).

This idea of annulment is associated directly with the term "covenant" or "treaty" in I Kings 15:19 (cf. II Chron. 16:3). In these verses Asa of Judah bribes Ben-Hadad of Syria to "nullify" his covenant with Israel. The context implies not so much that Ben-Hadad simply would violate the provisions of his treaty with Israel at a particular point. Instead, he is being encouraged to make null and void his treaty-relationship with Israel in favor of a different treaty-relationship with Judah.

The usage of the term in contexts relating to God's covenant with his people also suggests the idea of "nullification" rather than simply "violation." The uncircumcised male in Israel has "annulled" the covenant (Gen. 17:14). The person who sins defiantly has "nullified" the covenant, and so shall be cut off from God's people (Num. 15:31). After Israel has entered the land of promise, they will forget the Lord and "annul" the covenant (Deut. 31:16, 20). In each of these cases the idea seems to be one of "annulment" rather than simply of violation. Other passages in the Old Testament in which the term occurs in association with God's covenant with his people are: Ps. 119:126; Isa. 24:5; 33:8; Jer. 11:10; 31:32; Lev. 26:15; 26:44; Ezra 9:14; Ezek. 16:59; Zech. 11:10; Judg. 2:1; Jer. 14:21; Ezek. 44:7. In all of these places, it is quite likely that the concept "annulled" rather than "broke" is involved.

Quite obviously, such an annulment must be considered in relative terms. So far as the beneficent intention of the covenant is concerned, it may be annulled by the disobedience of the vassal. Since the primary intention of the covenant is to provide blessing for the subject of the covenantal relationship, it would appear quite appropriate to speak of an "annulment" of the covenant when the persistent disobedience of the vassal has the effect of making null and void the promises of blessing associated with the covenant relationship.[16]

The radical newness of the new covenant may be appreciated fully only from this perspective of the annulment of the old covenant. By removing Israel from the land of promise, the Lord dramatizes the end of the old covenant relationship. How could they be considered as God's people if the whole process of promised blessing has been reversed to the extent that they are cast once more into the same position that they were before God summoned Abraham out of Ur of the Chaldees? An entirely new covenantal history must begin. A people to be God's own must be constituted afresh. That is the meaning of Jeremiah's reference to a "new" covenant.

When the parallel passages to Jeremiah 31 speak of this new covenant as being "eternal" in character, the concept best may be understood as referring to the "irrevocable" or "definitive" aspect of this covenant. No possibility exists for an annulment of the new covenant. It cannot fail to achieve its intended goal of heaping redemptive blessing and restoration on its participants.[17]

Yet a proper balance must be maintained. While "annulment" and "newness" are contrasted in the prophecy of Jeremiah, it must not be forgotten that the old covenant also is characterized as an "eternal" covenant. While the form of the old covenant administration may pass away, the substance of blessing which it promises remains. God's torah will be written in the hearts of his people. God shall redeem his people in an ultimate sense, as it was done typo-

---

16. Von Rad, op. cit., p. 212, is quite correct when he asserts that ". . . the old covenant is broken, and in Jeremiah's view Israel is altogether without one."

17. Buis, op. cit., p. 6.

logically under the old covenant. That forgiveness of sins which was foreshadowed under the old covenant shall find consummate reality in the new. The new covenant can be understood in no other way than as a bringing to fruition of that which was anticipated under the old covenant. Continuity as well as newness must be recognized in the relationship of the new covenant to the old.

Corporateness versus Individuality in the New Covenant

Another question of significance with respect to the new covenant centers on the relation of corporateness to individuality. Both of these elements have their proper role in Jeremiah's prophecy. But how do they relate to one another?

It is rather tempting to set the individualistic dimension of this covenant over against a corporate concept, and to find the distinctiveness of the new covenant in this specific area. One commentator speaks representatively for a large constituency of evangelical Christianity today when he says:

> In acclaiming this new form of covenantal relationship both Jeremiah and Ezekiel saw that it changed the older concept of a corporate relationship completely by substituting the individual for the nation as a whole.
>
> Probably the most significant contribution which Jeremiah made to religious thought was inherent in his insistence that the new covenant involved a one-to-one relationship of the spirit. When the new covenant was inaugurated by the atoning work of Jesus Christ on Calvary, this important development of personal, as opposed to corporate, faith and spirituality was made real for the whole of mankind.[18]

This perspective recognizes appropriately a focal aspect of the new covenant as conceived by Jeremiah. A one-to-one relationship of the spirit certainly is a key factor in the new covenant.

---

18. R. K. Harrison, *Jeremiah and Lamentations* (Downers Grove, Ill., 1973), p. 140.

But this passage of Jeremiah should not be cited to prove the substitution of the individual for the people of God as a whole in the new covenant. Jeremiah does not set a personal faith-relationship in the new covenant in opposition to a corporate relationship. He maintains both of these features with equal emphasis. The prophet explicitly states that the new covenant shall be made corporately. Not just with individuals, but fully in accord with the whole pattern of God's dealing with his people throughout redemptive history, this new covenant shall be made "with the house of Israel and with the house of Judah" (Jer. 31:31).[19]

One effort to resolve this tension between the corporate and the individualized aspects of the new covenant suggests that the new covenant functions individually in the church age, but that it shall function corporately only with respect to ethnic Israel in the age to come. According to the "old" Scofield Bible, the new covenant "secures the perpetuity, future conversion, and blessing of Israel." But at the same time, it secures the personal revelation of the Lord to every believer.[20]

Such a dichotomizing of the prophecy of Jeremiah would have the effect of destroying the unified message of the prophet. If the new covenant is being fulfilled today, it should be expected that both the corporate and the individualistic elements currently are finding realization. The corporate dimension which played such a vital role in God's old covenant dealings with his people must not be omitted from the present realities of the new covenant.

Relief from the tension between individuality and corporateness

---

19. It is not necessary to suppose some textual corruption to explain the distinction between the reference to the covenant "with the house of Israel and with the house of Judah" (v. 31) and to the covenant simply "with the house of Israel" (v. 33). The more abbreviated designation of God's people simply as "Israel" may anticipate the united condition of the people of God at the time of new covenant establishment. Judah and Israel shall be joined into one.

20. "Old" Scofield Bible, op. cit., p. 1297, n. 1. Essentially the same treatment is found in the "new" Scofield Bible, op. cit., p. 804, n. 2: "Although certain features of this covenant have been fulfilled for believers in the present church age, . . . the covenant remains to be realized for Israel according to the explicit statement of v. 31."

in the new covenant may be provided by considering two questions: Who is the corporate community called "Israel"? and What is biblical corporateness?

Who is the corporate community called "Israel"? The question "who is Israel" plays a vital role in resolving the tension between individuality and corporateness in the new covenant. "Israel" in its very essence represents the corporate dimension of the covenant. But who is to be understood by the term "Israel"?

Though often overlooked, it should be plain from the beginning of the chosen nation's history that an Israelite could not be defined simply as a person ethnically descended from Abraham. Throughout Israelite history, any Gentile could become a full-fledged "Jew" by professing the faith of Abraham. At the same time, any one of Abraham's racial descendants could be declared not a part of the covenant nation of Israel by the violation of the covenant. The biblical perspectives on this question stubbornly resist efforts to force a definition of "Israel" along purely ethnic lines.

On the other hand, it is an oversimplification of the problem to suggest that Israel from the biblical perspective is to be identified with the elect people of God. While the ethnic aspect of this question does not resolve the whole problem, it is a feature that must not be overlooked. Certainly from an Old Testament perspective, the ethnic community of those descended from Abraham essentially were incorporated as the covenant people of God.

Part of a solution to the problem of the identification of "Israel" involves recognizing that the term has more than one use in Scripture. No effort will be made at this point to explore or define more carefully the various shades of meaning attaching to the term "Israel" in Scripture.

However, one significant usage of the term that may be helpful for the question of Jeremiah's prophecy should be noted. Old Covenant Israel may be regarded as a typological representation of the elect people of God. This assertion does not intend to suggest that Israel functioned merely in a typological role. But from an old covenant perspective, one significant aspect of Israel's existence was the nation's typological representation of the chosen of Yahveh.

The old covenant "serpent of brass" typologically anticipated the new covenant Christ cursed on the cross. The old covenant tabernacle typologically anticipated the new covenant dwelling of God in the midst of his people. The old covenant nation of Israel typologically anticipated the new covenant reality of the chosen people of God assembled as a nation consecrated to God.

When Jeremiah specifically indicates that the new covenant will be made "with the house of Judah and with the house of Israel," this perspective must be kept in mind. If the new covenant people of God are the actualized realization of a typological form, and the new covenant now is in effect, those constituting the people of God in the present circumstances must be recognized as the "Israel of God." As a unified people, the participants of the new covenant today are "Israel."

What is biblical corporateness? Biblical corporateness must be understood first of all as an essential reality of the covenant. God covenants corporately and not simply individually. The concept of the covenant inherently presupposes a people with whom the covenant is established. The communal aspect of the covenant relationship is forever present.

Secondly, biblical corporateness refers to a gracious promise to be claimed by faith. The promise-dimension of biblical corporateness appears plainly in the provisions made along genealogical lines. By entering into the covenant relationship, God not only makes promise concerning the salvation of the individual believer; he also offers promises with respect to the "seed" of the covenant participant.

This genealogical dimension of the corporate concept of the covenant occurs repeatedly with respect to the various covenants of Scripture.[21] It is not lacking in the prophetic development of the new covenant. In Jeremiah 32:39, the genealogical promises of the covenant find explicit repetition with respect to the "everlasting covenant." This particular verse appears in the context which parallels most closely the new covenant prophecy of Jeremiah 31. This

---

21. See above, pp. 34ff.

section restates essentially every element of the new covenant found in Jeremiah 31. According to Jeremiah 32:39, the Lord promises that he will give Israel one heart and one way that they may fear him forever, "for the good of them, and of their children after them." The promise of the covenant relates to a community of people. It includes not only the participant himself, but also his children.

Corporateness obviously is a part of the new covenant community. The genealogical principle is an integral aspect of biblical corporateness. It is a gracious promise to be claimed by participants in the new covenant. It is an essential reality of the covenant.

A third aspect of biblical corporateness simply has to do with the fact that corporateness functions as a complementary feature to individuality. Corporateness and individuality are not mutually exclusive principles. Problems arise in the covenant community when either corporateness or individuality is excluded from an understanding of the covenant relationship. Presumption occurs when corporateness is recognized apart from individuality. Isolationism occurs when individuality is recognized apart from corporateness.

Jeremiah in his new covenant prophecy gives full recognition to both of these principles and their roles in the new covenant community. Unless both these principles are understood aright, a true appreciation of the promise of the new covenant by Jeremiah cannot be comprehended.

Internal Reality versus External Substance in the New Covenant

A third point of tension in the new covenant has to do with the relation of internal reality to external substance. Unquestionably the internal transformation of the heart of man plays a most vital role in the new covenant. This particular dimension of new covenant emphasis has tended to lead interpreters to propose a purely spiritual or internal as over against a material and external realm of operation for the new covenant.

However, it is necessary to see these two aspects of the new covenant in a balanced perspective. The one does not necessarily exclude the other.

Internal realities are emphasized in the new covenant. Employing the added emphasis provided by poetic parallelism, Jeremiah declares God's word concerning the inward realities associated with the new covenant:

> I shall put my law
> in their midst
> and on their heart
> I shall write it (Jer. 31:33).

Unquestionably the immediacy of this inward transformation constitutes the very heart of the new covenant relationship when contrasted with the old. Says one commentator:

> . . . the difference between the two consists merely in this: that the will of God as expressed in the law under the old covenant was presented externally to the people, while under the new covenant it is to become an internal principle of life.[22]

A full appreciation of the radicalness of this provision of the new covenant may be seen only in the context of Jeremiah's strong emphasis on the wickedness of the human heart. Only as man is seen as unchangeable from Jeremiah's perspective can the hope of a new covenant be appreciated fully.[23]

Of course, it must be remembered that the old covenant also expected a change of heart. The law of God was to be in the heart of old covenant participants (cf. Deut. 6:6; 11:18; 10:12, 16; 30:6, 14). However, only in the new covenant is provision made for the writing by God himself of the law in the human heart.[24]

---

22. C. F. Keil, *The Prophecies of Jeremiah* (Grand Rapids, 1960), 2: 38.
23. Cf. von Rad, op. cit., p. 215. Many references in Jeremiah point to the wickedness of the human heart, including Jer. 3:17; 7:24; 9:14; 11:8; 12:2; 17:1.
24. Other Scriptures speak of a "purification" of the heart (Jer. 4:14; Ps. 51:12; 73:1, 13). Reference also is made to a "contrite" heart (Jer. 23:9; Isa. 57:15; Ps. 51:19)

By this imagery, Jeremiah emphasizes the im-mediate aspect of this law-writing. The substance of the law itself, apart from any externalized ritualistic details, becomes directly a part of the heart of the new covenant participant. All mediatorial externalities are removed, and the substance of the law itself lives in the heart of the new covenant participant. The putting of the law "in their midst" stands over against the "setting of the law before them," a phrase often used of the administration of the Sinaitic law (cf. Jer. 9:12; Deut. 4:8; 11:32; I Kings 9:6).

Is it to be assumed that Jeremiah implies that there was no regenerating activity of the Holy Spirit under the administration of the old covenant? Is it only under the new covenant that a renewed heart became the possession of covenant participants? John Calvin has provided what may be the clearest statement on this somewhat perplexing question:

> To this I answer, that the Fathers, who were formerly regenerated, obtained this favor through Christ, so that we may say, that it was as it were transferred to them from another source. The power, then, to penetrate into the heart was not inherent in the law, but it was a benefit transferred to the law from the gospel.[25]

Nothing under the old covenant had the effectiveness necessary actually to reconcile the sinner to God. Only in anticipation of the finished work of Christ could an act of heart-renewal be performed under the provisions of the old covenant.

The form of the old covenant's administration was in accord with its pre-messianic context. The messianic King had not yet overcome his enemies. He had not yet been anointed with the Holy Spirit. Under the old covenant, the king was not in a position to pour out the spirit of his anointment on his people. But in anticipation of the day in which all of these prospects would become realities, the

---

and to the circumcision of the heart (Jer. 4:4; 9:25). Cf. also reference to the law of God being in the heart (Ps. 37:31; 40:8; Isa. 51:7).

25. John Calvin, *Commentaries on the Book of the Prophet Jeremiah and the Lamentations* (Grand Rapids, 1950), 4: 131.

shadowy form of the old covenant administration participated in the powerful realities of the new covenant substance.

Jeremiah concentrates on one aspect of this heart-renewal. He says that under the new covenant no one would teach his neighbor or his brother to know the Lord. All would know him from the least to the greatest (Jer. 31:34).

This absence of teachers under the new covenant has been explained in a variety of ways. It has been suggested that the reference is to the replacement of men who taught from their own resources with men who would teach only what God had communicated to them.[26] Others have referred the contrast to the ultimate situation which shall prevail in heaven, in which no teachers shall function. Calvin suggests that Jeremiah has extended this picture hyperbolically. The prophet has made use of a mode of expression that goes beyond what may be expected to occur literally.[27]

However, the most natural interpretation in context would point to the fact that the new covenant situation would be one in which the need for people *to mediate* the covenant would disappear.

The teacher's office was that of covenant mediator. Moses in particular is presented as the "teacher" (מוֹרֶה) of Israel (Deut. 4:1; 4:14; 6:1; 5:31 [28]; 31:19, 22). In addition, the levites, the priests and the prophets were presented in the old covenant Scriptures as the teachers of God's people (II Chron. 17:7–9; Ezra 7:10; Jer. 32:33). These people held the office of covenant mediator.

But under the new covenant, no mediator would be necessary for the communication of the will of God to his people. From the smallest to the greatest, all would know the Lord, im-mediately.

The immediate knowledge of God by each and every participant of the covenant gives expression to the idea of the essence of the covenant relationship which runs throughout Scripture. What is the point of the covenant? It is to establish a oneness between God and his people. That oneness which was interrupted by the entrance of

26. Hengstenberg, op. cit., p. 442.
27. Calvin, op. cit., p. 134.

sin must be reconstituted through the covenant of redemption. "I shall be your God and you shall be my people," functioning as the central unifying theme of the covenant, underscores the role of oneness as the essence of the goal of the covenant.

A recognition of the goal of oneness as lying at the heart of the covenant relationship uncovers the inherent limitation of a form of covenant administration built on mediators. So long as the administration of God's covenant transpires through a system of intermediaries, covenant oneness essentially has been negated.

So the radicalness of Jeremiah's perspective on the new covenant hinges on his denial to a role for mediators. Contrary to the total experience of Israel under the Mosaic administration of the covenant, no series of teachers shall mediate the knowledge of God to the people of the covenant. The knowledge of God shall be the immediate possession of every participation in the new covenant.

The cryptic statement of the apostle Paul in Galatians 3:20 may be understood from this perspective. In the midst of his contrast between the promises of the covenant given to Abraham and the law mediated through Moses, Paul abruptly asserts: "Now a mediator is not of one; but God is one."

This passage of Scripture has been subjected to perhaps as many varied interpretations as any other verse in the Bible. In echoing Galatians 3:17, it has been suggested that as Israel was 430 years in coming out of Egypt, so interpreters have offered 430 understandings of Galatians 3:20.[28]

The key to Paul's statement resides in the essential purpose of the covenant, which is to establish oneness between God and his people. A covenant speaks of oneness. By God's covenant with his people, he intends to achieve unity.

But "a mediator is not of one." As long as intermediaries function in the covenantal relationship, the intention of oneness cannot be achieved.

---

28. Herman N. Ridderbos, *The Epistle of Paul to the Churches of Galatia* (Grand Rapids, 1953), p. 139.

The original establishment of Moses as mediator between God and Israel implied an absence of covenantal oneness. The people were terrified. They did not want to see God again. They pled with Moses to serve as their "mediator." By the establishment of a mediatorial office, the gap between sinful Israel and holy God was emphasized. Moses participated in a fellowship with God which was denied the rest of Israel.

The entire Mosaic dispensation built on the concept of the mediator. If it was not Moses who was mediating the covenant to God's people, the task reverted to a whole series of priestly or prophetic mediators.

Inherent in the Mosaic administration of God's covenant with his people was this visible indicator of its limitations. The ultimate oneness intended in the covenant never could be achieved through Moses. Some better administration had to be introduced. Some system without mediators had to be manifested, for "a mediator is not of one." The presence of a mediator denied the realization of the essential oneness intended by the covenant.

"But God is one," continues Paul. If God could be broken down into greater and lesser components, then perhaps one of these lesser components could be identified with the mediator of the covenant relationship. By such a process, perhaps it would be possible to achieve some limited form of oneness with God through covenant mediatorship.

"But God is one," insists Paul. The godhead does not contain in itself an elaborate system of mediators that might make room for covenantal oneness as well as for mediatorial office. God's people cannot be one with him by achieving a oneness with some "extension" of his person that is less than the wholeness of God himself. Either the covenant achieves an essential oneness of God immediately with his people, or the covenant fails in its purpose. Oneness must be achieved with the wholeness of God and with nothing less. "God is one," and oneness with some mediatorial figure will not substitute for oneness with God. Only when the mediatorial office is abolished altogether, when every man "knows" God in the ultimate sense, will the purposes of the covenant be realized.

Paul proceeds to indicate that this covenantal oneness is achieved in the person of Jesus Christ. He thereby affirms indirectly but unequivocally the full deity of Jesus Christ. Because God is one, and because oneness with God in the fullest sense is found in union with the person of Jesus Christ, then Jesus Christ must be essentially and totally God. He is not a sub-divine mediator, somewhat less than God and therefore somehow closer to man. Because covenantal oneness is achieved through oneness with the person of Jesus Christ, then Jesus Christ must be God. Oneness with an intermediary being cannot substitute for true covenantal oneness with the living God, for "God is one."

It is true that elsewhere Paul speaks of God as one, and Christ as the one mediator between God and men (I Tim. 2:5). This statement does not contradict Paul's affirmation in Galatians 3 concerning the oneness of God. It simply underscores the fact that a person cannot say everything at once.

From Paul's perspective, the day anticipated by Jeremiah in his prophecy respecting the new covenant now has been realized. God's people truly are one with him in the unity of the covenant which bypasses all mediatorial relationships. Through oneness with Jesus Christ, the people of the new covenant experience that immediate knowledge of God which makes a series of mediatorial teachers altogether unnecessary. In the present stage of the fulfillment of the new covenant, teachers function within the covenant community. In a limited sense they serve as mediators of the covenant.

However, the presence of teachers today in the context of the new covenant does not deny the principle propounded by Jeremiah and underscored by Paul. Every believer today is his own priest and his own interpreter of Scripture. Teachers function in this interim period only to assist every believer in realizing the direct oneness they now experience with God through the provisions of the new covenant.

Such is the dramatic message of the uniqueness of the new covenant. An actual oneness with God himself is achieved through Jesus Christ the son of God. He realizes the essential oneness between God and his people which throughout history has been the ultimate goal of the covenant. The participant in the new covenant experiences a depth of fellowship with God hardly conceivable under the provisions of the old covenant.

But external substance also receives stress. The new covenant lays a significant stress on internal transformation. A new heart in perfect communion with God epitomizes its blessings.

Yet the context of the prophetical message concerning the new covenant resists a pure "spiritualization" of the blessings of this covenant. The language of the prophets contains far too much in terms of materially defined benedictions. The return of Israel to the land, the rebuilding of the devastated cities, the reconstitution of the nation—even resurrection from the dead—play a vital role in the prophetical formulation of new covenant expectations.

How is this various data respecting the new covenant and its realization to be evaluated? How is the tension between internal reality and external substance in the new covenant to be resolved? Several possible ways of dealing with this problem may be suggested:

1. One possibility is the postponement of the actual fulfillment of all aspects of the new covenant to the future. This resolution of the problem commends itself because it leaves intact the various aspects of the promise of this covenant. Its immediate problem is dramatized by the fact that Christ formally inaugurated the new covenant by the institution of the Lord's Supper (cf. Luke 22:20). From that moment his people have celebrated regularly the present reality of the new covenant (I Cor. 11:25).

2. A second option is the full realization of the new covenant in the present. This perspective on the fulfillment of the new covenant has the advantage of treating seriously affirmations in the New Testament itself that the new covenant is in effect today (see in particular Heb. 8:8ff.; 10:15ff.; II Cor. 3:3ff.; I John 2:27).

However, from virtually any eschatological perspective, it must be recognized that portions of the new covenant redemption of God's people still are outstanding. At the very least, it is clear that the resurrection from the dead in bodily form yet remains as a future hope for new covenant participants.

3. One other suggestion is a two-staged fulfillment of the new covenant, based on a two-purpose scheme of God in history. The obvious advantage of this perspective is that it takes seriously the various dimensions of the new covenant prophecy of Jeremiah, while at the same time giving recognition to the application of new covenant prophecies to the present age by the New Testament. The problems with this approach arise from the rather arbitrary manner in which the various provisions of the new covenant are distributed between God's work with the church in the present age and God's work with ethnic Israel in the age to come. Nothing in the text of new covenant prophecy itself suggests that the internalized renewal of new covenant participants refers to one group of people identified as the church today, while the blessing of material prosperity awaits the reestablishment of ethnic Israel in a future millennial kingdom. The prophecy of Jeremiah appears as an integrated unit.

It has been suggested that the new covenant prophecies of Jeremiah simply are being "applied" to the present age, although their "fulfillment" *in toto* awaits the future restoration of Israel. But Christ in the institution of the Lord's Supper was not merely "applying" the new covenant prophecy to the present age. He was formally inaugurating the age of the new covenant. Paul the apostle in I Corinthians 11 indicates that the death of Christ for the sins of his people is an integral aspect of the new covenant age, and that its blessings are shared by all believers in Christ today.

4. Still another possible resolution lies in a multi-staged fulfillment, based on the typical/actual contrast of Scripture. Jeremiah's new covenant prophecy includes as an integral aspect of its fulfillment the return of Israel to the land of promise after the Babylonian captivity. But still further, Jeremiah specifically indicates that the return of Israel to the land of promise was to occur within 70 years (Jer. 25:12; 29:10). The consequent "mini-realization" of the new covenant promise inherently indicates that some typological factor must be involved in the fulfillment of new covenant prophecy. Obviously the return of Israel to Palestine in 537 B.C. at the decree of

King Cyrus of Persia did not meet all the requirements laid down in prophecy concerning the new covenant. Yet it symbolically represented the reestablishment of the people of God in accordance with the provisions of the new covenant.

A much fuller realization of the provisions of the new covenant is being experienced by the people of God in the present age. A new Israel of God has been constituted on the basis of the heart-revitalization of Jews and Gentiles through the new covenant provisions made possible by the death and resurrection of Jesus Christ, our covenant Lord.

Each time a group of believers in Christ celebrate the Lord's Supper, they rejoice in their current experience of the blessings of the new covenant because of their fellowship with God achieved by the "blood of the new covenant" (Luke 22:20; I Cor. 11:25). These current covenant participants are in a more exalted position than Moses, because with unveiled face they always behold the glory of God, and so pass from glory to glory (II Cor. 3:18). In experiencing the fulfillment of the new covenant, they now have the law of God written in their hearts (II Cor. 3:3, 6-8). It is "to us" that the Holy Spirit bears witness concerning the forgiveness of sins and the once-for-all cessation of offerings as promised in the new covenant (Heb. 10:15-18). Those who have received the anointing of the Holy Spirit today in fulfillment of the promise of the new covenant are the ones that have no need that anyone should teach them (I John 2:27).

Furthermore, it cannot be said that these blessings of the new covenant as experienced currently have no material benefits attached to them. To the contrary, in one sense it may be said that all material benedictions which fall to the lot of the people of God today come as a result of the provisions of the new covenant.

Yet at the same time, just as the people in the days of Israel's restoration looked forward to a more consummate realization of new covenant promises, so also participants in the new covenant today look forward to its consummate fulfillment at the time of the resurrection of the body and the rejuvenation of the whole of the earth.

Some might insist that "literal" fulfillment of new covenant prophecy requires the return of ethnic Israel to a geographically located Palestine. Yet the replacement of the typological with the actual as a principle of biblical interpretation points to another kind of "literal" fulfillment.

The historical return to a "land of promise" by a small remnant 70 years after Jeremiah's prophecy encourages hope in the final return to paradise lost by the newly constituted "Israel of God." As men from all nations had been dispossessed and alienated from the original creation, so now they may hope for restoration and peace, even to the extent of anticipating a "land of promise" sure to appear in the new creation, and sure to be enjoyed by a resurrected people.

Scripture Index

Genesis

1:14—20
1:16—21
1:20—111
1:24—110
1:24-26—111
1:25—110
1:27—76, 80
1:28—80, 110, 111, 207
1:28-3:6—205
1:30—110, 111
2:3—68
2:4—113
2:9—86
2:15—80
2:15-17—25
2:16—81
2:17—81, 86
2:18—74, 76
2:20—76, 77
2:22-24—75
2:24—75
3-11—109
3:6—207
3:14-15—93-103
3:14-19—93
3:15—25, 44, 97, 98, 100, 207, 208
3:16—103-104
3:17-19—105-107
3:19—176
3:22—86
4—98
4:1—208
4:7—104
4:15—116
6:5—207
6:5-7—112, 114

6:8—112, 113
6:9—112, 113
6:17-22—109
6:18—3, 18, 21, 113
6:20—110, 111
7:1—113
7:7—113
7:13—113
7:23—113
8:16—113
8:17—111
8:18—113
8:20-22—109, 114
8:22—19, 44
9—6
9:1—110, 116
9:1-7—109
9:2—110
9:3-6—115
9:5—117, 118
9:6—117, 118, 124, 176
9:7—110
9:8-17—110
9:9—111, 113, 122
9:10—6, 111, 120, 121
9:12—6, 113
9:17—6
10:1—113
11:10—113
11:27—113
12:1—30, 127, 146, 176
15—8, 9, 128, 129, 132, 133, 135, 145, 146, 147, 247
15:1—131
15:2—128
15:3—128
15:4—128
15:6—131

15:7—131, 174
15:8—128, 131
15:9—128, 131
15:10—7, 131
15:11—129, 132, 135
15:13—33, 129, 211
15:14—33, 129
15:16—129, 211
15:17—130
15:18—3, 7, 8, 9, 30, 32, 33, 35, 130
16—147
17—147
17:1—82, 127, 146, 148, 176
17:2—127
17:6-8—148
17:7—151, 277
17:9—148
17:9-14—148-149
17:12—39
17:13—39
17:14—146, 176, 284
18—97
21:23—7
21:24—7
21:26—7
21:27—8
21:28-32—7
21:31—7
21:32—8
22:17—96, 103
25:12—113
25:19—113
25:23—40
25:26—101
26:28—8
26:28-30—7

31:44—7, 8
31:53—7
31:54—7
36:1—113
37:2—113
39:4—112
40:13—269
44:42—269
46:3—211
46:4—211
49:8—96
50:4—112

Exodus

2:24—29, 171, 281
3:16—29
3:17—29
4:24-26—176-177
6:4—281
6:4-8—29, 30
6:6—46
6:7—46
6:8—7
12:43-49—154
16:4—264
19:4—46
19:5—46, 187, 216, 217
19:6—187
19:8—7
20-24—134, 169
20:1—31
20:5—35, 37
20:6—35, 37, 38
20:8—69
20:10—69
20:11—69
21:1-3—134
21:12—118
21:28—118
23:12—69
23:22—96
23:31—32
23:32—8
23:34—8
24:1—187
24:1-8—134
24:3—7

24:4—31, 187
24:7—7, 135
24:8—3, 7, 8, 51, 135
24:11—7
25:8—49
29:12—7
29:42-44—49
29:45—49
31:17—69
32:9—267
32:10—247
32:13—32
32:14—32
33:3—267
34:10—8
34:12—8
34:15—8
34:17—8
34:28—172
34:29-35—195-196
40:15—277

Leviticus

1:14-17—129
4:12—144
4:17—144
4:18—144
4:29—144
4:30—144
4:34—144
8:15—144
9:9—144
11:44—49
11:45—46
16:34—277
17:4—144
17:10-14—115
17:13—144
24:8—273
25:1-7—70
25:4—70
25:8-22—70
25:39-43—134
26:9-13—49
26:15—284
26:33-35—71
26:44—284

Numbers

14:28-35—35
15:31—284
24:10—96
25:12—27
25:13—27
26:63-65—35
30:8—284
30:12—284
30:13—284
30:15—284
32:5—112
35:16-21—118
35:21—96
35:22—96

Deuteronomy

2:14—35
2:15—35
4:1—293
4:8—292
4:13—172
4:14—293
4:20—47
4:23—8
4:26—10
4:37—36
5—72
5:2—8, 35
5:3—8, 35, 36
5:12—73
5:31—293
6:1—293
6:6—190, 291
6:19—96
7:2—8
7:8—7
7:9—14, 35, 37, 38
7:12—7
8:3—85
9:9—8, 173
9:11—173
10-16—267
10:12—291
10:16—153, 291
11:18—291
11:32—292

12:5—33, 50
12:9—71
12:10—71
12:11—33, 50
12:14—33, 50
12:18—33
14:22—50
15:1—134
15:12-18—134
16:2—50
16:6—50
16:7—50
16:11—50
28—136
28:15-68—218
28:25—136
28:26—136
29:1—8
29:11—36
29:12—8
29:13—7, 47
29:14—8, 36
29:25—8
29:29—8
30—218
30:3—218
30:6—153, 291
30:14—190, 291
31:16—8, 284
31:19—293
31:20—284
31:22—293
31:27—267
33—13
34—13

Joshua

1:3—32
3:16—22
5:9—155
6:26—259, 262
9:6—8
10:22-25—101
24—134
24:25—8
24:27—7

Judges

2:1—284
2:2—8
19:29—10

I Samuel

11:1—8, 9
11:2—8, 9
11:7—10
16:12—30
17:26—156
17:36—156
20:16—9
22:8—9
31:4—156

II Samuel

1:20—156
3:12—8
3:13—8
5—230
5:3—235
6—230, 250
7—6, 18, 230-234, 242, 245, 253-254
7:1—30
7:6—31
7:12—35
7:13—277
7:13b-16—245
7:14—236, 237
7:16—277
7:23—31
17:14—284
23:5—18, 220

I Kings

2:1-4—178, 254-255
2:3—32, 267
2:4—267
5:12—8
8—254
8:9—9
8:57-58—267

9—254, 255
9:6—267, 292
9:7—267
11:9-13—256
11:11—20, 237
11:13—237
11:31—256
11:32—237
11:34—237
11:35—256
11:36—237
12:1—240
12:13-15—256
12:25—240
12:32—257
13:1-10—256-257
13:11-32—258, 259
14:10—259
14:11—136, 259
14:14—259
14:17—241
14:21—238
15:4—238
15:19—284
15:21—241
15:28—259
15:29—259
15:33—241
15:1-4—259
16:4—136
16:6—241
16:8—241
16:9—241
16:10-12—259
16:15—241
16:23—241
16:24—241
16:34—259-260
17:13-16—260
18:45—241
21—241, 261
21:17-24—260-262
21:19—260
21:24—136
21:27-29—261
22:10—261
22:34—260
22:35—260

22:37—261
22:38—260, 261

II Kings

1:16—262
1:17—262
2:19-22—262-263
4:42-44—263
6:15-18—263-264
7:1—264
7:2—264
7:15—8
7:16-20—264-265
8:7-15—265
8:19—238
8:29-10:11—241
9:1-9—261
9:10—136
9:21-26—261
9:26—261
9:30-37—261
9:36—262
10:10—261
10:17—261
10:30—265
10:32—265
10:33—265
11:2—240
11:4—7
11:17—9, 47
12:18—265
13:3—265
13:7—265
14:25—265
15:12—265
16:5—240
17:7-41—266-267
17:13—34
17:14—266
17:15—20
19:34—238
20:6—239
20:12-18—266
21:4—239
21:7—239
23—134
23:1-3—235

23:3—9
23:15—256, 257, 258
23:16—256, 257, 258
23:26—239
24:1—265, 268
24:2—265, 268
24:10-17—266, 268
25:27-30—269

I Chronicles

11:3—8
16:15-18—34
16:16—7
17—18
17:5—231
29:22—250

II Chronicles

6:11—8
7:18—9
16:3—284
17:7-9—293
21:7—8
23:16—47
24:3—240
29:10—9
36:21—71

Ezra

4:5—284
7:10—293
9:14—284
10:3—8

Nehemiah

4:15—284
8—134
9:8—8

Job

9:17—100
31:1—8
40:8—284

Psalms

2—234
2:1—251
2:2—251
2:6—251
2:7—233
19:2-4—122
19:4—122
37:31—190, 292
40:8—190, 292
45:7—234
50:5—7, 8
50:16—20
51:12—291
51:19—291
56:6—100
73:1—291
73:13—291
78:23-27—264
78:60-72—229
79:2—137
79:3—137
89:3—3, 7, 8, 18, 220, 277
89:4—7, 277
89:34—6, 7
91:11—101
91:12—101
91:13—101
95:11—71
105:8—14
105:8-10—7, 37
105:8-12—29
105:9—7, 9
105:10—20, 277
105:42-45—29
106:45—29
110:6—101
119:11—190
119:97—178
119:126—284
132:11—220, 277
132:12—220
132:17—238
139:11—100

Proverbs

5:19—112

5:22—284
31:30—112

Song of Solomon
7:11—104

Isaiah
7:6—240
7:14—251
9:6—234, 251
11:1-10—251
24:5—277, 284
28:15—8
33:8—284
39:6—266
42:6—51
42:9—280
43:19—280
44:25—284
48:6—280
49:8—51
51:7—292
54:9—6
55:1-5—274
55:3—8, 51
55:4—51
57:15—291
59:21—39
61:1-3—70
61:1-9—274
62:2—280
65:17—280
66:22—280

Jeremiah
2:5—281
2:8—282
2:13—281
2:20—281
2:32—281
3:11-18—274
3:14—282
3:17—276, 291
4:4—156, 292
4:14—293

7:24—293
7:26—267
7:33—137
9:12—292
9:13—282
9:14—291
9:25—156, 292
9:26—156
11:8—291
11:10—8, 284
12:2—291
14:21—284
16:4—137
17:1—291
19:7—137
23:5—251
23:6—251
23:9—291
24:7—48
25:12—298
26:4—282
26:5—282
29:10—298
30—274
30:3—274, 279
31—21, 274, 278-279, 282, 285, 289, 290
31:3—17
31:27—279
31:31—3, 8, 41, 277, 279, 287
31:31-34—273, 274, 278, 282
31:32—280, 281, 282, 284
31:33—8, 48, 275, 276, 281, 284, 290
31:33-34—190
31:34—276, 282, 293
31:35—20, 21
31:38—279
31:38-40—275
32—43, 275
32:23—282, 293
32:27-44—274
32:37—48, 274
32:39—41, 289, 290
32:40—41, 276
32:50—274

33—20, 21
33:1-26—274
33:8—276
33:15-26—251
33:20—6, 19-21, 24
33:21—19-21
33:25—6, 19-21
33:26—19-21, 274
34—8, 132, 134, 136, 137
34:8—235
34:8-12—134
34:17-20—132, 136
34:18—10, 132, 133
34:19—132, 133
34:20—10, 132
50:4—277
50:5—274, 277
50:6-18—274
50:19—274
50:20—276
61:8—277

Ezekiel
11:19—280
16:8—7
16:59—284
16:60-63—274
16:63—276
17:13—8
17:19—7
20:37—7
25:15—96
28:10—156
31:18—156
32:19-32—156
33:6—118
34—24
34:1-31—274
34:10—118
34:13—274
34:20—42
34:23—42, 277
34:24—42, 48, 251
35:5—96
36:24-28—280
37:12—275

37:14—276
37:15—277
37:15-28—274
37:21—274
37:23—276
37:24—275
37:24-26—42
37:25—275
37:26—8, 17, 274, 275, 277
37:26-28—50
44:7—284

Daniel

9:1—72
9:21—72
9:24-27—72

Hosea

1:11—251
2:18—6, 8, 111
2:18-23—111
3:4—251
6:4—23
6:7—22-25
10:14—265
14:1—265

Amos

1:3-5—265
9:11—251

Micah

4:1-3—251
5:2—251

Haggai

2:5—8, 9, 281

Zechariah

2:11—48
8:8—48
8:16—49

11:10—8, 284

Malachi

1:2—40
1:3—40

Matthew

3:15—157
4:1—85
5:17—198
5:17-19—179
5:22—198
5:32—78
5:45—105
7:24-27—184
14:16—263
14:20—263
17:2—199
17:5—199
19:4—76
19:5—76
19:6—76
22:30—77
25:41—98
26:28—51, 138, 144-146
26:39—86
26:42—86

Mark

2:27—69
10:6-8—76

Luke

1—97
2:21—157
3:7—98
4:18—70
4:19—70
4:25—260
4:26—260
18:11—86
22:20—3, 17, 30, 43, 51,
    138, 144-146, 297, 299

John

1:14—50
1:17—173
6:9—263
7:22—151
7:23—151
8:44—98

Acts

2:30—220
2:30-36—252
2:32—220
2:34-36—220
3:25—38
7:51—267
10:44-48—158
15:1—158
15:8-9—158
15:20—120
15:29—120
16:3—158

Romans

1:3—233
1:4—233
1:26—79
1:27—79
2:21-23—180
2:25-29—160-161
3:20—180
3:21—179, 180
3:27—180
4:3—159
4:9-12—159
4:11—40, 161
4:12—40
4:16—183
4:17—183
5:18—85
5:19—85
6:4—165
6:14—179, 182
7:6—179
7:7—179
7:12—179

8:3—216
8:22—122
9:6—40
9:13—40
9:22—102
10:12—122
10:18—122
11:17—39
11:19—39
12:4—199
13:1—121
14:14—120
15:22—183
16:20—44, 183

I Corinthians

4:4—92
7:1—77
7:7—77
7:15—78
7:26—77
9:22—158
10:25—120
11:9—76
11:11—78
11:12—78
11:25—43, 297, 299
11:30-32—185

II Corinthians

1:22—161
3—191
3:3—297, 299
3:6—17
3:6-8—299
3:7—193, 195
3:7-9—192
3:10—192
3:11—193
3:12-15—193-199
3:18—197, 299
6:16—49
11:3—95

Galatians

2:14-16—58

3—296
3:1—58
3:8—59
3:9—59
3:13—39
3:15-19—59, 141
3:17—33, 60, 173, 174, 294
3:19—61, 188
3:20—294
3:23—58, 59
3:23-25—179
3:23-26—189
3:24—181
3:25—58
3:28—77
3:29—39
4:4—157
4:21—180
4:25—60, 181, 252
4:26—252
4:31-5:2—58
5:2—60, 158

Ephesians

1:7-14—166
1:13—148, 162
1:14—148
2:1—113
2:2—113
2:8-10—113
2:10—56
2:21—50
4:25—49
4:30—162
5:25—77
5:31—76
6:1-3—184
6:12—95

Philippians

3:3—161

Colossians

2:8—162
2:9—162

2:10—162
2:11—162, 166
2:12—162, 166
2:14—102
2:15—102

II Thessalonians

3:10-12—81

I Timothy

2:5—296
2:14—95-96
2:15—97

Hebrews

1:1-14—236
1:5—234
2:20-25—111
3:5—199
3:6—199
3:7—217
3:14—217
3:15—217
4:1—217
4:2—217
4:8—71
4:9—71, 74
4:10—74
4:11—217
5:5—236
5:6—236
5:8—86
5:13—36
5:15—48
6:4-6—217
7:18-19—216
8:6—43
8:6-13—43
8:8—17, 223, 297
8:10—49
9—138, 142
9:15—17, 43, 139, 140,
   141, 142
9:15-20—14, 138
9:16—14, 141, 142

9:17—14, 141, 142, 143,
  144
9:18-20—140, 141, 143
9:22—10
10:15—43, 223, 297
10:15-18—17, 43, 299
11:14-16—215
11:17-19—215
12:6—184
12:22-24—252
12:24—17

James
1:22—184

I Peter
2:13—121
2:14—121

II Peter
3:3-10—123
3:4-6—115
3:5-7—183

I John
2:27—297, 299
3:12—98

Revelation
4:3—124, 125
7:15—50
12:7-9—98
21:1—51
21:3—50
22:2—86